# ADVANCE PRAISE
## THE WRITER'S GUIDE TO PSYCHOLOGY

"Thoughtful, scholarly, comprehensive, and a boon to writers aiming for accuracy when depicting the world of abnormal psychology and clinical treatment."

—**Jonathan Kellerman**, psychologist and author of the best-selling Alex Delaware mystery novels

"I wish Carolyn Kaufman had written *The Writer's Guide to Psychology* years ago! Every writer who even thinks about creating or explaining a character with a psychological disorder should have a copy on their desk, right next to their dictionary and thesaurus. A well-written, easy-to-read guide to understanding the most complicated of psychological disorders that's sure to help writers abandon the stereotypes and develop realistic characters."

—**Jilliane Hoffman**, former felony prosecutor with the Miami-Dade State Attorney's Office and best-selling author of *Retribution, Last Witness, Plea of Insanity*, and *Pretty Little Things*

"As a psychologist, a novelist, and a reader, nothing stops me reading faster than flat characters, phony fictional shrinks, and false diagnoses. Fiction writers can get all the help they need with these problems and more in Carolyn Kaufman's excellent reference, *The Writer's Guide to Psychology*."

—**Dr. Roberta Isleib,** clinical psychologist and author of *Deadly Advice, Preaching to the Corpse*, and *Asking for Murder*

# THE WRITER'S GUIDE TO PSYCHOLOGY

## How to Write Accurately About Psychological Disorders, Clinical Treatment and Human Behavior

### by Carolyn Kaufman, Psy.D.

Quill
Driver
Books
Q

Fresno, California

*The Writer's Guide to Psychology*
Copyright © 2010 by Carolyn Kaufman. All rights reserved.

Published by Quill Driver Books
an imprint of Linden Publishing
2006 South Mary, Fresno, California 93721
559-233-6633 / 800-345-4447
QuillDriverBooks.com

Quill Driver Books and Colophon are trademarks of
Linden Publishing, Inc.

ISBN 978-1-884995-68-2

135798642

Printed in the United States of America
on acid-free paper.

Library of Congress Cataloging-in-Publication Data

Kaufman, Carolyn.
  The writer's guide to psychology : how to write accurately about
psychological disorders, clinical treatment, and human behavior /
by Carolyn Kaufman.
    p. cm.
  Includes bibliographical references and index.
  ISBN 978-1-884995-68-2 (pbk. : alk. paper)
  1. Psychology, Pathological. 2. Psychotherapy. 3. Psychology,
Pathological in literature. 4. Psychotherapy in literature. 5. Fiction-
-Technique. I. Title.
  RC454.4.K42 2010
  616.89--dc22
                              2010039077

# Acknowledgments

Many thanks go to Jenifer Takats, MD, not only for connecting me with several other psychiatric professionals, but also for so generously sharing her time and expertise on medications. Thank you also to Trupti Patel, MD, who gave me a fantastic inside scoop on ECT and VNS. Thanks to Sharon Hawk-Carpenter, RN, BSN, MSA and John Tilley, PsyD, for answering oodles of questions and showing me around private and state-run psychiatric wards, respectively. David Tom, PhD was also kind enough to answer questions on institutionalization, and to read the entire manuscript in search of errors.

Thank you to my beta readers, the first four of whom have been my partners in crime on the QueryTracker Blog (querytracker.blogspot. com)—Suzette Saxton, Mary Lindsey, Heather Dyer, MD; and Patrick McDonald. And Annie Louden's sharp editorial eye is very much to thank for the polish on the manuscript I initially turned in to the publisher.

Thank you to my agent, Kate Epstein, and to Quill Driver founder Steve Mettee, both of whom believed in this project in the midst of a brutal economy. Also at Quill Driver, editor Kent "we need more examples" Sorsky helped to make the book much stronger, and both he and publicist Jaguar Bennett provided guidance and assistance as I worked on book-support projects like the website, WritersGuidetoPsychology.com.

Thanks to Lori Moomaw, who helped keep me sane through this process.

And a special thanks to Sue Kaufman, who not only believed in this project from Day 1, but also provided support and assistance throughout the process of conceptualizing, developing, and writing this book.

Finally, thanks to my family and friends, as well as to my readers who have become advocates, cheerleaders, and fans along the way. I couldn't have done it without you.

For my mom, Sue Kaufman, and my dad, Dennis Kaufman, who have always supported and encouraged my dreams—including this one.

# Contents

# *Foreword*

Every writer—be he or she a novelist, journalist or screenwriter—has at one time or another attempted to create, explain or define in their work a complicated character who is afflicted with mental illness. We hear and see the slang medical terminology— "OCD," "manic," "schizo," "psycho," "PTSD"—casually tossed about in conversations, literature, movies, and on TV everyday. Sometimes the words are used interchangeably; oftentimes they are used incorrectly, but their frequent overuse has led many writers to believe they understand a disease or affliction when they really don't. Unfortunately, most writers aren't psychiatrists and very few have earned a doctorate in psychology. Save for a few who might've spent some time in a psych ward or on a therapist's couch, most writers have had no interaction with the schizophrenics, sociopaths, manic-depressives (aka bi-polarites), borderlines, post-traumatically-stressed-out, or otherwise mentally ill characters we yearn to write about. Without a clinical background or field experience, most writers have thus relied on the same old misinformed stereotypes we've heard or seen through the years to create characters that are inaccurate, or in some cases, actually atypical of an individual suffering from a particular psychological disorder.

I'd love to say, "If you need a psych degree to truly understand the nuances of a particular mental illness, then but for psychiatrists and those with a doctorate on their walls, who's the wiser if you rely on outdated or misinformed stereotypes?"—but it doesn't work that way. All writers worth their salt know that once a reader or a filmgoer catches on that an author or screenwriter hasn't done their homework, they lose credibility with that audience. From there, it's all downhill. But it's not just the misuse of slang terminology that immediately identifies you, the writer, as a person who didn't do his or her character research. It can be the situations you put your character in, how you make your character speak, what she looks like, how she dresses, what career choices she's made, and the type of men she dates. While mental illness is unique in how it may affect an individual, each diagnosis has certain defining symptoms that will shape a character's thought processes and how that character interacts with others.

I pen legal thrillers, and so the characters that I try to create, define or explain are usually diabolical psychopathic killers. As a former Miami prosecutor, I have some real life experience to help guide me in the killer department, but I'm no Sigmund Freud or Jennifer Melfi when it comes to understanding why my nasty characters do what they do. When it came time to tackle a different psychological disorder in my third thriller, *Plea of Insanity*, I actually had to read whole treatises on schizophrenia just so I could create an accurate depiction of a schizophrenic character. Of course, before digesting such exciting reads as the *Diagnostic and Statistical Manual of Mental Disorders-Version IV* (DSM-IV) and *Surviving Schizophrenia*, I first scoured the shelves of bookstores and libraries alike in search of an easy-to-understand guide to Psych 101. Unfortunately for me, there was nothing.

Until now.

I wish Carolyn Kaufman had written *The Writer's Guide to Psychology* a few years ago. She not only defines the most complicated of mental illnesses in an easy-to-understand manner, but she actually thinks like a writer, offering her invaluable insight as a seasoned clinician in character development. She debunks the myths and dismantles the stereotypes, gives an insider's view as to what really happens when a client lies down on that proverbial therapy couch (that is most likely a therapy chair nowadays), and in the end even helps you medicate your crazed character properly. She draws upon the past mistakes of other writers to provide readers with cautionary tales of what not to do and lauds the ones who hit a Hannibal Lector home run in an effort to better illustrate how a writer can get it right.

And that's what it really comes down to in the end—getting it right. Because even in works of fiction, the reader and the audience expect nothing less.

—Jilliane Hoffman, former felony prosecutor and author
of *Retribution*, *Last Witness*, *Plea of Insanity* and *Pretty Little Things*

# Introduction

It doesn't matter what kind of story you're writing—if it involves people, it involves psychology. There's just one problem: What you think you know about psychology may not be accurate. In fact, many common beliefs are misguided, outdated, or just plain wrong.

How does something like that happen?

Well, research shows that most of us get our knowledge about psychology from the mass media. And although most of us assume that writers, directors, and producers turn to psychological experts when they're doing their research, few actually do. Instead, their knowledge comes from the books, television, and movies they've seen. Myths and misconceptions about psychology are thus perpetuated, one storyteller to the next, like urban legends. As psychology and psychotherapy become more a part of people's everyday lives, however, readers are increasingly savvy—and increasingly aware of the embarrassing mistakes some writers make.

It seems like it should be simple to ferret out accurate information in the Internet age, but the truth is that the abundance of information can just be confusing. For example, television and movies regularly portray electroconvulsive ("electroshock") therapy as a terrifying, painful process that sends the person into massive convulsions. (In fact, as we'll discuss in Chapter 11, patients undergoing electroconvulsive therapy are neither awake nor in pain, nor do their bodies convulse.) If a writer even thought to question the validity of such portrayals, she would find that there are websites that describe the treatment very differently...but she would also find that there are just as many sites that continue to push grossly outdated and inaccurate information. In such an environment, even dedicated researchers may be hard-pressed to know what to believe.

In addition to the problems created by so much conflicting information, add the fact that it can be hard to obtain (and understand) the best resources to double-check that information. The books and journals that contain the latest experts' facts are not only expensive, they're aimed at professionals, which means they're jargon-laden and reliant on background information that the average reader just doesn't have. Think maybe a college psychology textbook would help? While you'd probably find it much easier to understand, a single book can also set you back $140 or more.

Psychology has struggled for years with the problem of how to make accurate, expert-based information widely available to the public. Misconceptions are such a problem that professional psychological groups have been formed just to try to put a dent in them. Even though such groups often provide expert consultation, those consultants are not nearly as easy to find and reach as, say, the information you can get from Wikipedia, the evening news, or that great psychological thriller you just finished reading.

To me, at least, it seemed clear what needed to happen. Someone needed to put together an interesting, affordable, easy-to-understand guide for writers to help them get their psych right!

Though authors who write books like this one are usually experts first and writers second, I actually started as a writer. In fact, writing is what led me to psychology.

When I reached college, I had no idea what I wanted to be when I grew up. What I did know was that I loved to write fiction, so I picked up English/writing as a major. When a friend raved about a psychology class she was taking, I decided to try it. Maybe, I thought, I'd learn something useful for my stories.

Well, I did. I learned so many useful things that I eventually added psychology as a second major. Yet I knew that the knowledge base I was building as I got my bachelor's degree was only the tip of the proverbial iceberg. I wanted more. By the time I headed off in pursuit of my doctorate, my fascination with psychology for writing purposes was my dirty little secret. Of course I wanted to help people, but I also wanted to understand them…because I could write better stories that way.

And with the help of this book, so can you.

While it would be erroneous to suggest that we can break down an entire profession in a few hundred pages, psychologists do develop thinking and interaction patterns that are counterintuitive to what most of us learn at home. If you really want to develop characters as fascinating, complex, and contradictory as real people, integrate accurate psychological information into your stories, and sound like you understand human behavior, you need to learn to think like a shrink.

To that end, we'll explore the core theories of human behavior, talk about what therapists really do in therapy sessions (and how!), and replace colloquial (mis)conceptions of deviance with fresh, accurate information. Once you understand how our biological heritage equips us all with predictable behavior tendencies and how those tendencies are modified by the environment, you'll also know why villains kill, victims suffer, and heroes rescue.

Along the way we'll also poke some of the skeletons in psychology's closet, look at what medications like Prozac really do, walk through psychological emergencies, and explore villains' brains.

So, let's get started! It's going to be fun....

# 1
# Common Myths and Mistakes
## *A Look at Fictional Portrayals of Psychological Problems, Professionals, and Treatments*

Most of us learn about psychological disorders and treatments from the mass media. Unfortunately, these media portrayals are often misguided if not downright wrong. Writers, directors, and producers rarely consult experts about psychological problems, but since most of us assume they do, myths are inadvertently perpetuated, one storyteller to the next. In other words, most writers believe they have a good understanding of psychology, even as they rely on outdated and inaccurate stereotypes, many of which were generated by their equally uninformed peers.

At the same time, readers and viewers are becoming savvier about what is realistic and are less tolerant of mistakes. By incorporating accurate psychological information into your writing you will make your work more authentic and appealing to today's increasingly knowledgeable and critical audiences. You will also distinguish your work from the average writer's confused and error-riddled portrayals of psychological concepts.

Let's test what you think you know about psychology: Which of these statements do you believe are true and which are false?

1. All psychotherapists call the people who see them "patients."

2. Everyone is diagnosable with something.

3. The clinical name for "split" or multiple personalities is schizophrenia.

4. Most therapists expect people to lie on a couch while they talk about their problems.

5. Most mental illnesses look similar.

6. People with mental illness are more likely to be violent than other people.

7. Most therapists believe that examination of one's childhood is crucial to therapy.

8. Psychologists analyze everyone they meet.

9. Most therapists are diagnosable with a psychological disorder.

10. Lobotomies are no longer performed on people with severe, chronic schizophrenia.

11. Sex therapists do not engage in sexual activities with their patients.

12. Serial killers are almost never psychotic.

13. It's fairly hard to get committed to a psychiatric ward against your will.

14. During electroconvulsive (electroshock) therapy, the person lies still.

15. Mental illness is usually invisible to the casual observer.

In the quiz you took, statements one to nine are false; statements ten to fifteen are true. Each statement taps a common myth, so don't feel bad if you got quite a few wrong. You've spent most of your life bombarded by outdated or just plain false information.

## 1. Many psychotherapists call the people who come to see them "clients."

Until the 1950s, many psychotherapists were trained as medical doctors, not as psychology practitioners. As the profession of "psychologist" developed, psychologists began working to differentiate themselves from psychiatrists and the medical model of mental illness, under which psychological problems are seen as diseases and the person needing care is allegedly a passive recipient of the doctor's expertise. Part of this differentiation process included a shift away from the term "patient" and toward the term "client." Present-day trainees are usually taught that *client* is the most appropriate, caring term, and one that implies that the person in treatment must be an active participant if he wants to get well. Therefore, many if not most therapists trained in the last ten to twenty years feel strongly about calling the people in their care clients.

Psychologist and bestselling thriller author Jonathan Kellerman, however, who was trained in the 1970s, feels just the opposite. Having seen the political shift in terms, he says, "I prefer patient because it implies a healing process and greater caring, emotion and intimacy. Client, to me, has a cold, impersonal 'business-model' ring."

So which term should you use? Well, it depends on two things. When your therapist was trained and where he works. Psychiatrists, who are medical doctors with specialized training in psychology, still use the term *patient*, but most psychotherapists working outside of a hospital setting and trained in the last twenty years say *client*. If you're writing about a psychiatrist who holds an actual MD, a psychologist who works in a hospital, or someone who's been practicing therapy for three decades or more, use the term *patient*. Otherwise, use *client*.

So let's say your character is headed to her weekly visit with her therapist or to a couples session with her partner. In both cases, her therapist will think of her as a client. If she's visiting a psychiatrist for medications or a hospital because she's afraid she might hurt herself, however, she'll be referred to as a patient.

For more information on the differences between psychiatrists, psychologists, counselors, and social workers, check out Chapter 3.

## 2. *About a quarter of the population is diagnosable with a disorder at any given time.*

If you were to look at psychology's "bible," the *Diagnostic and Statistical Manual of Mental Disorders-Version IV-Text Revision* (*DSM-IV-TR*), you'd find that the entries are deceptively easy to understand. So easy, in fact, that students and casual browsers often develop "intern syndrome," or the belief that they have half of the disorders they're studying.

For example, in the DSM, Generalized Anxiety Disorder (GAD) is described as "excessive anxiety and worry…[that] the person finds difficult to control, accompanied by tiredness, muscle tension, restlessness, [and] difficulty concentrating." Though just about everyone who has ever gone to school, worked, or been in a romantic relationship can relate to such a broad description, only about 3 percent of people have GAD.

What most people don't realize is just how important that word "excessive" is. To be diagnosable, the symptoms must consistently interfere with one's ability to go to school, to work, and/or to have meaningful social and romantic relationships. Feeling anxious about everything you have to get done at work is normal; being so anxious about work that you can't keep a job is diagnosable. Someone suffering normal anxiety might consider seeing a therapist and might be helped by therapy, but would not receive a diagnosis of a disorder. Instead, the normal diagnostic code would be replaced with a V code, which indicates a normal reaction to a given situation. In other words, the problem is not due to a psychological disorder.

### 3. Schizophrenia and multiple personalities are completely different problems, with different causes and different symptoms.

Multiple personality disorder was renamed Dissociative Identity Disorder (DID) for the DSM-IV, which was released in 1994. The disorder is caused by multiple sadistic, traumatic experiences, each of which is so overwhelming that the mind walls them off from the rest of their personality. Each of the walled-off parts then begins to develop into its own personality. Therefore, the more unique traumas the person experiences, the more personalities she will have.

One of the hallmark symptoms of DID is amnesia. If a particular personality is not "out" (not presently in control of the person's body) the person usually has no memories of what went on. Since the personalities take turns being "out," they all suffer amnesia to some extent.

By contrast, schizophrenia is a biological disease caused in part by too much of the brain chemical dopamine. People with schizophrenia may hallucinate, have strange ideas called delusions, behave oddly, or become catatonic. They do not feel like more than one person or identity lives in their bodies, and they don't have problems with amnesia the way people with multiple personalities do.

The reason people confuse DID and schizophrenia is that "schizophrenia" literally means "split personality." Eugen Bleuler, the person who first came up with the name, noticed a "split" in schizophrenic behavior. Sometimes people with schizophrenia are agitated, talkative, and have odd ideas; other times, they have little or no energy and may become catatonic. Chapter 6 discusses schizophrenia in more detail, and Chapter 8 looks at DID.

> **DON'T LET THIS HAPPEN TO YOU!**
>
> In *Unshapely Things*, Mark del Franco's detective says, "We have a disassociative personality acting out anger against victims who represent some kind of psychological trauma from the murderer's past." It sounds good, but there's no such thing as a disassociative personality— only a dissociative personality. There's also no indication in the book that the killer is dissociating; that is, experiencing a split in identity. The writer would have been better off suggesting the killer had an anti-social or narcissistic personality.

### 4. *Most therapists are uncomfortable if clients lie down on the couch.*

Modern therapy clients don't lie on a couch; in fact, some therapists' offices don't even *have* couches. So where did the idea come from? Sigmund Freud had his patients lie on a couch so he could sit in a chair behind their heads. He argued that this let people talk without being influenced by his appearance or reactions.

Good contemporary therapists try to establish a meaningful connection with clients, and that requires face-to-face discussion. Since most therapists are used to doing therapy with both people sitting up, if a client lies down, the therapist feels the same way an accountant would if her client lay down during an appointment! You can use this in your fiction the same way Jake Gyllenhaal did when he played a client in the film *Donnie Darko*. His character lounges back on the couch like he's in his bedroom, refusing to make eye contact and making his therapist visibly uncomfortable. Likewise, given that most modern audiences appreciate that nobody lies down in therapy anymore, you can use the couch for comedic effect if your story calls for it.

### 5. *Though some mental illnesses have symptoms in common, each disorder looks different from the others.*

Though there are about 300 different diagnoses in the *DSM*, writers often refer to characters as "crazy" or "mentally ill" and leave it at that. The problem is that without researching a particular diagnosis, they may create a constellation of "symptoms" that don't make sense together, or blame a disorder for symptoms that particular disorder never causes. For example, a client cannot have both schizophrenia and Parkinson's disease because schizophrenia is caused by too much activity in the dopamine system and Parkinson's is caused by too little. Likewise, psychosis cannot be caused by an anxiety disorder, so it would be silly to explain your psychotic character's behavior with an obsessive-compulsive diagnosis.

Also, be careful not to name a diagnosis without researching what the symptoms are. In the movie *The Cell*, Vincent D'Onofrio plays a serial killer who drowns women in glass cells. The therapist in the film claims he's schizophrenic when no real symptoms of schizophrenia appear in the movie. Instead, the symptoms point to completely different disorders; likely, sadomasochism and antisocial personality disorder.

It's best to use only one or two diagnoses in your story so you can consistently show the relevant symptoms in the character's behavior. Because mental illness does not appear and disappear randomly, you must be vigilant about consistently portraying your character's symptoms.

Symptoms that are vague to the point of uselessness or are so jumbled that they defy any clinical logic are confusing and unsatisfying for your audience. To make your character stand out from all the other "mentally ill" characters, choose symptoms from the disorders chapters of this book that fit your character's diagnosis. Since similar symptom patterns are grouped together by chapter, you can also work from the opposite direction, choosing a diagnosis that fits your character's symptoms. A specific diagnosis with accurate symptoms makes your story more credible and your character more compelling.

## 6. *Most people with mental illness are no more likely to be violent than the average person.*

Many of the modern associations between mental illness and evil are residuals of historical beliefs. Early societies saw madness as proof of possession by evil spirits, so doctors and spiritual leaders used severe treatments including starvation and beatings to drive out these demons.

In modern times, when people with mental illness do commit violent crimes, they tend to make headlines. Killers who talk about hearing voices or who have other bizarre ideas make for fascinating news.

We all have a tendency to estimate how valid information is based on the examples we most easily call to mind. Though you have a 1 in 84 chance of dying in a car crash and a mere 1 in 5,051 chance of dying in

## DON'T LET THIS HAPPEN TO YOU!

The heroine of Charles Stross's fantasy novel *The Family Trade* finds herself in a parallel world, chased by a knight bearing an M-16. She quickly finds her way back home, but worries it all means she's going crazy. She "wrack[s] her memory for decade-old clinical lectures… *Well, whatever this is, it ain't in the DSM-IV*," she concludes. "No way was this schizophrenia. The symptoms were all wrong, and she wasn't hearing voices or feeling weird about people. It was just a single sharp incident, very vivid, realistic…[plus] the walls aren't going soft, and nobody is beaming orbital mind control lasers at me."

Stross is making a mistake many writers do: relying on half-remembered assumptions about a disorder rather than taking the time to research actual diagnostic symptoms to make the passage more coherent and believable. No heroine who really understood schizophrenia would be reassured by how realistic her experience seemed. Hallucinations and delusions are, by definition, vivid, realistic, and inseparable from reality. Also, while many people with schizophrenia hear voices, so can people with other disorders, so assuming the problem isn't in the *DSM* just because she's pretty sure she's not schizophrenic isn't a good bet. Finally, someone having "weird feelings about people" while the "walls [are] going soft" sounds more like drug use than a psychological disorder.

a plane crash, a lot more people are afraid to get on an airplane than to get in a car. Because plane crashes are so much rarer, they're more likely to be reported in the news and remembered when it's time to fly. The same thing happens when people with psychological problems commit violence. The stories are so bizarre, we remember them well and assume violent behavior is more common among the mentally ill than it is.

According to forensic psychologist John Tilley, who works regularly with violent offenders, active psychopathology *can* make some people more violent. Still, *some* is not *all* or even *most*. Unfortunately, writers like to explain violence with mental illness. One study found that a whopping 75 percent of "mentally ill" television characters were violent!

Tilley argues that there are four specific psychological problems that make someone likely to be violent:

1.  First, "there is probably no single better predictor of future violence than psychopathy," he says. This is because the psychopath has no conscience or qualms about using or harming others to achieve his selfish aims. Though violence can land someone who has a psychological problem in a psychiatric ward, psychopathy isn't a mental illness as much as it is a problematic personality structure. Therefore, few psychopaths are hospitalized; instead, they end up in prison.

    We'll talk more about psychopathy in Chapter 10.

2.  Next, says Tilley, comes "anyone who is suffering from threat/control-override symptoms. These are specific symptoms of psychosis that involve the delusional belief that someone or something is controlling your mind or persecuting you in some fashion." For example, in the film *A Beautiful Mind*, the psychotic John Nash is plagued by delusions of grandiosity and persecution—he thinks, in essence, that the U.S. government hired him to be a code-breaker and that other agencies such as the Soviets are conspiring to do him harm. Another example would be someone who believes that the next-door neighbor is using some kind of technological device to implant 'voices' inside his or her head. This group, those demonstrating what are called TCO's, are probably the next most likely to be violent statistically, though from a clinical/anecdotal perspective, this category and the two below are about even in terms of dangerousness potential."

3.  Third is "anyone who is actively intoxicated on some substance and/or is substance dependent." Once in a while a study will find that people with schizophrenia are more violent than others, but once you take into account their substance abuse and other factors that contribute to violence, such as poverty, *schizophrenia* isn't usually what's actually causing the increased violence.

4.  Finally, "anyone who is displaying an active and severe disturbance in mood, with those demonstrating mania being the most likely among this sub-group to be violent."

For more information on both mania and psychosis, check out Chapter 6.

In many cases, using "mental illness" to explain wicked behavior is less a plot device than it is laziness on the writer's part. And lazy or careless writers make silly mistakes. For example, in James Neal Harvey's *By*

*Reason of Insanity*, the antagonist's murderous behavior is blamed on cyclothymic disorder, which is an extremely mild form of bipolar disorder. So mild, in fact, that it's rarely recognized as a problem at all.

## 7. Not all therapists believe the examination of the patient's childhood is crucial to therapy.

Only one branch of psychotherapeutic theory emphasizes how our childhoods affect us—the rest don't. Most modern practitioners assume that what's happened since childhood is at least as important, if not more important, than what happened to us as children. Some therapists actually believe that discussion of the past is an attempt to escape responsibility for current life problems. Others believe that the social and cultural environments we live in are what cause problems.

In the film *The Dark Knight*, District Attorney Harvey Dent is committed to cleaning up Gotham, and his heroic efforts to that end earn him the nickname "The White Knight." When love interest Rachel Dawes is killed by the Joker, Dent stops thinking straight. The Joker convinces Dent to seek revenge on Batman and Commissioner Gordon. Watching Dent deteriorate into Two-Face, based on the movie's events, is far more interesting than a quickly-mentioned abusive childhood.

The movie's writers even take a mocking stab at the cliché of childhood abuse causing villainy. The Joker explains that his father's abuse made him what he is, only to turn that explanation on its head and tell a completely different lie later. We realize that the Joker was joking, and we believed him because we're so accustomed to writers using the abusive childhood cliché.

Check out Chapter 2 for more information on the different types of therapy.

## 8. Psychologists rarely analyze the people they meet socially.

Psychoanalysis is Freud's lie-on-the-couch-and-free-associate-about-your-childhood-on-a-daily-basis approach. Today, most therapists have been trained in more goal-oriented approaches to get the client done with therapy in eight to twelve sessions. That's far too few sessions to go into deep analysis of one's childhood or unconscious.

Since Freud *did* analyze people and *did* find what he believed were hidden meanings in everything from jokes to slips of the tongue, psychologists got a reputation for having an insatiable urge to analyze and diagnose everyone. Because modern psychologists are trained to understand human behavior better than the average person, many people worry that therapists have a kind of psychological x-ray vision that will expose their darkest secrets.

Since his training allows him to see and name psychological quirks, the therapist may *seem* to be analyzing when he notes something people around him couldn't put a finger on. At the same time, a smart therapist always checks out his impressions with the client and adjusts them as needed. So while characters like *The Mentalist*'s crime investigator Patrick Jane make uncannily accurate assessments based on things like cologne and clothing cut, the therapist knows that he's likely to gather better information if he asks tentatively about an interpretation rather than if he makes a snap assumption and lobs it into the room like a grenade. Also remember that your therapist character gets paid to do therapy, and it most likely feels like work to him, so he's not going to want to do an in-depth "analysis" of someone he doesn't even know. Plus, it's unethical to do therapy outside the office, where the client and therapist have agreed to work together, privacy agreements have been signed, and closed doors protect the client's interests.

### 9. *Most therapists are not diagnosable with a psychological disorder.*

Though some therapists do struggle with psychological disorders, most don't. A therapist with a serious untreated mental illness not only isn't able to provide good therapy, he's in violation of the American Psychological Association's ethical code *because* he can't provide good therapy.

In fiction, the psychologically disturbed therapist is usually either flaky and useless or volatile and dangerous. For example, in Dean Koontz's novel *False Memory*, a psychopathic psychiatrist creates false memories that induce such "severe cases of demonophobia"—the fear of demons and devils—that he's able to "[shatter] his patients' lives." Like most evil therapists, Koontz's finds "such sport highly entertaining." And like most fictional psychopaths, he's somehow able to get away with his behavior without anyone reporting him.

In real life, real people with serious problems have trouble hiding them, and that includes therapists. Add that to the fact that therapists are mandated to deal with their personal problems and to stop seeing clients if they can't do so. Plus, truly crazy therapists who aren't smart enough to stop seeing clients will get caught thanks to their crazy behavior. Therefore, you end up with far more psychologically healthy therapists than not.

For more information on therapist stereotypes, check out Chapter 2.

### 10. Lobotomies, which are the destruction of the frontal areas of the brain, are no longer performed on people with severe, chronic schizophrenia (or anyone else!)

The frontal areas of the brain are important for judgment, planning, decision making, troubleshooting, creativity, time management, and dealing with new situations. Destroying them with a lobotomy therefore changes the patient's personality and capabilities. The practice gained popularity in the U.S. in 1936 thanks to a psychiatrist who performed lobotomies indiscriminately on everyone from people with schizophrenia to children who defied their parents. Shamefully, one likely reason 40,000 lobotomies were performed in the United States alone is that they rendered difficult patients quiet and passive, making them easier for frustrated caregivers to work with.

Effective antipsychotic drugs were discovered and prescribed in the 1950s and, because they reduced psychotic symptoms so dramatically, lobotomies became less common. Still, it wasn't until Ken Kesey's *One Flew Over the Cuckoo's Nest* was made into a movie in 1975 that there was a true outcry against lobotomies in the United States. Thereafter, the practice declined and finally stopped completely in the 1980s.

Lobotomies still sneak into fiction frequently enough that many people are unclear about when they were first and last performed. In the film *From Hell*, which is set in the mid-1800s, a physician performs a lobotomy with a hammer. In reality, Gottlieb Burckhardt performed the first surgery on a living patient's frontal lobes in 1890.

We'll talk more about lobotomies in Chapter 11.

### 11. Ethical sex therapists do not engage in sexual activities with their patients. Ever.

During sex therapy, the therapist and client talk about sex, and the client may have homework to try with a partner, but there's no hanky panky in the office itself.

If a therapist sleeps with a client, he is not only taking advantage of his power over her, he also irrevocably changes the nature of their relationship from a professional one to a personal one. Some therapists manage to get away with this kind of unethical behavior, and usually the client is in need of even more therapy after she has been exploited. Her new therapist is obligated to report the unethical one, and psychology's governing associations can take away the unethical therapist's license to practice. In more and more situations, the client sues the former therapist for negligence or even assault. Sex with clients is swiftly becoming a criminal offense, and a number of states now classify it as a felony.

We'll look at the ethical obligations for therapists in more detail in Chapter 3.

## 12. Serial killers are almost never psychotic, especially the ones that don't get caught for a long time.

Psychosis is a loss of contact with reality as most people experience it. The most common symptoms of psychosis are hallucinations and delusions. Hallucinations can be visual, tactile, or auditory, but "hearing voices" is most common. Delusions are strong and often strange ideas that go against cultural norms and are not supported by reality.

Once in a while a serial killer does have a psychotic disorder, but that's rare for a couple of reasons. First, psychotic behavior draws attention to itself, making it difficult for people to disguise what they're doing. Second, to get away with multiple dangerous crimes, planning and forethought is necessary. The deterioration of organized thought and behavior associated with psychosis makes successful planning nearly impossible.

By contrast, serial killers *are* diagnosable with Antisocial Personality Disorder (APD), which is an ongoing carelessness for and violation of others' rights. People with severe APD don't experience normal guilt when they break rules or hurt people, so they lie, cheat, con, steal, and behave aggressively without qualms.

People with severe APD can fall into two categories. Members of the first group are born with brain abnormalities that make them more likely to be adrenaline junkies, more likely to be aggressive, and less likely to feel guilt. This group—the one most serial killers fall into—is sometimes called *psychopathic*, a term often confused with *psychotic*.

The second group, referred to as *sociopathic*, develops antisocial traits due to severe abuse or neglect. For reasons we'll discuss further in Chapter 10, the abuse interferes with the normal development of a conscience.

### 13. It's fairly hard to get committed to a psychiatric ward against your will in the United States.

In the United States, people can't be forced into treatment just because they have a psychological condition and don't want to go. The classic fear that "the men in white coats" will drag someone off and "put them away" for odd behavior just isn't realistic. At least one of the following three things must be true:

- The person is an immediate danger to herself; in other words, she is not only suicidal, she has a plan, the means to carry out the plan, and a time set.

- The person is an immediate danger to others.

- The person's life is in danger because she is unable to provide for basic personal needs like food, clothing, shelter, or personal safety due to psychiatric illness.

Even some people who want to commit themselves voluntarily have trouble doing so. Because commitment is so much more expensive than weekly appointments with a therapist, insurance companies will sometimes try to persuade their subscribers not to go to the hospital, or they might even refuse to pay for a hospital stay.

We'll look more closely at emergencies and hospitalization in Chapter 12.

### 14. During electroconvulsive ("electroshock") therapy, the person lies still.

When most people think of electroconvulsive therapy (ECT), they imagine someone strapped to a table while painful electrical currents are directed through his body, causing him to jitter and shake.

Electroconvulsive therapy works by triggering a seizure, but early instances of the treatment were "unmodified," which means the person wasn't given any medication to control the associated convulsions. Because in some cases the convulsions were so extreme that patients fractured or broke bones, treatment teams began to use muscle relaxants. Since it's scary for most people not to be able to move, they also administer a general anesthetic. Brain activity caused by the seizures is monitored on a screen.

ECT is typically used as a last resort, and only when the potential benefits (a quick normalization of mood) outweigh the potential side effects (usually temporary memory deficits). Chapter 11 explores ECT in more depth.

## 15. Mental illness is usually invisible to the casual observer.

Caricaturists intentionally exaggerate their targets' distinctive physical features to make them recognizable. Likewise, film directors may originally have given people with psychological disorders bizarre appearances and habits to demonstrate that those characters are different from others.

The truth is that just as religious beliefs, sexual orientation, and ethnicity can be inconspicuous, psychological disorders are usually invisible to the casual (and sometimes even the careful) observer. While disorders are evident to those closest to the people struggling with them, sufferers often become adept at hiding their symptoms from strangers.

### FINDING IDEAS IN NEW RESEARCH

A lot of great fiction is born of new research. Just like medicine and technology, psychology is constantly evolving. Some interesting news and research items include the following:

- A preliminary study led by R. Robert Auger, M.D., at the Mayo Clinic linked certain drugs to acting out violent behavior from dreams. Sample plotline: A woman murders her visiting mother but frames her husband, who has a history of violent dreams.

- Jordan Grafman and colleagues from the National Institute of Neurological Disorders and Stroke have shown that damage to certain parts of the brain reduce the likelihood that the person will develop Posttraumatic Stress Disorder (PTSD). Sample plotline: A mercenary group intentionally damages their soldiers' ventromedial prefrontal cortexes in a risky experimental plot to keep them from developing PTSD; instead, the damage causes the soldiers to revolt during a dangerous incursion.

- Christophe Pierre Bayer and colleagues at University Clinic in Hamburg, Germany, found that children with PTSD are more likely to grow up seeking revenge on those they believed were responsible for what happened to them than those who never exhibit PTSD. Sample plotline: Discarded by society thanks to their childhood problems with PTSD, a group of misfits plot to overthrow the regime that killed their parents.

You can track cutting-edge research on websites like the American Psychological Association's Psych Port (www.psycport.com), WebMD (www.webmd.com), Science Daily (www.sciencedaily.com), Scientific American (www.scientificamerican.com), or on most major newspaper and television network websites. Many sites will even send you health news alerts tailored to your interests.

Since articles you find through these sites are written with the layperson in mind, they're easy to understand. Usually they present one or two interesting new research findings like the ones above. Use the articles as springboards for your stories.

And rather than saying your vengeful adult villain has PTSD and leaving it at that, check out the PTSD section in Chapter 8 so you understand what causes the disorder and how the symptoms look. An overactive startle reflex, social withdrawal, drug and alcohol abuse, and nightmares are common for people with PTSD, so it wouldn't make sense to blame the character's vengefulness on PTSD unless you are also showing *symptoms* of PTSD.

Now that your character is no longer lying on the couch with a generic mental illness in danger of being subjected to anesthetic-free ECT by her salacious, lobotomizing therapist, let's dig into the realities of modern psychology, starting with why people do what they do.

# 2
# Why People Do What They Do
## *Learning to Think Like a Shrink*

Because no one has taught them how to "think like a shrink," many writers are forced to rely on worn therapist stereotypes. Their psychologist characters practice old-fashioned Freudian psychoanalysis, talk more than they listen, or give so little feedback that they may as well not be there. From time to time, they launch into stilted, jargon-laden descriptions of human motivation without ever actually touching a legitimate psychological theory.

By avoiding common therapist stereotypes, and by acquiring a basic understanding of the five theoretical frameworks within which therapists operate (discussed later in this chapter), you'll be able to create compelling and realistic psychologist characters who will lend authenticity and credibility to your work.

## THERAPIST STEREOTYPES

The four most common therapist clichés in fiction are Dr. Evil, Dr. Dippy, Dr. Wonderful, and Dr. Sexy. Sometimes, as with Thomas Harris's serial killing psychiatrist Hannibal Lecter, one of these stereotypes is fleshed out in a way that captures the imagination of audiences. More often, stereotyped therapists are flat and predictable, and they rarely if ever step out of the therapist role and develop into interesting characters.

1.  *Dr. Evil* is the psychological version of the mad scientist. He uses diagnoses as a rationale to imprison hapless victims and run tortuous experiments on them. In Nate Kenyon's horror novel *The Reach*, a group of psychological professionals have given a patient

a false diagnosis of schizophrenia so they can keep her locked up and manipulate her paranormal abilities. In the thriller film *The Jacket*, the malicious psychiatrist drugs his patient, binds him in a straitjacket, locks him in the body drawer of a morgue, and calls it therapy.

2. *Dr. Dippy* is the useless head-shrinker, the self-important windbag, and ultimately the butt of the joke. He encourages useless ongoing therapy, often based on his own egotistical theories. He makes tons of money and tells clients they need more sessions just so he can have a bigger house. In the film *What About Bob?*, Dr. Leo Marvin is a self-important psychiatrist whose theories about treating patients have just been published in a book he calls *Baby Steps*. Though he sees himself as a peerless therapist and a brilliant father and husband, he is of course brought low by one difficult patient: Bob. Another famous Dr. Dippy? *Frasier* sitcom psychiatrist Frasier Crane, who in spite of his high opinion of himself is ultimately crazier than any of his patients.

3. *Dr. Wonderful* is too good to be true. Not only is he endlessly patient and available, he always knows exactly the right treatment and he makes astonishingly accurate interpretations. Once in a while, Dr. Wonderful acts as a kind of *deus ex machina*, sweeping in with a treatment that cures all of the hero's ills. More often, Dr. Wonderful is a mask for the writer who wishes to espouse his own philosophies and insights. In Ted Dekker's Christian thriller *Three*, the "wise" and "wonderful" Dr. John Francis not only pontificates on the importance of good Christian values, he also provides spot-on insight into the main character's problems whenever the other characters get too stumped.

4. *Dr. Sexy* is almost always female. Though in most real life cases of sexual misconduct male therapists are taking advantage of female clients, in fiction it's usually Dr. Sexy falling for her male client. In the 1993 film *Mr. Jones*, for example, Lena Olin's character violates ethics left and right to be with her bipolar patient, whom she ultimately helps not with medication, but with her undying love. Interestingly, even when female therapists aren't reduced to sex objects, they're almost unanimously incompetent. A notable exception is Dr. Jennifer Melfi in HBO's series *The Sopranos*.

In reality, therapists are people just like anyone else; the only difference is that they have specialized training in human behavior and thought processes. With a solid understanding of the frameworks therapists use to understand people, you can not only write rounder, more realistic therapists, but also gain a better understanding of why your characters do what they do.

# THERAPIST ORIENTATIONS

Every experienced therapist is guided by a theoretical framework, called an "orientation." This orientation guides the therapist's entire approach to therapy—the types of questions she asks, the treatment approaches she prefers, and the types of changes she expects to see. Once you understand psychology's five major orientations, you can build on them to create realistic dialogue, show realistic techniques, and, if it's appropriate, portray realistic insight and change.

## ORIENTATION 1. PSYCHODYNAMIC THERAPIES

### Core Principles

All psychodynamic therapies emphasize the importance of the past, especially childhood, on social and relationship problems in the present. The unconscious is believed to influence current choices and behavior. Therapy is intended to help the client gain insight into why she is the way she is; change is seen as following naturally from insight.

### Background

Psychodynamic therapies are directly descended from Freudian psychoanalysis. Freud believed that every child moved through five stages of psychological and sexual development that later influenced the adult personality. When things went wrong during those developmental stages, people developed psychological problems. He found that when people talked about their problems, they often felt better and were subsequently able to make changes in their lives. He trained many of the famous therapists who came after him, but one by one those therapists decided Freud had placed too much emphasis on sexuality and aggressive instincts, and each developed his or her own theories.

Most modern psychodynamic therapists believe that as a child interacts with his environment, he forms a blueprint of how the interpersonal world works and how he should behave in response to that world. For example, by watching his caregivers' relationships, he learns what friendship is, how men and women "should" relate, and how to react when things go wrong. Now, if we all were aware that we have blueprints and knew the contents of those blueprints, there would be less need for therapy. But the blueprint is stored mostly in the unconscious, and we assume that the world we see in the blueprint is objective reality.

When someone comes into therapy as an adult, the psychodynamic therapist assumes that the psychological blueprint that guides the client's current behavior is faulty or lacking in some way. The therapist's goal is thus to learn what's in the blueprint, help the client understand how the blueprint is influencing him, and restructure areas in the blueprint that aren't working.

### In Therapy

To help the client gain insight into how his past (and the blueprint he built based on it) influences his current concerns, the therapist uses "interpretations." For example, she might draw parallels between past experiences and current behavior, or between two seemingly unrelated things going on in the client's life. For example, the therapist might say, "I wonder if you worry so much that your boyfriends will leave you because your father left your mother when you were young." Or, "It seems to me that you're in the same sort of power struggle with your boss that you are with your wife." Or, "I wonder if you're actually angry with me, or if you're angry with your father."

Interpretive statements always target an unconscious process, and they usually start out with phrases like:

- It may be that…
- Could it be that…?
- Is there any possibility that…?
- I wonder if…
- It seems to me that…
- Maybe it's because…
- I get the feeling that…
- It's almost as if…

Writers usually show their client characters responding in one of two ways to interpretations. Either they have a *eureka!* moment during which everything suddenly becomes clear, or they're disgusted by the therapist's cluelessness. It's more realistic to show the client talking through the interpretation with the therapist, saying things like, "Maybe that's why I..." or "You mean I...?" or "No, that doesn't feel right; maybe..."

If your character is constantly saying "No, I don't think so," especially about connections that are pretty obvious, the therapist might decide the client is displaying "resistance." She can address the resistance by saying something like "I get the feeling you have something on your mind that you're reluctant to talk about" or "I've noticed that when your sister comes up, you talk less than usual."

### When Your Therapist Should Use Psychodynamic Therapy

Psychodynamic therapy is good for when you want to explore your character's motivations or push him to realize something he can't see for himself. In the film *Ordinary People* the therapist, Dr. Berger, makes interpretations that linger in the main character Conrad's mind long after the session ends. Eventually, Conrad is able to realize that it's not his mother who must forgive him for the accident that caused his brother's death—instead, he must forgive himself. Psychodynamic therapy is also a good choice for an individual who is having relationship problems. However, if the client comes in with the person or people he's having trouble with, you may want to consider portraying a systems approach instead (we'll look at this approach later in the chapter).

### How Understanding Psychodynamic Therapy Can Help You Understand Your Character

Ask yourself the following questions to better understand how your character's childhood and unconscious are affecting his current life choices.

- Who were the most influential people, both good and bad, in your character's childhood?

- What significant events happened in your character's childhood?

- How did each of those people and events influence your character's understanding of the way the world works today? In other words, what rules, beliefs, ideals, expectations, and values does he live by, and where did he learn them?

- How is your character reliving old conflicts? For example, does he choose partners who allow him to have the same kind of relationship his parents did (even if that relationship was unhappy)?

Or, approach it from the opposite direction:

- What are your character's most significant traits?

- How was each of those traits shaped by his relationships with other people? Let's say, for example, that your character is especially cynical. Perhaps when he was a child his parents often made promises they never planned to keep. As a result, he might grow up believing that other people are selfish liars who never keep their word.

---

**Don't Let This Happen To You!**

In fiction, bad psychodynamic therapists are usually pushy, elitist, and off-base. They ask about characters' childhoods so abruptly the question feels like a non sequitur. In the action film *Blade Trinity*, Dr. Vance is the consummate Freudian cardboard cutout. First he provides a disdainful analysis of Blade's beliefs in vampirism, and then he adds, "You have to ask where that [business about vampirism] comes from. I'm wondering, for instance, what your relationship was like with your mother. Were the two of you close?" Blade eyes Vance as though *he's* the crazy one—and can you blame him?

---

## Orientation 2. Cognitive-Behavioral Therapies

### *Core Principles*

According to cognitive-behavioral therapies, irrational thoughts—which stem from a natural tendency to blow things out of proportion and personalize them—and learned ("conditioned") behaviors cause people to behave in dysfunctional ways. Though everyone has *some* dysfunctional behaviors thanks to irrational thinking and conditioning, a few people's are exacerbated by life experiences or chemical imbalances. Treatments often target both thoughts and behaviors.

## Background

Cognitive-behavioral therapy (CBT) is based on two ideas. First, many of our behaviors are simply learned responses to particular things in the environment. Second, the way we consciously think about things—rather than an unconscious dynamic—creates and maintains problems. For example, people with mood disorders often fall prey to "dichotomous thinking," which means they see things in all-or-nothing terms. If your character wanted a job that went to another candidate, rather than appreciating that only one person can step into the desired position (and that adapting his interviewing approach might be helpful in the future), he might decide he is an abject failure and that he can't do anything right. Likewise, if your character has a problem with social anxiety, he might use emotional reasoning to conclude that because he *feels* awkward around other people, he must *be* completely inept.

Over time, unhealthy behaviors and thinking become habits, and cognitive-behavioral therapy helps clients become more aware of those habits so they can change them. This approach is particularly effective with mood and anxiety disorders. CBT is intended to be short-term therapy, and it operates on that old assumption that "if you give a man a fish you feed him for a day; if you teach a man to fish you feed him for life." The goal of CBT is to make the client self-sufficient and send him on his way.

## In Therapy

CBT is much more present-focused than psychodynamic therapy. The cognitive-behavioral therapist doesn't necessarily care where the client learned to think and act a certain way; she just cares that he's working to change those patterns in the present. Though cognitive-behavioral therapy can be broken down into two parts—cognitive (thoughts) and behavioral (actions)—they are often used together, which is why you find them here in one category.

### The Cognitive Part of CBT

CBT often uses activities and homework assignments to help the client identify and dismantle irrational thinking.

A person is thinking irrationally when he evaluates himself, others, or the world using unrealistic expectations. Irrational thoughts are usually automatic, and because they're heavily tainted by emotion, they rarely seem irrational to the person having them. Words that indicate irrational thinking include absolutes like "always" and "never" and judgments about what "should," "shouldn't," "must," or "mustn't" be.

For example, it's reasonable to be sad and frustrated if someone you're interested in doesn't ask you out; it's irrational to declare that this means no one will *ever* love you. The original event is uncomfortable, but the catastrophized result (as a cognitive-behavioral therapist might refer to it) is awful, terrible, and unbearable. Another example: It's reasonable to be upset if you make a mistake on something important; it's irrational to say that you can't do *anything* right.

To help clients combat irrational thinking, CBT therapists often use an Automatic Thought Record. The thought record consists of five columns, one for each letter:

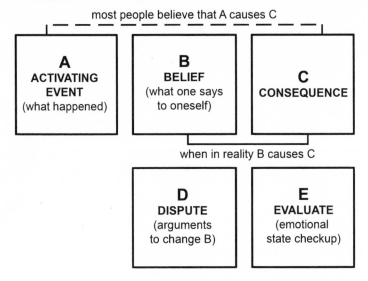

**Fig 2.1. Cognitive-behavioral therapy automatic thought record.**

When the client catches himself feeling bad, he writes down what happened (the Activating event), what he thought to himself (the Belief), and how he felt as a result (the Consequence). The Belief invariably includes an irrational thought, because rational thoughts don't make people devastatingly anxious or depressed.

Next, the therapist teaches the client to Dispute his irrational thoughts. During this process, the therapist teaches the client to ask himself questions like the ones below. These questions confront the irrational thought and help the client construct one that's more realistic.

- What evidence do I have that _____ is true? What evidence do I have that it isn't true? (For example, if the client is saying "I'm a failure," is he a failure in *everything*? The therapist helps him identify places in his life in which he is a success—with friendships, other classes or jobs, etc.)

- If the feared statement is true, then *realistically* what's the worst thing that can happen? And so what if that happens? Why would that be so terrible? (In other words, am I being melodramatic? How?)

- What would I tell a friend if she said these things about herself?

- Is it really reasonable for me to be so hard on myself for this? Is it helping the situation or just making it worse?

- If I had to prove my statement in a courtroom, could I really provide enough evidence to convince a judge or jury?

- What would happen if I changed the way I was thinking? How might my life improve?

- If it's really a problem, what can I do to make it better?

After the client has Disputed the irrational thought, he Evaluates how he feels. Better, even a little? Worse? Why? (If the client feels worse, the irrational thought either hasn't been properly identified, or it hasn't been effectively disputed, in which case he needs to back up and try the process again.)

The thought record does at least three things. First, it makes the client more aware of his thought patterns. It's hard to change an irrational thought that's so automatic the person doesn't even consciously hear it! Second, the thought record teaches the client how to change the thought patterns himself. That way he won't have to rely on the therapist long-term. Third, it allows him to practice his new thinking patterns at home.

In spite of the fact that CBT is one of the most common (and empirically best-supported) approaches to therapy, few writers understand the underlying principles the way you now do. Therefore, most fictional therapists not only try to Dispute clients' irrational thoughts themselves, they do it without helping the client to identify what's going on in his head first. The client then experiences the therapist as a pushy, insensitive dolt who's supplying a pat, off-target answer to the problem. To portray an effective CBT therapist, show her helping the client attack the problem with the logical tenacity of a good attorney.

For example, if your client character's wife just left him for another man, he might be convinced that he has not only failed in his marriage, but that he will never find someone else who will love him. Those are pretty depressing thoughts, but see that little giveaway word "never"? That also means the thoughts are irrational. Have your therapist choose one of the questions above and use it to expose how unrealistic and damaging the thoughts are. "What would you tell your best friend if he was saying this about himself?" she might ask. Later, after she and the client have talked about that, she might wonder aloud, "Is thinking this way helping the situation or just making it worse?"

### The Behavioral Part of CBT

The behavioral part of CBT focuses on faulty learning or conditioning. From a strictly behavioral perspective, people do things for two reasons: because those things are rewarding, or because those things help them avoid unpleasant consequences.

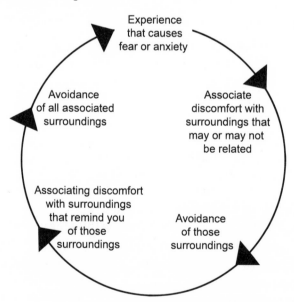

**Fig 2.2. How avoidance behavior develops.**

Behavioral therapy techniques are focused on helping the client unlearn his problematic behaviors and/or find healthier behaviors that are more rewarding than the unhealthy behaviors. For example, most phobias are learned. Perhaps someone got trapped in an elevator once, and while he was in there he became (irrationally) convinced that the cables would break. Or let's say one of the cables on his elevator *did* break. Now he's terrified of all elevators.

Two things have happened. First, the way the client is thinking about the elevator is causing fear. (And yes, it's *still* irrational for him to avoid *all* elevators even if a cable really did break, because the reality is that most elevators are perfectly safe.) Second, the client has learned to avoid elevators because they make him feel uncomfortable.

To help the client change the irrational *thinking*, the therapist might use an Automatic Thought Record like the one discussed above. To address the avoidance *behavior*, the therapist can use exposure-based techniques like systematic desensitization. After the client has gotten good at using relaxation techniques, the therapist helps him work through a hierarchy of increasingly stressful situations during which he is exposed to the feared thing without being allowed to run away. For example, if he's terrified of elevators, the bottom of the hierarchy might be talking about elevators; at the top of the hierarchy would be actually riding in one. In between are steps like standing in an elevator lobby, pressing the button to call the elevator, stepping close to the doors when they open without getting on, getting on but getting back off before the doors close, and so forth.

Flooding or implosion therapy is a similar but much more extreme form of behavioral desensitization in which the client is exposed to the feared stimulus in a massive dose; eventually he either becomes numb to the stimulus or realizes he doesn't need to be afraid. In the film *Batman Begins*, Bruce Wayne has been afraid of bats since he was a child. Upon entering a cave filled with bats, he forces himself to stand still and tolerate their presence until he's able to conquer his fear.

## When Your Therapist Should Use Cognitive-Behavioral Therapy

Cognitive-behavioral therapy is especially helpful for situations in which your character is thinking negative things about himself, so characters with low self-esteem, depression, or anxiety would be good targets.

CBT is also one of the most directive therapies, so if you want a therapist who's actively doing something to help your client character, and/or who talks a lot, CBT is the approach you want to take.

If your character is psychotic, you might be tempted to have a therapist use CBT to attack his delusional beliefs because they seem so irrational. Delusions are generally impervious to logic, however; CBT is best used to either alter unacceptable behavior or to improve the client's ability to *cope* with his psychosis. Also remember that because antipsychotic medications alter the brain chemistry causing psychosis, they are enormously helpful.

### How Understanding CBT Can Help You Understand Your Character

- Think about the way your character customarily behaves toward other characters. How is each of those tendencies rewarding for your character, or how does it help him avoid unpleasantness? For example, if your character is a jokester, does he crack jokes because he finds other people's amusement or attention rewarding or because making jokes lets him avoid dealing with something unpleasant? Be careful not to focus too much on how something was rewarding in the past—how is it rewarding *now*?

- Oftentimes when writers create a character with a psychological problem, they forget (or don't know how) to consistently show that disorder affecting the character's life. Connecting behavior to thought and vice versa will help you make the disorder pervasive in a character's life. For example, let's say your character has a major depressive disorder. What kinds of things is he thinking to keep him depressed? Does he discount positive experiences by insisting they "don't count"? Does he tell himself he's a loser every time something goes wrong? Does he temper good news with a dose of negativism? What kinds of things does he say or do that reflect those depressing thoughts?

## ORIENTATION 3. HUMANISTIC AND EXISTENTIAL THERAPIES

### Core Principles

Humanistic therapies emphasize personal growth, self-fulfillment, and meaning. According to humanistic therapists, problems occur when the innate tendency toward psychological growth is blocked. Rather than trying to "fix" a client the way psychodynamic and cognitive-behavioral therapists do, the humanistic therapist believes that the *client* is the foremost expert on what needs to happen. The therapist's job is to create an open, honest environment where the client can figure out what's blocking his natural tendency toward growth. Humanistic therapy is extremely non-directive. The client guides the course of therapy and the therapist's job is to listen, accept, and appreciate the client's journey.

## Background

In the 1950s, psychologist Carl Rogers decided he'd had enough of the idea that patients should be "fixed" by their therapists. He argued that therapists needed to focus on listening and offering open, nonjudgmental acceptance of who the client was. He was the one who started calling patients "clients," and he viewed the client as an equal. Rogers's ideas were so influential that they affected the way *all* therapies are practiced. Thanks to Rogers, the core elements of any modern therapeutic relationships are rapport, trust, dignity and respect, empathy, and genuineness.

## In Therapy

Rather than interpreting a client's mental constructs the way a psychodynamic therapist does, or challenging thoughts and providing guidance the way a cognitive-behavioral therapist does, the humanistic therapist summarizes and paraphrases what she hears the client say in an open and accepting way. She also asks questions to help the client get more "in touch with" himself. (This is where the infamous "And how do you feel about that?" comes from.) More than any other type of therapist, she turns the question back to the client. Doing so prompts the client to explore further.

Humanistic therapy can be particularly useful for dealing with existential issues, which are problems of existence. According to psychiatrist Irvin Yalom, the issues people struggle with most are death, freedom, isolation, and meaning (or meaninglessness, depending on whether you're an optimist or a pessimist). In other words, everyone must face certain realities of existence, such as the reality that we all die sooner or later. A humanistic therapist can help the client explore what death means to him.

## When Your Therapist Should Use Humanistic Therapy

Humanistic therapy is especially good for characters who need to sort out what's best for *them*. Though in real life humanistic therapists do talk back and forth with their clients, in writing it can seem as though the humanistic therapist is simply parroting back the gist of what the client said, so have your client do most of the talking. If you want your therapist to just ask a question here or there without interpreting or providing direction, keep the humanistic therapist in mind.

## How Understanding Humanistic Therapy Can Help You Understand Your Character

Most people respond well to genuine interest in their lives and an appreciation for their point of view. If you have a character that just doesn't want to open up to you (or other characters), try taking a humanistic approach. Imagine that you have all the time and patience in the world and just be okay with whatever your character brings to the table, even if it's reticence. With clients who don't want to talk, you can even go so far as to say, "Sometimes we just don't feel like talking to other people, so we can sit quietly for as long as you need."

### DEALING WITH DIFFICULT CHARACTERS

The main character in Jenna Black's Morgan Kingsley urban fantasy series is abrasive and difficult with everyone she encounters. It's hard to imagine her going to therapy under any circumstances, but let's pretend for a moment that she did. She'd probably mock a psychodynamic therapist's attempts at interpretation and balk at all the things a cognitive-behavioral therapist wanted her to do. She might actually find herself talking with a humanistic therapist, though.

A humanistic therapist would never attempt an interpretation to explain why Morgan is doing what she is or give her tips on how to change it. Instead, he would convey a genuine interest in understanding where she's coming from and accept *her* without necessarily accepting her *behavior*. If she insisted on being abrasive and antagonistic with him, he would honestly share the way she's impacting him and ask whether this was her intent. Given no one to fight with, and honest feedback on how she affects others, Morgan might actually feel a bit like sharing whatever's bothering her most, in spite of herself.

> People like Morgan usually test the waters by throwing out things they expect will shock the therapist. When the therapist isn't horrified or repelled and continues to relate openly and genuinely, the person is left without her regular defenses and can begin to trust and interact more genuinely with the therapist.

## ORIENTATION 4. SYSTEMS THERAPIES

### Core Principles

Imagine a mobile, the kind that hangs over a baby's bed. If you tap one of the toys on the mobile, the entire thing begins to spin and sway. Family therapists see families the same way. The actions of each member of the family affect the other members. Therefore, systems therapists always view the individual in the context of his social environment. They assume that he constantly influences and is influenced by things like family, peers, and culture. Disorders are seen as indicative of a problem within a larger group or context. Therefore, the system itself is the client.

### In Therapy

In each of the other orientations, the focus is on what's going on *inside* the individual; in systems theory, the focus is on what is going on *between* individuals in a system. Individual motives and intentions are less important than how each individual's behaviors affect the rest of the group's interactions. According to this perspective, if the therapist can expose the patterns of interaction among the family members, the system will change. *What* the system is doing is far more important than *why* the system is doing it.

Because psychological problems are seen as the result of hostile or unclear communication and blocked needs among family members, the therapist's goal is to help them communicate clearly and effectively. She does this by interfering with the family's normal (unhealthy) communication and showing them how to use more appropriate behavior. The goal is not to figure out who is to blame for the problem, but to increase the family's ability to work together as a problem-solving unit.

A systems therapist isn't going to focus on what happened in each family member's past and explore how that past is affecting the family; rather, her focus is going to be on changing family members' interactions with one another right now.

31

## When Your Therapist Should Use Systems Therapy

Systems theories are used for family, marital, and to a lesser extent, group therapy. Be careful to keep your therapist's or co-therapists' eyes on the interactions among members rather than taking sides or focusing on one member to the exclusion of the rest. The family or couple is the client, not any one individual. Also be careful not to let your group or family therapist become passive: her job is to act as a teacher and model.

## How Understanding Systems Therapy Can Help You Understand Your Character

Sometimes characters seem to operate in a vacuum. We never see their parents, their bosses, or their friends. If you step back and look at your characters the way a systems therapist would, you'll remember that humans are social animals, constantly influencing and being influenced by other people. Remember the mobile over the baby's bed? Look at the way the lives of your characters are intertwined and how each character's actions create ripples in the other characters' lives. When the main character in the film *Cool Hand Luke* is sent to a prison camp for drunkenly cutting the heads off parking meters, he isn't in prison alone. His tenacity, sense of humor, and irrepressible independence inspire the other prisoners, whose enthusiasm in turn feeds his determination to beat the system. The prison guards are also influenced by Luke's antics, which force them to work harder and harder to beat Luke down. In other words, each character's choices are influenced by the choices of those around him.

A systems therapist also knows that people are always going to try to maintain homeostasis; that is, they are going to try to make sure the world continues to operate the way they think it should. If your main character sees himself as a kind person, he is going to struggle to "prove" that he is kind, even if someone else points out evidence of how badly he is treating others. Likewise, if your villain sees herself as powerful, she is going to make moves that will allow her to continue to feel that way about herself.

---

**Q & A**

**Q:** My main character is trying to work through why she's always choosing men who hurt her. She tells her psychologist that her first boyfriend hit her, but only once, and it doesn't count because she taunted him to do it. How would a psychiatrist/psychologist respond?

---

**A:** The therapist's approach will depend on his orientation and how long he's been seeing your main character. If your character and her therapist have a pretty good relationship, he might just ask what compelled her to taunt her boyfriend in the first place: "Why do you think you were trying to get him to hit you?"

If the therapist was psychodynamic, he might also make interpretations like, "I wonder if you believe you deserve to be hit" or "It's almost as if you believe all romantic relationships involve violence and you were trying to get him to conform to your expectations."

At some point, the therapist might ask your character, "How did you feel when he did it?" Relieved? Disgusted? Angry? Depressed? Something else?

The therapist probably wouldn't focus on piecing out whether it was abuse—that could lead to an argument that serves no purpose. *Without blaming the client*, he'd be concerned about how and why the client was trying to elicit abuse from her boyfriend. Did she think abuse was inevitable and she was trying to get it over with? Had she done something she believed deserved punishment?

At some point she's likely to ask, "Was it still abuse because I taunted him until he hit me?" Many therapists would respond with something like, "It's never okay for a partner to hit another partner, and he shouldn't have hit you even if you did taunt him."

The therapist might also point out that there are lots of kinds of abuse, and go over a handout that describes types of abuse. Your character might then point out other things the same boyfriend had done, and she and the therapist could talk about any other ways he was abusive.

## ORIENTATION 5. BIOLOGICAL THERAPIES

### *Core Principles*

Biological approaches emphasize genetics and biology. Unlike other approaches, which are practiced by all types of therapists, psychiatrists specialize in biological treatments. That means that in most U.S. states, only a psychiatrist or another medical doctor can prescribe psychiatric medications.

## *In Therapy*

Some psychiatrists provide therapy in addition to handling medications, but many stay busy enough just prescribing. In the latter situation, the patient sees both the psychiatrist and a separate therapist. The patient is usually responsible for keeping each professional up-to-date on how the other is helping. Direct communication between professionals requires the patient to sign release forms for each.

The first session with a psychiatrist is usually between an hour and an hour and a half long. During that time, the psychiatrist gathers the same kind of information any other therapist would, with extra emphasis on medical history and problems. Psychiatrists who provide therapy in addition to monitoring medications, use one of the orientations above for the therapy itself, and sessions run about fifty minutes. If the psychiatrist is primarily handling medications, however, as is the case when a patient has a separate psychotherapist, regular medication checkup sessions are typically about fifteen minutes long.

Since different brain chemicals do different things, a good psychiatrist can identify which brain chemicals are functioning incorrectly by listening to the patient's symptoms. Depression, for example, is associated with inadequate levels of serotonin and norepinephrine, while psychosis is associated with abnormally elevated dopamine levels. Since there are numerous medications available to treat each of these conditions, and because each one affects the brain in a slightly different way, there may be some trial and error in finding the best fit for each patient. As noted above, psychiatrists therefore schedule regular checkup appointments until the medications have stabilized the condition. Psychiatrists also take medication side effects under consideration based on individual patient characteristics. For example, a depressed person who is having trouble eating enough to maintain a healthy weight might be prescribed a different medication than someone who regularly overeats. Finally, the psychiatrist must balance the risks of any medication, including potential side effects, with the potential benefits.

Remember, medications treat the biochemical aspect of the problem. They can't improve a client's coping mechanisms or help him figure out how to get out of an abusive relationship. They can, however, improve the client's ability to function enough that he is *able* to improve his coping mechanisms or better work on his problems.

### *When Your Therapist Should Refer to a Psychiatrist*

Not every client who visits a therapist for problems with depression is referred to a psychiatrist for medication. Instead, therapists estimate how much brain chemistry and biology are contributing to a problem based on things like family history and symptoms; only if those things seem to be a significant factor do they refer.

For example, if a client comes in for anxiety and that client's mother, sister, brother, and aunt all have problems with anxiety, there's a good chance the problem is at least partly biochemical. If they've all been helped by a drug like Paxil, there's a good chance the client would benefit from Paxil, too. Likewise, if your client is so sick that he can't benefit from therapy, a medication can help him improve enough to really start working on his problem.

We'll look more carefully at medications and other biomedical treatments such as electroconvulsive therapy (ECT) and innovative surgical implants in Chapter 11.

## MIXING IT UP: THE INTEGRATIVE APPROACH

Few modern therapists are purists. Instead, most therapists mix and match therapies and techniques based on how they understand the world and their perception of what the client needs. As a result, they are considered "integrative" or "eclectic" therapists. Integrative therapists appreciate that problems are not caused only by the past, or by thoughts, or by interactions among family members. They recognize that every human being is influenced by biology, social environment, *and* psychological factors.

Don't worry about whether your therapist consistently sounds psychodynamic enough. These days, a therapist who thinks psychodynamically may still use cognitive-behavioral techniques.

Clients sometimes wonder how to pick the type of therapist to see, but the most important factor in whether therapy is effective is that the therapist-client relationship is a positive one.

## GROUP THERAPY

Group therapy is run by one or two therapists and may be used, for example, to educate clients, help them develop better social skills, validate each other's experiences, work on interpersonal issues, or provide support. Therapy groups usually include five to eight clients, though educational groups may be larger.

Many people enter group therapy believing they are the only ones experiencing particular problems. By sharing and listening, they learn that they are not alone. Sooner or later, every member of a therapy group also plays out his or her problem in front of the group, giving the group opportunities to provide feedback.

A lot of fictional groups focus on the supportive aspect of group therapy, with writers portraying them as maudlin and pathetic. In real life groups are usually tenser and more contentious because group members tend to confront each other, sometimes without tact, and dish out advice that isn't always helpful or wanted. You can also make your fictional group more interesting and authentic if you show your character doing the very thing that's causing him problems and the other group members reacting to it.

The therapist's (or co-therapists') role in the group is facilitator, and as a facilitator she has two basic functions. First, she's a technical expert who helps to shape group norms, which are expectations about things like how to indicate one wants to speak and how to phrase feedback to other group members. Second, she models appropriate behavior within the group. When two therapists work together, a female-male pair is ideal because group members experience them as mother- and father-type figures. This helps group members act out behaviors they learned in their families of origin.

Early in the life of a group, members wonder how they'll benefit or question their places or roles in the group. Over time, they begin to vie for positioning on the pecking order, usually by judging and criticizing each other and the therapist. Eventually, however, conflict evolves into cohesiveness, with group members bonding and trusting each other enough to talk about their concerns.

# 3
# The Therapist's Profession
## *Degrees, Training, and Ethics*

In this chapter, we're going to talk about choosing the best degree for your therapist character, the kind of training he'll have gotten to achieve that degree, and the ethics he must follow when he begins to practice. Just as you wouldn't want a pediatrician doing an orthodontist's job of straightening teeth, you don't want your social worker doing a psychiatrist's job of prescribing medications!

## PSYCHOTHERAPY DEGREES FOR YOUR CHARACTERS

Psychiatrists, psychologists, counselors, and social workers are all trained to do slightly different jobs, but there's a lot of overlap. Though some universities award social work degrees at the bachelor's level, most psychotherapists have at least a master's degree, and many have a doctorate. Regardless of degree, if your therapist is legit, he should be either licensed or practicing under a supervisor who is licensed.

## PSYCHIATRIST (MD)

Psychiatrists are, first and foremost, medical doctors. Just as a cardiologist is a physician who specializes in heart health and a pediatrician is a physician who specializes in young people's health, a psychiatrist is a physician who specializes in mental health.

This training in medicine is what makes psychiatrists unique among psychological professionals. With the exception of a few specially-licensed psychologists in the state of New Mexico, they are the only ones who can prescribe medication. While some psychiatrists enjoy doing therapy, others primarily prescribe. Therefore, it's entirely possible for your character to be seeing both a psychiatrist and another type of counselor, such as a psychologist.

Oftentimes, psychiatrists use medications "off-label." In other words, the FDA has not approved the medication for a particular problem, but the psychiatrist still prescribes it. Off-label use is typically based on experience, current research, and colloquial knowledge. For example, a stimulant like Adderall, which is typically used to treat ADHD, may be used in conjunction with an antidepressant to help with treatment-resistant depression. To stay up-to-date on the ever-changing world of psychotropic medications, be sure your character reads journal articles, attends professional conferences, and takes continuing education courses.

Writers often make their clinicians psychiatrists because they believe that psychiatrists are at the top of the psychological food chain; in fact, psychologists have at least as much training in therapy. If your character doesn't need to prescribe medications, consider using a type of therapist other than a psychiatrist.

The psychiatrist profession is a good choice for characters who need expertise on brain and body chemistry, for example because you want them to be able to write prescriptions or perform electroconvulsive therapy. It was important, for example, for Jack Nicholson's doctor to be a psychiatrist in *As Good As It Gets* since the character is prescribed medication.

## PSYCHOLOGIST (PHD OR PSYD)

Psychologists can be broken into two main groups: research psychologists and applied psychologists. Research psychologists are *not* trained to do therapy. Many of them teach at a college or university, in addition to doing research.

Applied psychologists have one of two degrees—a Doctorate in the Philosophy of Psychology (PhD, established in 1949), or a Doctorate in Psychology (PsyD, established in 1973).

PhDs and PsyDs are either clinical or counseling psychologists. (Even forensic psychologists graduate from a clinical or counseling program.) The clinical model of psychology assumes that people who need treatment are sick in some way, so clinical psychologists are trained to treat severe disorders—things like schizophrenia, dissociative identity disorder, and bipolar disorder. Counseling psychologists are trained to work with "everyday life" issues like career and relationship problems. As a result, they believe that problems are not necessarily sicknesses. If your character is working in a hospital or another setting where the patients have more extreme disorders, give him a clinical degree; if he's focusing on things like marriage or career therapy, give him a counseling degree. If he's in private practice, you can decide based on how extreme your client character's problems are. In the film *Mr. and Mrs. Smith*, for example, the hero and heroine see a therapist for marital problems. A counseling psychologist would be a good choice for that situation.

Most psychologists talk about their degrees by saying things like "I got my PhD in counseling psychology from _____ University" or "My PsyD is in clinical psychology." Psychologists spend a lot of time learning about psychological assessment, so if your character is being given an IQ test

## PSYCHIATRISTS VS. PSYCHOLOGISTS

Writers often confuse psychiatrists with psychologists, so here's a quick cheat sheet to help you out!

|  | Psychiatrist | Psychologist |
|---|---|---|
| **Degree** | MD, sometimes also a PhD | PhD or PsyD |
| **Schooling** | After the MD, four years in psychiatric residency | Five to seven years to complete the doctorate; some pursue additional post-doctoral training |
| **Prescription Privileges** | Yes | No |
| **Emphasis on Therapy** | Prescribe and evaluate medications, sometimes do therapy | Focus on psychotherapy |

like the Wechsler Adult Intelligence Scale (WAIS), a personality test like the Minnesota Multiphasic Personality Inventory (MMPI), or a projective test like the Rorschach inkblots, a psychologist should probably be the one doing the testing.

Though most of the principles in this book apply to all forms of psychotherapists, psychologists are the "default" practitioner. Unless I state otherwise, I'm writing with psychologists in mind.

## PROFESSIONAL COUNSELORS (USUALLY MA, MS) AND SOCIAL WORKERS (MSW IS MOST COMMON)

Most people pursuing an advanced degree in psychology get a master's degree first. Due to the time and expense required to get a doctorate, many stop at the master's level. Those who go on to a doctorate do so because the doctorate provides them additional specialized training, increased prestige, better academic positions, and in some settings, more power. If your therapist supervises other therapists or does a lot of psychological testing, you'll probably want to make him a psychologist. If he works in a primary or secondary education school, a college, or a social service agency, consider using a master's-level practitioner. Counselors and social workers in private practice may do work that is virtually indistinguishable from that of psychologists; however, they often have additional certifications in niches like marriage and family therapy (MFT), sex therapy, alcohol and drug counseling, or hypnotherapy.

Social workers in particular are well-versed in helping people function better in the community. If your client character has a problem that makes it hard for her to keep her day-to-day life organized, get or hold jobs, take her medications, or get herself to regular group and individual therapy sessions, a social worker can help her get and stay on track. Social workers also do things like provide child welfare assessments to law enforcement agencies, advocate for women and children trying to escape domestic violence situations, and work with clients in the prison system.

### THERAPIST TRAINING

If you're going to write about a therapist trainee, talk with someone who's currently going through training in an accredited program. You can find accredited programs and their contact information in the book *Graduate Study in Psychology*, by the American Psychological Association. Call the main number and ask if the school has contact information for students who would be willing to talk about the program with you.

In addition to taking classes, your therapist character may have been required to do some or all of the following:

- *Practice placements.* For all intents and purposes, practice placements are carefully supervised apprenticeships, which makes them an indispensible part of therapist training. Practice placements can be in any setting that provides psychological services, including Veterans' Administrations, hospitals, community mental health centers, college counseling centers, domestic violence centers, military bases, prisons, crisis centers, and private practices.

- *Teaching and/or research.* In some programs, students teach or help teach undergraduate courses. In others, especially in PhD programs, students are expected to do research, both as part of their training and to help pay for their schooling.

- *Thesis or dissertation.* To graduate, each student must produce a paper that provides a "unique contribution to the field of psychology." The paper is called a "thesis" for master's-level students and a "dissertation" for doctoral students. When the paper is done, the student defends it in front of a committee. Doctoral students sometimes get everything done but their dissertation, leaving them "All But Dissertation" or "ABD." While most students *do* eventually finish their dissertations, those who don't never receive the degrees they were pursuing, which means they can't get licensed or practice independently as doctors.

Though most programs do *not* require their students to get therapy as part of their training, some classes may begin to *feel* like therapy to those taking them.

## ETHICS

Every type of therapist is bound by the ethical code of a governing association—the American Psychological Association, for example, governs psychologists—as well as by the laws set forth by each state's psychology board. Because most writers aren't familiar with these codes and laws, they create therapists who blithely violate them without consequences.

The ethics of psychology are complicated, even for the people who are bound by them. In some cases, the therapist must choose between a client's well-being and the law. For example, imagine that a woman and her children are regularly beaten by her spouse. If the woman believes her husband will eventually kill her or her children, and she's unable to get the help she needs from the law, she might take her children and flee. Legally, this is called kidnapping, and the woman's therapist can be subpoenaed and asked under oath where she went. The therapist must then decide whether to divulge this information and thereby put the client and the children in danger, or refuse to answer, risk perjuring himself, and face the possibility that he'll end up in jail. (Therapists who deal regularly with domestic violence avoid this dilemma by asking clients not to tell them where they are going.)

## CONFIDENTIALITY

Everything that's said in the client-therapist relationship is confidential unless the client is in immediate danger of harming herself or someone else or reports that a child or elder is being abused. Then the therapist is obligated to protect whoever is in danger.

Though what happens in therapy sessions is confidential, therapy records can be subpoenaed by a court. Child custody battles are particularly likely to elicit such requests. Most therapists won't hand over notes just because they've been subpoenaed, even if the client has agreed to release the files, and even if there isn't anything that can be used against the client in the file.

First, the therapist offers to write a summary of some kind. Though he does have to be honest and make the summary accurate, it's much easier to gloss over things that could hurt a client in a summary. If the court continues to insist the files be handed over, the therapist encourages the court to request a specific *part* of the file. Once in a while, the attorney or judge is insistent, and the therapist has to make a choice: does he want to hand over the notes, or does he want to go to jail?

Though it's unethical, some therapists do keep two sets of notes—the official notes and personal, private notes that are theirs alone. Other therapists write vague or illegible notes, assuming that if the files are ever requested by another party, that party will need the notes translated, and the therapist can translate broadly. Finally, many therapists keep information that might be used against a client in their heads. The types of things in the mental file are usually few and never the presenting problem or a major issue. For example, a therapist seeing a client in an Employee Assistance Program might decide not to include notes on significant drug use during college, a colorful sexual history, or a client's sexual orientation if those things are not immediately relevant to the presenting problem.

One other group has the right to know what goes on during sessions: the parents of minors. The problem with this setup, of course, is that the child is usually in therapy either because the parents don't know how else to help or because the parents *are* the problem. To maintain the child's confidentiality, the therapist and parent may agree that, for example, the child's sessions are private unless she says she is being abused, is going to hurt someone or is a danger to herself, or is using drugs. If the child is in the room during the discussion, she knows exactly what the boundaries are.

## DUTY TO WARN AND THE TARASOFF RULE

The Tarasoff Rule says that if a client "poses a serious danger of violence to others," the therapist has a *duty to warn* (some prefer the term *duty to protect*) the potential victim if he or she is identifiable. In theory, the therapist has done his duty if he notifies the police, notifies the potential victim, and/or has the client committed. However, there's a lot of gray area around Tarasoff. In 2004, a therapist committed a dangerous client who, after he was discharged, killed another man and then himself. The court ruled that both the therapist and the hospital were liable for committing the man without *also* warning the identified victim (*Ewing v. Goldstein*, 2004).

Not all states uphold the Tarasoff Rule. To determine whether Tarasoff or some variation thereof is used in a particular state, enter the state name and the term "Tarasoff Rule" into your favorite search engine.

## DUAL OR MULTIPLE RELATIONSHIPS

A therapist is only allowed to have one relationship with her client—the therapy relationship. She cannot also be her client's friend, relative, teacher, student, or exercise buddy. Nor can she be a friend, relative, teacher, student, or exercise buddy to someone who's very close to her client. She can, however, see clients who know each other, as long as that doesn't interfere with her ability to be objective about each individual's treatment.

When the therapist in the movie *Prime* realizes that her client is also her son's serious girlfriend Rafi, she's not sure what to do and sees Rafi for several more sessions. A real therapist would know right away that a dual relationship is unacceptable and would help Rafi find a new therapist.

---

### DON'T LET THIS HAPPEN TO YOU!

In Nate Kenyon's novel *The Reach*, therapist-in-training Jess Chambers is handpicked by a professor to work with Sarah, a little girl who has been institutionalized with schizophrenia. Strangely, Jess has no other patients, practices without direct clinical supervision, and spends a lot of time sitting around taking notes on Sarah while Sarah does nothing. What a way to make Sarah feel like an object! Worse, Jess seems to have neither personal nor professional boundaries. She spends huge blocks of her free time with Sarah and gives her inappropriate personal gifts, like a teddy bear that once belonged to her.

In reality, someone like Jess would see a variety of patients and meet regularly with a supervisor. She absolutely would not be allowed to spend her free time with a patient or bring her gifts. In the story, Jess's behavior is supposed to be sweet, but to someone trained in psychology, it looks obsessive and a little creepy.

---

## PERSONAL PROBLEMS

Psychologists shouldn't let personal problems or worries interfere with their work. If the therapist is going through a divorce, for example, and a new client reminds him so strongly of his soon-to-be-ex wife that he can't treat her objectively, he should first seek supervision to help him work through his own issues. If that doesn't resolve the problem, he should transfer the client to someone who can be objective.

## SEX

Ethical therapists—including sex therapists—neither have sex with their clients nor watch their clients having sex. They talk frankly about sex, but that's all. Carefree disregard for this particular ethical standard abounds in fiction. For example, in the movie *Tin Cup*, Roy McAvoy introduces his girlfriend, Molly Griswold, to his friends. "Meet Dr. Griswold," he says. "This is Molly. She's my shrink." Molly cheerfully adds, "Ex-shrink. We're sleeping together now, so I can't be his therapist."

It's even unethical for a therapist to discontinue therapy so he can date or have sex with a former client. Technically, a psychologist can date a client he hasn't seen in therapy for at least two years, but that is *very* much frowned upon. A therapist also doesn't conduct therapy with someone he previously was involved with, nor can he become sexually or romantically involved with the close friend or family member of a client.

Why so many rules about dual relationships and sex? Well, clients with relationship or sexual issues, especially those related to abuse, are least likely to recognize inappropriate behavior from a therapist. They are also the most likely to pursue an inappropriate relationship with the therapist. Therefore, a therapist who engages in sexual activity with a client is taking advantage of problems he is only privy to *because* he's the therapist. Afterward, clients feel used, guilty, ashamed, angry, and depressed. Over 10 percent are hospitalized as a result, and even more consider suicide. Post-traumatic stress disorder is common, just as it is in rape survivors.

A therapist's role is to be an objective authority, and nobody can provide objective observations and suggestions to someone in whom he's personally interested. Sexual interest destroys the therapist's ability to do therapy. There is also a huge power differential because the therapist doesn't (or shouldn't) reveal many personal details about himself in therapy, while the client shares a great deal of intimate information.

## VIOLATIONS OF THE ETHICS CODE

Since many ethical code violations are also violations of the laws set down by state psychology boards and the courts, punishments can include legal repercussions. According to the American Psychological Association, "compliance with or violation of the Ethics Code may be admissible as evidence in some legal proceedings." Depending on the type and severity of the offense, the therapist's license to practice can be suspended or revoked, or he might find himself embroiled in a legal case that leads to fines and/or incarceration.

## THE ETHICS OF DUAL RELATIONSHIPS IN THE SOPRANOS

The psychological and psychiatric communities have lauded the HBO series *The Sopranos*, which ran from 1999–2007, as an excellent representation of real therapy. In the series, Tony Soprano regularly visits Dr. Jennifer Melfi, a psychiatrist who practices psychodynamic therapy. Unlike most fictional female therapists, Dr. Melfi avoids developing a dual relationship with Tony, despite his feelings for her. There are times when she wants to, but she doesn't.

For example, during season three, Dr. Melfi is brutally raped, and she struggles with the knowledge that if she would only ask him, Tony would kill her attacker. She resists, a decision that frustrated many fans. But Dr. Melfi is a principled practitioner, and asking Tony to kill someone would be criminal. It would also have been an exploitation of his feelings for her and thus the end of their therapeutic relationship.

# 4
# Behind Closed Doors
*How Real Therapy Sessions Work*

M any writers create characters who have no desire to go to therapy, yet show up religiously every week. That's just not realistic. According to the oft-quoted 1999 *Surgeon General's Report on Mental Health*, about 80 percent of people with diagnosable problems avoid going to therapy. Most often, what's holding them back is fear. People are afraid:

- of change
- of what they'll learn about themselves
- of what the therapist will do to them as part of treatment
- that seeking therapy means they're crazy or weak
- that others will find out and think poorly of them for needing help
- that therapy is always a long-term commitment
- that the therapist will uncover some hidden or forgotten part of their past they'd prefer not be revealed
- that the therapist will judge them.

As for those who do go to therapy, many leave before they resolve their problems. Sometimes the client's financial situation changes and money becomes a problem. Sometimes the client simply doesn't click with the therapist. And sometimes people terminate therapy prematurely for psychological reasons. For example:

- Some clients report that they're suddenly, miraculously cured of the problems for which they entered therapy. Psychodynamic therapists in particular view this "getting better" as a defense mechanism called a "flight into health." The sudden improvement is a subconscious attempt to avoid the anxiety and discomfort of additional self-disclosure and exposure to the problem.

- Feeling stuck can be a normal part of dealing with a problem, but some clients are impatient. When change doesn't happen immediately, they quit rather than work on what's keeping them stuck.

- Therapists sometimes point out things that are difficult to hear. If they hit too close to home, some clients will begin to avoid sessions to shield themselves from the pain.

- Therapy can be hard—and sometimes uncomfortable—work. Sometimes it feels easier to live with the problem than to make meaningful changes in how one approaches life.

Many clients enter therapy hoping—even expecting—the therapist to provide a treatment that will miraculously eradicate the problem. What they may be disconcerted to learn is that psychotherapy, like physical therapy, can be difficult and even painful *work*. All clients reach a point where they have to decide to either leave their comfort zones and plow through the problems, or turn their backs on any new insights and choose to live with things the way they are. Many people would rather maintain an unpleasant status quo than shake things up and deal with all the uncertainty and discomfort that comes with the unknown.

Imagine, for example, that Jack is tired of his mother always demanding that Jack spend the holidays with her. Maybe Jack and his mother don't get along very well, and Jack would really rather spend his holidays with friends. What Jack comes into therapy *hoping* is that the therapist will tell him how to painlessly make his mother and her demands evaporate.

What the therapist would actually do, however, is suggest that Jack tell his mother that he can't or won't be joining her for Thanksgiving this year. That sounds simple enough, but it isn't, because people like Jack's mother inevitably know how to create consequences that wear the client down and make him feel bad. The therapist would work with Jack on why Jack feels so bad when his mother responds with anger, or sadness, or a guilt trip; and on how to deal with those bad feelings when they arise.

However, clients like Jack often decide that it's less painful to maintain the status quo and endure unhappy holidays than to upset the parent figure and deal with the consequences. In other words, it's easier for many people to deal with the known pain of an unpleasant circumstance than the unknown (but possibly catastrophic) results of standing up to the person in question.

What all of this means is that your character needs a truly compelling reason to start and continue therapy; otherwise, he has no incentive to go in the first place, or to talk once he's there.

By the time most people step into the therapist's office, they're at the end of their proverbial ropes. They don't know what else to do or who else to turn to, but they do know they want things to change. Make sure your character is in a similar situation. If you want him to stick with therapy when things get tough, make the stakes high enough that he *has* to change, or else.

In the film *Analyze This*, for example, mob boss Vitti has been having crippling panic attacks. He certainly doesn't want to go to therapy, but failing to get his anxiety under control contributes to additional problems like erectile dysfunction—something Vitti definitely doesn't want to continue! Add that to the fact that Vitti can't stay in control (and may have trouble staying alive) if he doesn't get treatment, and you have a fantastic *or else* situation.

You can also have your character enter therapy because someone else compels him to go: the court system, an employer, a parent, or a significant other. Someone who's ordered into therapy is usually resistant to treatment, but he too has something he wants—to be done with therapy. The therapist may point out that doing the work he's been sent to do will get him out more quickly, and sometimes that's enough impetus for the client to buckle down and deal with the problem. Since a client who's been forced into therapy must often complete a particular number of sessions and be able to parrot back the "right" responses to a particular scenario, real change may or may not actually take place. As for people who absolutely don't want to deal with therapy, they simply won't show up, regardless of the consequences.

## THE INTAKE

The first session with a potential client is called an intake interview or, more often, just an intake. Some therapists like the client to talk about whatever comes to mind, while others have a list of questions they like to ask. Regardless, every therapist has two goals during an intake: to gather information about the problem and to establish rapport and help the client feel accepted and understood.

Most therapists take notes during the intake. They may or may not take notes during regular therapy sessions. Fictional therapists resort to note-taking when the author doesn't know what else to have them say or do. Try to write your therapy sessions without a notepad in your therapist's lap. That will force your therapist to interact more genuinely with her client.

## CLIENT CONFIDENTIALITY

Before the intake begins, the therapist explains the limits of confidentiality. She might say something like "Before we get started, I want to let you know that everything we talk about is confidential. The only exception is if you tell me that you're going to hurt or kill yourself or someone else or that you know of a child or elder who's being abused." If someone is in real, immediate danger, the therapist must find a way to intervene. For example, she can hospitalize a suicidal or homicidal client or call Children's Services to look into child abuse allegations. We'll look more carefully at emergency situations in Chapter 12.

Assuming that the client is self-referred rather than, say, court-referred, and no one is in immediate danger, the therapist does *not* have to report a drug habit, theft, or other types of illegal or unethical behavior.

Though clients rarely ask spontaneous questions about confidentiality, the therapist watches for discomfort and reassures the client if necessary.

## THE PRESENTING PROBLEM

The problem that brought the client into therapy is the "presenting problem." If the client enters therapy because of a suicide attempt, then "suicidality" is the presenting problem. If someone is depressed because of relationship problems, the relationships issues are the presenting problem. A client can have more than one presenting problem, but one is usually more pressing than the others.

Most people are up front about their problems, but a few people come into therapy with a "cover" problem. They're afraid or embarrassed to talk about their real concerns, so they test the therapist with a more benign problem, or try to shock her with an outrageous story. The title character in *Good Will Hunting* takes the latter approach with multiple therapists, scaring them off before they can get to know him. When he finally begins to trust the therapist who gets through to him, he avoids the topic of abuse in his childhood by focusing on other topics.

Sometimes, the presenting problem is just one piece of a larger pile of issues. A client might enter therapy because he can't stand to be alone when his roommates are away. Here the presenting problem is anxiety about being alone. As time goes by, however, the therapist might learn that the client is also dealing with an overbearing boss, depression, and difficulty coming to terms with the fact that he's gay—enough to make anyone anxious!

## Problem Clarification and Background

Based on the information the client provides early in the session, the therapist decides what additional information she needs about both the problem and the client's life. The questions she asks help her "rule in" and "rule out" different diagnoses.

For example, if the client is reporting sadness, the therapist asks about and mentally checks off additional symptoms like changes in appetite, low energy, poor self-esteem, and feelings of guilt to make sure depression is the appropriate diagnosis.

If the therapist hasn't been able to fully rule out certain conditions, she'll make a note in her intake report to find out more later. Therefore, it's not unusual for the preliminary diagnosis to be followed by one or two conditions to "rule out."

---

### Intake Questions

The therapist's approach to intake will vary with his orientation, the clinical setting, and the client, but here are some preliminary questions your fictional therapist might ask your character as he gathers information. If you're actually writing about an intake interview, be sure your therapist follows up on each question and doesn't just jump from one to the next in a disjointed way. Also be sure that the conversation is logical and natural. A therapist shouldn't ask someone with career concerns about his romantic history, for example, unless it seems directly relevant.

#### *Presenting problem*
- What brings you in today? *or* Where shall we start?

---

- What happened that's brought you in *now* (rather than last week/last month/next week/next month)?

## Problem history and clarification

- How long has this been a problem? How often is it a problem?
- How is the problem affecting your life?
- What makes the problem better? Worse?
- What changes would help you most?
- What types of solutions have you tried? Have they worked?

## Gathering information about medical and psychiatric history

- Have you ever been to therapy before? Was it helpful? In what way?
- Have you ever been hospitalized? Attempted suicide?
- Do you take any medications?
- Do you have any medical conditions?
- When was the last time you used alcohol? Drugs? (Note that a smart therapist never asks "*Do you* use drugs?" but "*When* was the last time?")

## Relationships and relationship history

- How did you get along with the other people in your family?
- Did you ever see violence in your family? What happened? How often? How did it affect you?
- Have you ever been married? Are you involved in a romantic relationship? How would you describe your marriage/relationship?
- Do you have any children? How do you get along with them?
- Do you have close friends you can confide in about personal matters?
- How has your [presenting problem] affected your relationships with others?

*School, work, and recreation*
- Do you go to school or take any classes? Do you work?
- Did you miss or skip any classes/days of work in the last week? How come?
- Does your [presenting problem] cause problems at school/work? Like what?
- How much has your [presenting problem] affected your participation in hobbies?
- What have you done for fun over the last week?

## HELPING CLIENTS OPEN UP IN ANY SESSION

Blogger Jeff Atwood offers an excellent description of expertise: "Being an expert isn't telling other people what you know. It's understanding what questions to ask, and flexibly applying your knowledge to the specific situation at hand." In other words, effective experts spend more time asking questions and making sure they understand the responses than telling people what to do. If you can get a handle on this concept—that therapists are more inquisitive than they are prescriptive—your fictional therapy sessions will be leaps and bounds ahead of most people's.

If you want a feel for what a good therapy session looks like, watch a skillful television journalist interview a celebrity. Diane Sawyer is a master at balancing fantastic information-gathering questions with empathy and genuine interest. She is willing to wait while the interviewee thinks through an answer and avoids interrupting while the interviewee is talking. The interviewee has the floor. Sawyer is as comfortable with tears as she is with laughter, and she doesn't shy away from uncomfortable topics.

Ideally, therapists create a safe, supportive environment in which clients can share difficult or overwhelming emotions and experiences. They put themselves in their clients' shoes and try to appreciate their points of view. Further, a good therapist is herself; she doesn't play a role or act phony. She's nonjudgmental and respectful of the client and treats him with dignity and acceptance.

> ## The Ineffective Therapist
>
> What if you don't want to create an evil therapist, just an ineffective one? The trick is to have him fail—but not *too* miserably—at building an empathic relationship with his clients. Have him deny the seriousness of a problem, offer empty reassurance, dish out trite advice, or rely on some pat answer or treatment. Mark Sicherman's therapist character makes these mistakes in *Levels of Consciousness*, leaving the client frustrated with her "stupid, useless therapist who keeps telling her if she could only see how beautiful she was, she wouldn't do this to herself."
>
> For example, your ineffective therapist can say things like:
>
> - I'm sure it will all work out.
> - I know exactly what that's like.
> - You should try harder to see his point of view.
> - You don't really feel that way, do you?
> - Why can't you get along with her?
> - I bet you could deal with that if you really wanted to.
> - If you'd only _____, you'd get better.
> - Clearly you have a problem with _____.
>
> You can also have an ineffective therapist talk too much about himself, talk over the client's head, or convey verbally or nonverbally that he thinks the client should be wowed by his expertise. Show him needing too much personal validation: have him make the therapy session at least partly about him, when the focus should be completely on the client.

## Asking Questions and Active Listening

In the short story *The Letter*, Howard A. Losness's character mockingly says that "A good psychologist always turns a patient's question back to him." The implication is that therapists play mind games. In reality, many therapists *will* answer a direct question. When a question is returned to the client, it's usually because there isn't a right answer, and the therapist doesn't want to impose her opinions on the client.

Therapists rely on open and closed questions, clarification, paraphrasing, and reflection to double-check their understanding, gather more information, and help clients feel heard.

1.  *Closed* questions are used to get particular pieces of information. They often start with words like *are, do, is, did*, and *can* and can be answered with a few words.

For example:

- Have things been better since we last talked?
- Did you feel sad when that happened?

*Open* questions are more common in therapy than closed questions. They require more explanation, and usually begin with *what, how, why*, and sometimes *could, where*, and *who*.

To start a session, your therapist should use open questions like:

- How have things been since we last talked?
- What would you like to talk about today?
- Where should we begin today?

During the session, he might ask things like:

- Could you tell me more about that?
- Why do you think *x* happened?
- What happened then?
- What feels most scary about this?
- How did you feel when that happened?
- What did you do next?

2.  *Clarification* questions encourage the client to talk more about ambiguous statements, often with an example or illustration. For example, if the client says "So then I got in trouble," the therapist might ask with whom the client got in trouble and what happened. If the client says "I wish I could just get away from it all," the therapist will clarify what that means to the client. Changing departments at work? Taking a vacation? Suicide?

Clarification questions typically start with phrases like:

- Do you mean that _____?

- Could you describe _____?
- Could you give me an example of what you mean by _____?
- How do you feel about _____?

3.  When a therapist *paraphrases*, she translates the content of the client's message into her own words. Rather than parroting the client's words back, she's checking out her understanding, encouraging elaboration, and letting the client know he was heard. Paraphrases can start with phrases like

- It sounds like …
- It seems like …
- What you're saying is …
- What I'm hearing is …
- I have the feeling that …
- You wish that …

4.  *Reflection* emphasizes the emotional part of the client's message, which is often conveyed through nonverbals and vocal cues. Reflections can make clients more aware of their feelings, encourage them to talk about those feelings, and help them feel understood. Reflections may start with the same kinds of sentence stems as paraphrases, but they always include emotion words. For example:

- It sounds like you're angry about _____.
- You're feeling disgusted with _____.
- You're uneasy about _____.
- You're feeling _____ about _____.
- It really shook you up when _____.

Keep in mind that therapy is not a game show—the therapist doesn't get points for always being right. So when she asks questions, she's always ready for the client to say, "No, I actually feel _____" or "Well, that's true, but it's also that _____." Often the therapist learns *more* when the client disagrees with her.

## THE KINDNESS EXPERIMENT

One of the most effective ways to get someone to talk is to express genuine interest, kindness, and concern. I have my students do an assignment I call The Kindness Experiment to help them see how altering their behavior can change others' behaviors. Grumpy and unhappy people are often the most responsive because they're used to people responding poorly to them.

Here's the assignment:

> Spend at least one whole day going out of your way to consciously treat other people as well as you possibly can. Assume that everyone has a reason for the things they do, even if they're rude to you or cut you off in traffic. For example, assume they're having a bad day, or that someone broke up with them, or that they're late for work.

> Approach everyone as if you expect to be treated well in return, no matter how silly you feel. Go out of your way to smile at strangers on the elevator, hold doors for other people, let people out in front of you in traffic, greet cashiers in stores with genuine warmth, and just all around be as courteous, kind, and polite as you possibly can, in spite of how anyone treats you. If you're normally kind, kick it up a notch. (Note that being kind doesn't mean you put up with people mistreating you—it just means being kind and respectful in your approach, no matter what the situation.) If you make a mistake, just set it aside and go back to being as courteous and kind as you can.

> Now, write about your thoughts, feelings, and behavior before, during, and after your actions, as well as the reactions of the people around you. What did you learn about how your expectations affect others' behaviors? How did people respond differently to you than they normally do? Did anything surprising happen? Will this affect how you behave in the future?

I won't ruin the assignment by telling you what will happen if you do it, but I have had many students tell me it really impacted their understanding of how their behavior affects others.

## Therapist Impressions

Words make up 7 percent of communication. Paralanguage (vocal tone and inflection) makes up 38 percent of communication, and nonverbals (body language) make up the other 55 percent. Therapists are trained to pay particular attention to all aspects of communication, not just the words. They are also trained to listen "between the lines."

There's a persistent myth that therapists are mind-readers, but in reality they've just learned how important paralanguage and nonverbals are, so they pay close attention and trust their impressions. In everyday conversation, we don't normally point out that someone seems nervous because he's wringing his hands. Since gestures like that are often unconscious, the therapist seems particularly astute when she asks about them. Note that the therapist isn't necessarily making an interpretation when she remarks on body language; rather, she's pointing it out and then waiting for the *client's* interpretation.

Someone who comes into therapy wearing torn blue jeans and a ball cap and who mumbles and avoids eye contact is sending a completely different message than someone who comes in wearing a jacket and tie and grills the therapist on her training and education. Someone who arrives half an hour early for his appointment and becomes agitated if he's not seen immediately also sends a different message than someone who arrives half an hour late and seems disappointed when the therapist is still willing to see him for the time that's left.

Rather than thinking "that client who always comes late is a jerk" and forgetting about it, the therapist wonders what the behavior *means*—that is, what message is the client sending with it? And she doesn't just "analyze" and assume. She will remark upon it to the client. For example, "I notice that you've been coming to sessions later and later each week" or "I wonder if it's harder for you to come since we've started talking about your miscarriage?"

Throughout training, therapists watch videos of themselves practicing therapy so they can become more aware of their own habits, mannerisms, and nonverbal messages, and learn how to adapt them if necessary. They may also be asked to consider their personal "stimulus value." In other words, they learn how other people see them and what assumptions or projections people are likely to make. Part of this is becoming aware of how clothing, hair, makeup, and other appearance-based choices can affect how others see you.

## WHAT MESSAGES ARE YOUR CHARACTERS SENDING?

Imagine spending an afternoon with your main character. What messages is he or she sending through paralanguage and nonverbals? Is the message he or she is trying to send always the message other people receive? Here are just a few examples of the types of things you might want to notice.

- What does your character like to wear? What message is she *trying* to send with that clothing? Is she successful? Do others ever see her as unusual or trying too hard? If your heroine is a leather-wearing badass, for example, what do the people in the local grocery store think of her? Remember, your character may be sending messages she doesn't intend to.

- Does he have any tattoos or piercings? Why did he get those things? What was he hoping to convey to others?

- How does she wear her hair? Why?

- How does he carry himself? For example, does he swagger, slink, or tiptoe through life?

- What are her mannerisms? For example, does she twist her wedding ring, keep a vice grip on her purse, or dangle her shoe from the tips of her toes? What kinds of worries, needs, or hopes is she conveying with her mannerisms?

- What's his vocabulary like? Does he use a lot of slang, rely on intellectual jargon, swear a lot, or use clichés? What's he trying to convey with these speech patterns?

- What is her voice like when she talks? Do others have to lean close to hear her? Does she have an accent? Does she talk in a high, childlike voice or a husky smoker's voice?

- Does he ask questions of the other person or mostly focus on his own interests? Does he pay attention when the other person talks, or does he interrupt or get distracted?

- What is the emotional "flavor" of the afternoon? Is she basically an upbeat person? Or does another word fit her better? For example, she could be cynical, whiny, apprehensive, jittery, nonchalant, unemotional, moody, bad-tempered, gloomy, self-critical, self-pitying, shy, or childlike. How do others react to her attitudes?

- How does he treat other people? Is he sarcastic, rude, exasperated, flirty, overly friendly, pushy, or needy?

- What sorts of information does she share about herself? Is she reticent or secretive? A chronic provider of Too Much Information?

- How does he use technology, and what do those things say about him? Does he use an email signature? What desktop wallpaper does he use on his computer? What's the ring tone on his cell? Will he answer his cell if it rings while he's in the middle of something?

## CLIENT RECORDS

Therapists keep records for a variety of reasons, the most obvious being to track treatment and progress and help the therapist remember pertinent information. If a client is transferred to another therapist (because the client moves, for example, or because the therapist-in-training finishes her practicum year), the notes can help the new therapist get up to speed.

The therapist should document all important information, but interventions around suicidal ideation, anger management, and other situations in which the client may be dangerous to himself or others are particularly important from a legal standpoint. If a client does harm himself or someone else, the therapist is likely—rightfully or wrongfully—to be dragged into court. If the records make it clear that she has fulfilled all of her duties, the lawsuit is unlikely to be successful.

Client records include:

- The initial client contact form, which usually includes very brief notes taken by an office assistant regarding the client's name, age, insurance information, social security number, and sometimes a few words explaining the presenting problem.

- The intake form containing notes taken during the first session.

- The intake summary, which is a formal report reviewing what the therapist learned during the initial interview.

- Treatment plans, which are an explanation of how one is going to treat the presenting problem and any associated problems. As treatment progresses, the therapist and client create additional plans to meet the client's changing needs. Treatment plans are required by insurance companies so they can authorize sessions; therapists who don't take insurance or who have private-pay clients usually don't do treatment plans for those clients—it's just extra paperwork.

- Progress notes, which are summaries of what happens during each session.

Charts may also include:

- Updated treatment plans.

- Phone log. Some therapists incorporate these into the progress notes and may not have a separate phone log.

- Any relevant letters, notes, or other information from other health-care professionals, including physicians and hospitals. These are particularly important if a client is hospitalized for mental health reasons.

- Copies of any disability documentation.

- Client emails and other communications.

- Any psychological tests, results, and write-ups.

## How Much Therapy Is Enough?

The standard therapy "hour" is fifty minutes, and early in the course of treatment the therapist and client typically meet once a week. If the client is in crisis, they might meet twice a week for a short time; as the client's symptoms improve, sessions might move to every other week, once a month, or even longer periods of time between check-ins.

Though early psychodynamic psychotherapy regularly involved exhaustive long-term analysis, the overall duration of modern treatment is often dictated by insurance companies. Better insurance policies will help pay for twenty, thirty, or sometimes even more sessions each year, while more stringent policies require extensive therapist documentation in the form of treatment plans for even a handful of sessions. Some insurance policies don't cover therapy at all.

To keep the number of sessions down and make them affordable, many therapists practice brief intermittent therapy. In other words, rather than trying to fix everything that could possibly be wrong, the therapist sees the client long enough to shore up his coping skills and help him find new ways to deal with the most pressing presenting problems. Though the problem may not be completely resolved by the time the client leaves therapy, he will certainly have more tools to deal with life than he had when he arrived. None of this is to imply that the therapist is pushing the client out of therapy; rather, the client and therapist agree to end treatment when the client feels like his issues have been resolved and he is better able to deal with his problems. Still, he may return weeks, months, or years later to deal with new or similar problems.

Just as insurance companies dictate how many days in the hospital a patient can stay for a physical condition, they also dictate how many days they will pay for care when psychological hospitalization is needed. Insurance companies allot a certain number of days based on the diagnosis the client is given when he is admitted; for example, someone who is displaying psychosis might be allowed to stay for a few more days than someone who is diagnosed with a major depressive disorder.

Some insurance companies dictate how many sessions a client gets with a therapist based on his diagnosis. Someone with a major depressive disorder might get a few more sessions than someone with dysthymia (a more "minor" depression). In these cases, the therapist is typically required to fill out a treatment plan with concrete, behavioral markers that will indicate improvement. If you need to create a treatment plan for your character, check out the Practice Planners book series with Arthur Jongsma.

### WHAT HAPPENS WHEN SOMEONE DOESN'T HAVE INSURANCE?

Some therapy providers, such as community mental health centers, crisis centers, and state psychiatric hospitals, provide services at a much lower cost (usually on a sliding scale based on what the client can pay), or even for free. Because they tend to be inundated, they too focus on stabilizing the client in as few sessions as possible.

Though the people working in these centers strive to provide good care, they are dealing with the most severe problems—their clients are often people who can't even get insurance because their problems are so bad—and for abysmal pay. The lack of funding can make these places dreary, threadbare, and even downright depressing, and it's not unusual for them to be in unsafe parts of town. The burnout rate among staff is extremely high, which leads to lower-quality care for the people who need it most.

# 5

# Disorders and Diagnosis

## *When Does a Problem Become a Disorder?*

In the world of psychology, the line between normal and abnormal is fuzzier than most people think, just as it can be with medical problems. For example, everyone has moles, freckles, and other bumps and marks on their skin, and most of them are perfectly normal. While sometimes lesions are clearly malignant, other times doctors need to do a biopsy to learn whether a particular mark is benign or cancerous. Since psychologists can't do biopsies on mental illnesses, they have to rely on other indicators of abnormality.

Psychology students are often taught that there are four broad categories that can, depending on their severity and context, make therapy a good idea: distress, dysfunction, deviance, and/or dangerousness. Rather than acting as part of a formal assessment or diagnostic process, these four categories are a good starting point for people who are new to understanding why someone might seek therapy.

1.  *Distress* is subjective discomfort or unhappiness. People with phobias, for example, experience debilitating distress when confronted with anything that reminds them of the feared object or situation. In the classic Hitchcock film *Vertigo*, the hero has an incapacitating fear of heights. When his lover climbs a tower to commit suicide, he remains paralyzed and helpless on the ground.

    Sometimes people worry that their distress isn't serious enough to "bother" a therapist with, when the truth is that most therapists are happy to work with anyone who believes therapy might help them feel better. In some cases unhappiness or distress doesn't lead to a formal diagnosis, but rather to something called a V code, which we'll talk about later in this chapter. For example, if a college student is struggling to decide between the major she wants to pursue and the major her parents want her to pursue, she might visit her university's counseling center. If the conflict has been painful and ongoing, she might be diagnosable with something like depression or anxiety. In less intense circumstances, however, the therapist might use a V code (which indicates a basically normal reaction to a given situation) to indicate that she is in therapy to deal with something that's bothering her, but isn't causing enough problems to warrant a *disorder* diagnosis.

2.  *Dysfunction* is not being able to carry out normal day-to-day tasks. Examples of dysfunction include trouble sleeping, holding a job, or maintaining relationships. In the film *Finding Forrester*, Sean Connery's awkward titular character is so anxious he can't leave his apartment, even to get groceries. His fear of doing something embarrassing in front of others makes it impossible for him to live a "normal" life.

3.  *Deviance* refers to thoughts, feelings, or behaviors that are statistically uncommon and/or that differ greatly from accepted social standards, norms, or values. In the movie *The Fisher King*, Robin Williams's character, like many people with schizophrenia, displays deviant behaviors. For example, he runs around his hovel with an aerosol spray shouting at the "little people" to shut up. Note that in the United States people are rarely institutionalized for deviance alone—they have to be dangerous or unable to care for themselves as well.

4.  Dangerousness can be broken down into two categories: danger to self (suicidality) and danger to others (homicidality). In Andre Dubus's novel *The House of Sand and Fog*, recovering alcoholic Kathy tries to escape her depression by repeatedly attempting suicide. To help her as quickly as possible, many therapists would want Kathy to spend a few days in a hospital. You can read more about what her hospital stay might be like in Chapter 12. Meanwhile, in the film *Taxi Driver*, Travis Bickle is consumed by persecutory delusions that end in several murders. Contrary to popular belief, courts rarely find people like Bickle "not guilty by reason of insanity." If one did, Bickle would be committed long-term to a forensic mental institution.

To be considered serious enough to warrant a disorder diagnosis, each of these problems must be *beyond what is considered normal or reasonable given the circumstances*, and they should actually be causing significant problems for the person or society.

# IS IT NORMAL AND REASONABLE? OR IS IT SOMETHING ELSE?

To decide whether a behavior is reasonable or normal, we have to look at the problem's context. If someone close to your character dies, she is likely to cry, sleep too much or too little, lose her appetite, feel "on edge," and get overwhelmed by things that don't normally bother her. Your character can go to therapy if she needs extra support or help, but because grief is an appropriate reaction to loss, it's not a diagnosable *disorder*.

On the other hand, if your character were crying, edgy, sleeping too much and eating too little in the absence of any significant problem or tragedy, the behaviors would be out of proportion to the context and, would most likely cause problems in her life as well. When that's the case, a diagnosable disorder may exist.

Whether your character is dealing with a "normal" problem or a diagnosable disorder, it is possible for her to get well without visiting a therapist. If she gets plenty of support from people who are close to her, if the situation that's causing the problem changes, or if she's dealt successfully with a similar problem in the past, she may not need a therapist. We'll talk more about protective factors, which shield people from disorders, below.

## OTHER CONTEXTUAL CONSIDERATIONS

Sometimes the context that makes a behavior normal is cultural rather than situational. For example, carrying on conversations with dead relatives or supernatural entities is considered healthy in some cultures with indigenous world-views. In other words, in some places, it's not only okay to talk to God, it's okay if he talks back. If "he" tells you to kill someone and you try to do it, though, your behavior is going to be viewed as problematic regardless of culture.

Disordered behaviors that appear only in certain cultures are called culture-bound syndromes. For example, in Algonquian Native American mythology, a wendigo is a cannibalistic monster. When food is short, people from the Algonquian culture can (very rarely) develop an incapacitating fear that they are going to turn into cannibalistic monsters just like the wendigo. Because wendigo psychosis only appears in Algonquian groups, it is bound to that culture. Even among Algonquian groups, however, the behavior is considered abnormal and deserving of treatment.

If the same behavior appeared in a middle-class Caucasian businessman from Colorado, he would not be diagnosed with wendigo (a culture-bound syndrome), but instead with a delusional disorder (a Western diagnosis).

Culture also affects the way disorders manifest themselves. People with delusions in industrialized nations may be convinced that someone has hidden electronic bugs in their homes or that friends and family members have been replaced by robots. Whereas, someone with delusions in a developing country is more likely to talk about witchcraft, evil spirits, and curses.

## CULTURE-BOUND SYNDROMES

Culture-bound syndromes are widely recognized in some cultures but completely foreign in others. Some of these syndromes overlap with diagnostic categories in the *Diagnostic and Statistical Manual of Mental Disorders* and some don't. Because many of them have a supernatural element, they're usually treated with folk medicine in the cultures in which they appear. Here are a few examples:

- **Falling out:** Following extreme stress or a trauma, the person collapses. Though her eyes are open, she's unable to see. She usually understands what's happening around her, but can't move. This appears most often in the Southern United States and Caribbean groups.

- **Mal de ojo (evil eye):** Often thought to be caused by a look of envy from others, *mal de ojo* symptoms can include crying, vomiting, restless sleep, and fever. Because babies are so often praised, they are thought to be particularly at risk. People in Mexico and Central America may attribute a baby's illness to *mal de ojo* rather than something like colic.

- **Susto (fright sickness or soul loss):** After an accident, seeing a ghost, or experiencing another traumatic event, the soul is thought to leave the body, causing symptoms like insomnia, nervousness, listlessness, depression, and severe weight loss. This appears in some Latinos in the United States and among people in Mexico and Central and South America.

# THE DIATHESIS-STRESS MODEL

The *diathesis-stress model* describes the relationship between biology and context in the development of a disorder. *You* can use it to decide whether your character's problem should be labeled as a true disorder. For a disorder to develop, there must first be some kind of vulnerability (called a diathesis) to that disorder. That vulnerability can be biological, social, or psychological.

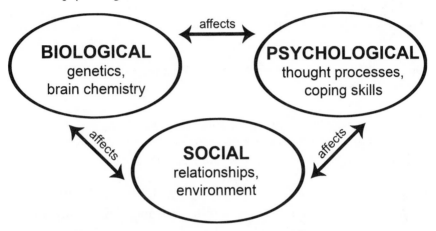

**Fig 5.1. Biological, psychological, and social factors should continuously interact and affect one another in your characters' lives.**

Each of these three areas affects the others. For example, social skills (psychological) can affect how an individual is treated by people she encounters (social). Likewise, optimism and pessimism (psychological) can affect brain chemistry (biological), and vice versa.

Let's say that your character inherited the genes for bipolar disorder. In most cases, inherited disorders are thought to be polygenetic; that is, several genes work together to cause the disorder. But just having the genes isn't enough to cause the disorder. It still has to be triggered by something in the environment. Otherwise, the genes lie dormant.

Things that trigger problems are referred to as *stressors*. Just like vulnerabilities, stressors can be biological, psychological, or social; they can also be positive or negative. For example, getting married is a happy occasion, but in most cases it's still extremely stressful. In someone who has a genetic predisposition toward anxiety, dealing with all the social pressures of getting married—relatives, caterers, florists, well-meaning acquaintances, and the future spouse—could be enough to trigger an anxiety disorder.

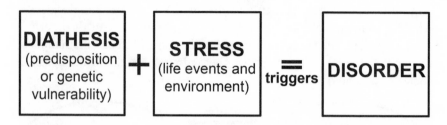

**Fig 5.2. The diathesis-stress model reminds us that it isn't enough to have the genes for a disorder. To appear, the disorder has to be triggered by environmental stressors.**

*Protective factors* can buffer or eliminate the effects of stress and reduce the intensity of or even prevent the disorder. Protective factors might include a strong network of people your character can count on when things are tough, an optimistic approach to problems, and the attitude that he is in control of his own destiny and can handle life's challenges. If your character's protective factors start to break down, she might break down as well!

In the 2010 thriller *Peacock*, John Skillpa has at least two different personalities—John, who goes to work every day, and Emma, who does chores around the house. The film repeatedly references the trauma young John suffered at his mother's hands. Like other people who develop multiple personalities, we can assume that John had a biological tendency to dissociate. This was his diathesis or vulnerability. His mother's abuse, however, was necessary for him to develop a full-blown dissociative identity disorder.

When the film begins, John has compartmentalized his personalities in such a way that they can both have time "out" without letting anyone in the community know. When a train comes crashing through a fence into John's backyard, however, the neighbors are determined to worm their way into his life. The resulting stress makes John's disorder worse, until the two personalities are fighting each other for dominance in John's life. This is a good example of how stressors can not only trigger disorders, but also exacerbate existing disorders.

Your therapist character can theorize using the diathesis-stress model regardless of his orientation. If he's psychodynamic, for example, he will believe that childhood stressors can trigger a disorder in someone with genes that make her vulnerable to that disorder. By contrast, a humanistic therapist might believe that blocked personal potentials are what create enough stress to trigger the disorder.

How severe the disorder is depends on how many of the contributing alleles (versions of a gene) you have, how those alleles influence each other, how many stressors you endure, and whether there are any protective factors against the genetic vulnerability and/or the stressors.

What this means to you as a writer is that psychological problems can be biological, social, or psychological in origin. Once the problem or disorder exists, biological problems like disease, social problems like relationship conflicts, and psychological problems like guilt over a past transgression can all make the problem worse. The more predisposing factors your character has, the more likely she is to develop the problem; the more stressors she experiences after she develops the problem, the worse it's going to be! Obviously that means that as she deals with the conflict built into your plot, her mental health is going to be affected.

## Beware the Disappearing Diagnosis

People who have psychological disorders have them all the time. Though they might have learned to hide their symptoms, they can't turn the disorder on and off just because they have a date or because it's inconvenient. Writers often emphasize their characters' disorders when they serve the story and ignore them when they don't. Instead, think about how a particular disorder would affect all aspects of your character's life and use the resulting conflicts to increase the stakes in your story.

For example, having social anxiety disorder might not be a big problem if your character works from home on her computer, but sooner or later she's going to have to deal with other people. Is she comfortable in chat rooms but tongue-tied on the phone? What happens when the guy she's had a crush on since the fifth grade finds her online and asks her to go on a date? What happens when she has to visit the store? Does she shop as quickly as possible because she can only stand to be around people for a few minutes, or does she spend half an hour in the parking lot working up the nerve to go inside?

The more stressors your character is dealing with, the worse her disorder is going to look, so imagine what her date would be like if she first had to talk on the phone to make restaurant reservations *and* go to the store to buy a new pair of shoes!

---

**Q & A**

**Q:** My character is a human clone in a future society. Humans believe that clones have no souls. Sometimes their genes mutate, and as a result some are born monsters. Based on this combination of genetic and environmental factors, what sorts of mental problems would clones develop?

**A:** When people are different from us, especially if we have a reason to dislike or hate them, we develop something called an outgroup bias. That is, we see everyone in the other group as exactly the same—inferior. If your clones are less than human because they have no souls, perhaps people also believe that makes them amoral, primitive, more dangerous, etc.—fill in the adjectives with what you know about your society. Since some clones also have the potential to be monsters, it's likely that people would generalize their fear to *all* clones, leading to discrimination at best and genocide at worst.

Therefore, if people knew your character was a clone, she would struggle with mistreatment and abuse, much of it so subtle she might wonder if she's just being paranoid. All these little stressors would affect her body's immune system, making it work more poorly than it might otherwise. Over time, this could also degrade the functioning of brain chemicals like serotonin and norepinephrine, possibly leading to depression.

In many cases, targets of hatred will start to act the way the discriminators expect them to act. This makes sense when you imagine how you'd feel if someone crossed the street every time you walked by just because you were different and they assumed you were hostile and dangerous. You'd probably start *feeling* a little hostile and dangerous!

If people *didn't* know she was a clone and she was hiding in human society, she would probably be anxious. She might also resent that humans can live without hiding who and what they really are. She might feel guilt for hiding what she is or not speaking up when she hears people speak badly of clones. Anxiety can lead to insomnia, feelings of dread, and fight-or-flight symptoms like sweaty palms, pounding heart, and feeling disconnected from one's surroundings.

---

# MAKING IT OFFICIAL: HOW REAL DIAGNOSES LOOK

Diagnosis is a type of shorthand between professionals, and in some cases it's used to help people put a name to what they're experiencing. If a therapist wanted to consult with a colleague about a client, he could say, "My client has a minor depression that's lasted for about three years. She's able to function, but she's not eating or sleeping well, and she just doesn't enjoy life—everything seems gray and hopeless." That's a pretty long description. Using the shorthand of a diagnosis, he could summarize all of that by saying, "My client has dysthymia." Much more efficient!

## THE MULTIAXIAL SYSTEM

Your therapist character has just finished meeting with a new client for the first time. The most important thing he will do when he writes his notes is give a diagnosis. Diagnoses include five levels of information. Each level is called an *axis*. Together, the axes provide an at-a-glance summary of the client's problems.

The five axes are:

*Axis I: Clinical or symptom disorders.* Axis I holds every disorder diagnosis except for two: personality disorders and mental retardation. That means that if your character has a mood disorder like depression, an anxiety disorder like a phobia, a lifespan disorder like dementia, an eating disorder, a psychotic disorder, or a dissociative disorder, those diagnoses belong on Axis I. These disorders tend to get better and worse depending on the amount of stress the person is under. Most of them also respond well to therapy and/or medications.

*Axis II: Personality disorders and mental retardation.* Though mental retardation is diagnosed on Axis II, when therapists mention "Axis II disorders" they almost always mean personality disorders.

Personality disorders are long-standing problems actually rooted in the person's character, which means you couldn't remove them without changing who the person is. Think about marble—if you removed the veins, it wouldn't be marble anymore.

People with personality disorders don't see a problem with their behavior. They don't take personal responsibility when things go wrong; instead, they see themselves as victims. They have trouble seeing other people's points of view and are manipulative and difficult to please. We'll talk in much more detail about personality disorders in Chapter 9.

*Axis III: General medical conditions.* Ongoing medical issues are recorded in this category. For example, if a client has cancer, both the diagnosis and the treatments can contribute to psychological problems like anxiety and depression.

*Axis IV: Psychosocial stressors.* Psychological and social problems that are *currently* causing stress are recorded on Axis IV. Examples might be the birth of a child, problems with a landlord or boss, or living in an extremely dangerous neighborhood.

*Axis V: Global Assessment of Functioning.* The GAF is a number from 1 to 100. Extremely low numbers are associated with severe psychosis or dangerousness. Numbers in the middle range of forty to sixty are associated with problems that are interfering significantly with day-to-day life. The higher the number, the better the person is dealing with the problem, with eighty and above being very healthy numbers.

---

### A Sample Multiaxial Diagnosis

Let's say your character recently returned from active duty in the military. He was injured when a bomb exploded under his group's Humvee, and all but one other person was killed. He had a serious head injury and was honorably discharged. Now that he's home, he has post-traumatic stress disorder and is having repeated episodes of major depression. While he was gone, his civilian friends all moved on with their lives, so he feels alone. He's trying to finish college, but he's finding the work overwhelming, especially since he isn't sleeping well and is having trouble concentrating.

His diagnosis might be written like this:

Axis I: 309.81 Posttraumatic Stress Disorder

      296.3 Major Depressive Disorder (these can go in any order)

Axis II: No diagnosis

Axis III: Traumatic brain injury

Axis IV: Inadequate support group, educational problems

Axis V: GAF current 45

---

Note that your client character's bill wouldn't include any of the information above; the multiaxial system is only for the therapist and the insurance company. The bill also wouldn't include the name of her diagnosis, only a numeric diagnostic code. The only ways your client character would know her diagnosis would be if the therapist told her or if she looked up the diagnostic code in a *DSM*.

---

**DON'T LET THIS HAPPEN TO YOU!**

In the film *Identity*, a group of therapists solemnly identify their patient's problem as an "Axis IV dissociative disorder" when there is no such thing. All clinical disorder diagnoses have to go on Axis I. And since all clinical disorders go on Axis I, it would be redundant to say "an Axis I dissociative disorder."

---

## V CODES

V codes indicate problems that don't fit the criteria for a psychological disorder yet are still a focus in therapy. For example, it's perfectly legitimate for your character to see a therapist to help her deal with the problems in her marriage, but because marital problems are not a *disorder*, a V code is used. In other words, there's nothing wrong with the client. She doesn't have a disorder or an illness, but she does have a problem that's being addressed in therapy. V codes belong on Axis I.

Insurance companies don't cover V code problems. There is, however, a loophole: The V code problem could be causing serious enough problems that a diagnosis of depression, anxiety, or another disorder might eventually be added to Axis I to suit insurance.

## NOT OTHERWISE SPECIFIED (NOS) CATEGORIES

One of the reasons clinicians get excited about "textbook cases" is that they don't see many. Think about how much variety there is in the way people express different emotions. It makes sense then that disorders can also look very different in different people.

In rare cases, the diagnostic categories in the *DSM* don't fit. Other times, for example during an emergency situation, the clinician may not have the time or information to make a precise diagnosis. In either case, a "Not Otherwise Specified" diagnosis can be made while the clinician gathers more information or finds a better fit.

So let's say that one of your characters has a disorder that nobody has ever seen before. First, make absolutely sure that the problem isn't covered by an existing diagnosis. Then choose the diagnosis that's closest to your character's problem and add the term "NOS."

For example, if your character had episodes that looked like full-blown mania—poor judgment, aggressiveness, extremely high energy—even though she didn't abuse substances and never displayed depressive episodes, the normal diagnosis of bipolar disorder wouldn't work. The therapist might tell a colleague, "I've never seen this pattern of symptoms, so I had to give her a mood disorder NOS diagnosis."

---

### COMMON DIAGNOSTIC TERMINOLOGY

- **Affect** Emotional state.

- **Age of onset** How old someone was when the disorder appeared.

- **Comorbid disorders** Two or more distinctly different disorders appearing at the same time and affecting one another in a negative way.

- **Etiology** Cause or origin of disorder.

- **Exacerbate** To make (a disorder) worse.

- **Insight** Client awareness that symptoms are abnormal; for example, that the voices she hears are not real. A client who insisted the voices were real would be displaying a *lack of insight*.

- **Mental disorder** A pattern that causes distress or dysfunction or significantly increases the likelihood that someone will die, experience pain, develop a disability, or lose freedoms. The pattern must not be a logical and appropriate reaction to a particular stressor.

- **Onset** The appearance of a disorder.

- **Predisposing factors** Stressors, problems, family issues, or genetics that make one more likely to develop a disorder.

- **Premorbid condition** What the client was like before the onset of the problem.

---

- **Presenting problem** Chief complaint or symptoms; the problem the client says she's come for.

- **Prevalence** How common a disorder is within a given population.

- **Prognosis** A prediction about the course and outcome of a problem.

- **Stressor** Anything that makes the client's life harder to cope with. Stressors are often associated with the onset or exacerbation of mental disorders.

- **Stimulus** Anything in the environment that affects the person. A stressor is a kind of stimulus.

- **Substance** Anything that, when taken, changes an individual's perceptions of the world. Alcohol or drugs, legal or illegal.

## DIFFERENTIAL DIAGNOSIS

Many disorders have overlapping symptoms, and that overlap is probably one of the reasons 70 percent of writers don't know the difference between schizophrenia, bipolar disorder, and dissociative identity disorder (multiple personalities)!

Research is constantly identifying new ways to tell similar disorders apart. For example, people with multiple personalities always have periods of amnesia, while people with bipolar disorder and schizophrenia don't. Likewise, people with bipolar disorder tend to understand and appreciate humor, while people with schizophrenia take everything so literally they have trouble appreciating humor.

I've detailed the differences between diagnoses that are commonly confused in the upcoming chapters to help you (and your characters!) differentiate among the diagnoses.

# 6
# The Disorders, Part I
## *Mood, Anxiety, and Psychotic Disorders*

In this chapter and the next three we'll focus on how different disorders might look in your characters' everyday lives. We'll also look at common misconceptions that you'll want to avoid in your writing. First up are mood, anxiety, and psychotic disorders.

Mood and anxiety disorders are the most common problems most therapists see. While psychotic disorders like schizophrenia are far less common, writers frequently reference them because of their vivid dramatic possibilities.

## MOOD DISORDERS

In a moment we'll look at each part of the mood spectrum, but first let's talk about what "normal" is. Someone without a mood disorder experiences different emotions throughout the day, but his overall emotional "climate" is fairly stable. More important, he's able to manage his life from one day to the next and feels extremely good, irritable, or sad only if something happens to cause those feelings. For example, if you won a multi-million dollar jackpot, you *might* feel as "high" as someone who's hypomanic. If someone close to you died unexpectedly, you *might* feel as low as someone with a major depressive disorder. Since you'd be reacting in a reasonable way to something in the environment, the emotions would not be considered abnormal.

There are two types of mood disorders: unipolar and bipolar. People with unipolar mood disorders get depressed and only depressed. People with bipolar disorders experience depression as well as an "up" state that includes euphoria or agitation.

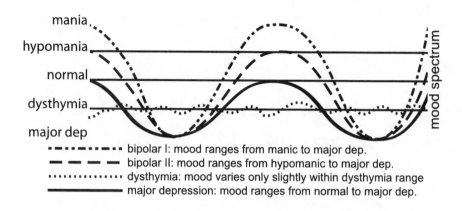

**Fig 6.1. Mood spectrum.**

## UNIPOLAR DISORDERS

Depression is caused at least in part by imbalances among brain chemicals like serotonin, norepinephrine, and dopamine. Because these chemicals affect appetite, sleep, concentration, and energy levels, someone with a true depressive disorder experiences much more than simple sadness.

### Dysthymia

People with dysthymia, the mildest form of unipolar depression, have a chronic case of the blues. Things may not be *bad*, exactly, but sufferers feel like they're going through the motions of life without getting much in return. They struggle with feelings of inadequacy and hopelessness, have trouble enjoying things, and are usually less productive and effective than other people. They may have poor appetites or tend to overeat, and either sleep poorly ("insomnia") or sleep too much ("hypersomnia"). Dysthymia tends to last, and last, and last; over time, dysthymia can become as debilitating as major depression.

Writes Andrew Solomon, the author of *The Noonday Demon: An Atlas of Depression*:

> Mild depression is a gradual...thing that undermines people the way rust weakens iron...Like physical pain that becomes chronic, it is miserable not so much because it is intolerable in the moment as because it is intolerable to have known it in the moments gone and to look forward only to knowing it in the moments to come.

One of the most outstanding literary depictions of dysthymia is Marvin, the chronically pessimistic and morose robot in Douglas Adams's *The Hitchhiker's Guide to the Galaxy*. Regardless of the situation, Marvin sees the negatives. Rather than having trouble functioning, Marvin slogs along through life complaining about pretty much everything. "Pardon me for breathing," he moans, "which I never do anyway so I don't know why I bother to say it, oh I'm so depressed."

Arguably the most famous dysthymic in fiction, however, is A. A. Milne's depressed donkey, Eeyore. Like Marvin, Eeyore plods along, expecting unhappiness, because that's all his experience consists of. He greets Pooh thus: "Good morning, Pooh Bear. If it is a good morning. Which I doubt."

Some people with dysthymia go on to develop major depressive disorder. Others have dysthymia *and* major depressive disorder, a condition colloquially called "double depression." These people are more likely to seek treatment than those with dysthymia alone.

Many people with dysthymia go untreated because they don't realize they're depressed. If a therapist asks about depression they say things like, "But I've always been like this" or "That's just the way I am." Some disorders tend to get better over time even if they're not treated, but dysthymia is not one of them. Most sufferers need active treatment with therapy and medications to improve.

**Additional Information**
- Dysthymia usually begins during childhood, adolescence, or early adulthood.

- Unlike adults, children and teens with dysthymia are often cranky and restless. Schoolwork and peer interactions are usually impacted.

- It's not uncommon to find other mood disorders, especially dysthymia or major depressive disorder, among the relatives of people with dysthymia.

**Misconceptions**
- There's no such thing as "severe dysthymia." If the depression is severe, the person is diagnosed with a major depressive disorder.

## *Major Depressive Disorder (MDD)*

People with major depressive disorder have far more debilitating symptoms than people with dysthymia. Rather than being chronic, their depressions come in waves that last weeks, months, or sometimes even years at a time. Between episodes, some people go back to feeling "normal," but others, who have a double depression, just become dysthymic.

"Large depression," writes Solomon in *The Noonday Demon*, "is the stuff of breakdowns. If one imagines a soul of iron that weathers with grief and rusts with mild depression, the major depression is the collapse of a whole structure." People with MDD don't just feel bad about themselves—they feel worthless and hopeless, swallowed by an abyss of emotional agony. They don't just feel indecisive—they slog through a mire of mental fog and mud that makes it difficult to think, concentrate, and make decisions. Because they believe they're a burden on others, they're often guilt-ridden. Some wonder what they've done to deserve such misery. Because motivation plummets, many stop participating in hobbies and social activities; some even lose their jobs. They may complain of mental and physical sluggishness ("psychomotor retardation"), waking up during the night and having trouble going back to sleep ("middle insomnia") or wanting to sleep all the time ("hypersomnia"). Recurrent suicidal thoughts are very common in people with major depression. Unable to see a way out of their pain, they turn to suicide as a last-ditch effort to escape. You can find more information on suicidal thoughts and how psychological professionals handle them in Chapter 12.

Major depression is noticeable to people who know the individual well because the person's speech and movements literally slow down, the sadness and lack of energy are obvious, and the person tends to complain about memory and concentration problems. In extreme cases, the person's hygiene and ability to care for himself may decline.

In *The House of Sand and Fog*, the main character, Kathy Nicolo, has had problems with depression for most of her life. Rather than a consistent, low grade unhappiness, Kathy's depression becomes excruciating from time to time. As a result, she lives a lonely, miserable life. The little chores of everyday existence—opening the mail, picking up around the house, fixing a dripping faucet—are more than she can handle. Weighted down by helplessness and hopelessness, unable to cope with losing her home, Kathy repeatedly attempts suicide.

A rare subset of people with severe major depressive disorders experience delusions and/or hallucinations. Paranoid delusions and delusions of guilt or sin are the most common. Some people also have nihilistic delusions and believe that their organs are rotting or afflicted with cancer.

**Misconceptions**

- Many people assume that those with depression feel blank and empty when the truth is that they drown in a deluge of guilt, hopelessness, and self-loathing. "Depression is a place that teems with nightmarish activity," claims Lesley Dormen in her essay "Planet No." "It's a one-industry town, a psychic megalopolis devoted to a single twenty-four-hour-we-never-close product. You work misery as a teeth-grinding muscle-straining job, proving your shameful failures to yourself over and over again." The misery can feel like a physical burden, one so heavy that even the therapist can feel it when the client enters the room.

- Someone who is grieving a loss but still able to function normally is not diagnosed with a major depressive disorder. Instead, he is given a V-code of "bereavement." V-codes indicate reasonable reactions to difficult situations but recognize that the condition may still benefit from therapy.

---

## THE COGNITIVE TRIAD OF DEPRESSION

Cognitive therapist Aaron Beck identifies three types of negative thoughts common in people with depression. That is, they feel bad about three things: themselves, the world, and the future. They feel inadequate, unlovable, and worthless with regard to themselves. They experience the world as overwhelming, punishing, and unpleasant. They expect only bad things to happen going forward, and believe they will be helpless to stop or change those things.

Fortunately, therapists can break through the cognitive triad with techniques like cognitive-behavioral therapy. The A-B-C-D-E model we looked at in Chapter 2 can be especially effective.

---

## Bipolar Disorders

In 1994, "manic depression" was renamed "bipolar disorder" in the *DSM*. There are three types of bipolar disorder: bipolar I, bipolar II, and cyclothymia.

### *Bipolar I Disorder = Major Depression + Mania*

People with bipolar I disorder struggle with devastating major depressive episodes; however, they also have recurrent spikes of mania. Be careful not to have your character swing back and forth from depression to mania too often, though. Bipolar disorder often cycles with the seasons, leaving the person depressed during the winter and manic during the summer, with Daylight Savings Time acting as a trigger. That means that a full cycle takes a year. "Rapid cycling" bipolar disorder, which means four or more episodes in a year, is rare and usually happens later in life.

Mania, like depression, is caused by a chemical imbalance. Imagine a house with a broken thermostat. To stay comfortable, you'd regularly need to adjust the temperature so you weren't too warm or too cold. The brains of people with bipolar disorder have the same problem—they can't seem to find the right mood "temperature" and stay there. Because it's a biochemical problem, medications are used to help regulate the moods and keep them within a normal range.

Some people who are manic feel euphoric and grandiose, while others become irritable and volatile. Sometimes they dress or behave more flamboyantly than usual, and they often make irrational, impulsive decisions. Some get so talkative they sound as if they're being "pressured" to keep speaking. Others go for days without sleeping. Most can't see any problem with their thoughts and behaviors, at least during the mania. Poor judgment leads them to harmful decisions they might otherwise never even consider—for example, outrageous spending sprees, careless sex, and dangerous risk-taking. Their lack of impulse control can lead them to say and do things that have long-reaching repercussions. Finally, they're more likely than someone with major depression to experience delusions and/or hallucinations. Once in a while, the combination of poor impulse control and psychosis can lead to violence. Substance abuse is also a big problem for people with bipolar disorder. About 60 percent "self-medicate" with alcohol and/or drugs in an attempt to regulate their moods and feel better.

Though some people find themselves feeling especially good for several days or weeks before a full-blown manic episode, more often mania begins suddenly, with symptoms getting worse over the following days. Triggers include illicit drug use, major stressors, sleep loss, starting a new antidepressant, and changes in the seasons, with mania being most common in the spring and summer due to increased sunlight. Manic episodes last between a few weeks and a few months. More than half the time, the person plunges into a major depressive episode right before or right after the mania. As with unipolar major depressive disorder, depressive episodes can last weeks, months, or years, though many people with bipolar disorder do return to "normal" functioning from time to time.

Poet Theodore Roethke described the euphoria and delusions of one of his manic episodes like this:

> "For no reason I started to feel very good. Suddenly I knew how to enter into the life of everything around me. I knew how it felt to be a tree, a blade of grass, even a rabbit. I didn't sleep much. I just walked around with this wonderful feeling. One day I was passing a diner and all of a sudden I knew what it felt like to be a lion. I went into the diner and said to the counter-man, Bring me a steak. Don't cook it. Just bring it. So he brought me this raw steak and I started eating it. The other customers made like they were revolted, watching me. And I began to see that maybe it was a little strange."

The difference between the euphoria of hypomania or mania and the agony of major depression puts sufferers at particular risk for suicide. Writer Virginia Woolf took her own life because, according to her suicide note, "I feel certain that I'm going mad again. I…can't go through another of those terrible times."

**Additional Information**

- Symptoms of bipolar disorder usually first appear in the teens or early twenties, though for some people they develop during childhood. The earlier the first symptoms of depression appear, the more likely it is that the person will later have a manic episode and be diagnosed with bipolar disorder. This is because bipolar disorder usually begins with depression and almost invariably appears at earlier ages than unipolar disorders.

- Most people with bipolar disorder are depressed far more often than they're hypomanic or manic.

- Bipolar disorder has a strong genetic component and often runs in families. Relatives of people with bipolar I disorder often have bipolar I, bipolar II, or major depressive disorder.

- Even with medication and therapy, people with bipolar disorders can be moodier than the average person because they're more strongly affected by the things going on around them. Most learn to manage their illness by doing things to help keep their brain chemistry as stable as possible. For example, they learn to get enough sleep, eat well, exercise regularly, and be careful with medications, including caffeine, over-the-counter cold medicine, appetite suppressants, and alcohol.

- Bipolar disorder is an extremely stigmatizing diagnosis, and people often take months or even years to accept it.

## MIXED EPISODES

Some people with bipolar disorder experience "mixed episodes," which means they're hypomanic or manic *and* depressed. The result is that the person feels awful but has lots of energy, which manifests as agitation, anxiety, irritability, and racing thoughts. For many people this is a jagged, frantic, terrifying experience, like being on a runaway train hurtling through a nightmarish landscape.

Researcher Kay Redfield Jamison describes her own mixed episode as "the most dreadful I have ever felt in my life." She goes on:

*There was a definite point when I knew I was insane. My thoughts were so fast that I couldn't remember the beginning of a sentence halfway through. Fragments of ideas, images, sentences raced around in my mind... I wanted desperately to slow down but could not. Sex became too intense for pleasure, and during it I would feel my mind encased by black lines of light that were terrifying to me. My delusions centered on the slow painful deaths of all the green plants in the world—vine by vine, stem by stem, leaf by leaf they died and I could do nothing to save them... At one point I was determined that if my mind... did not stop racing and begin working normally again, I would kill myself by leaping from a nearby twelve-story building."*

**Misconceptions**

- Delusions and/or hallucinations don't always indicate schizophrenia, but people with bipolar I disorder who have delusions or hallucinations are sometimes misdiagnosed with schizophrenia. The key difference is the predominant symptom—if the person primarily has mood problems, the diagnosis should be bipolar disorder; if the primary problem is psychotic thinking, schizophrenia is a better bet. A few other differences:

    - Many people with schizophrenia take everything literally, so they have trouble appreciating sarcasm and humor. People with bipolar disorder understand the humor even if they don't feel like laughing.

    - People with schizophrenia usually have bizarre mannerisms and speech.

    - The mental disorganization schizophrenia creates makes it difficult for people with schizophrenia to produce effective creative works. By contrast, creative people with bipolar disorder often produce good work.

## Bipolar II Disorder = Major Depression + Hypomania

Bipolar II disorder is less severe than bipolar I because while the person has major depressive episodes, he never actually gets manic. Instead, he experiences hypomania, which is an "up" or euphoric state without the emotional extremes and poor judgment of true mania.

Some clinicians and researchers argue that people diagnosed with major depressive disorder who don't respond to treatment may have bipolar II disorder. Others argue that this theory encourages clinicians to over-diagnose bipolar disorder. However, some people do have a good response to mood stabilizers when antidepressants alone weren't effective, suggesting that at least some of the time bipolar II disorder is actually the culprit.

## Cyclothymia = Mild Depression and Hypomania

Cyclothymia is the mildest form of bipolar disorder, and it may go undiagnosed unless it develops into bipolar I or bipolar II. People with cyclothymia experience neither mania nor major depression; instead, they have periods of hypomania and dysthymia. Since the problem may be exacerbated by seasonal changes in light, the person may alternately be diagnosed with seasonal affective disorder.

## TREATMENTS FOR MOOD DISORDERS

Cognitive-behavioral therapy and interpersonal therapy (a short-term psychodynamic-based approach that focuses on relationships) are particularly effective in treating depression. The automatic thought records described in Chapter 2 give the client something concrete to do to improve his symptoms as well as help him practice new ways of thinking.

When someone is having trouble functioning due to a unipolar depression, antidepressants can help. Meanwhile, medications are the cornerstone of treatment for bipolar I and bipolar II disorders. Sufferers are often on a "cocktail" of medications, including one or more antidepressants (to get rid of the depression), a mood stabilizer (to suppress hypomania and mania *and* to treat depression), and if necessary an antipsychotic (to reduce the delusions and hallucinations of extreme mania). Some atypical antipsychotics like Abilify, Geodon, Seroquel, and Zyprexa also have antidepressant properties. See Chapter 11 for more detailed information on these medications.

Many people with mood disorders are affected by the changes in light during the different seasons. This is sometimes called seasonal affective disorder, but it's actually diagnosed as a major depressive disorder or bipolar disorder "with seasonal pattern." For people who have particular problems during the winter months, the therapist may suggest winter phototherapy, sometimes called light therapy. The client sits in front of a light box that emits very bright (up to ten thousand lux) wide-spectrum light. He doesn't have to stare directly at the light, he just needs to have it shining over whatever he's doing.

In extreme cases, when nothing else seems to be helping, doctors may suggest electroconvulsive therapy (ECT) to a client. ECT can force mania or depression into remission, sometimes immediately. After several sessions, antidepressants are often more effective than they were before ECT. Treatment-resistant mood disorders may also respond to new approaches like Transcranial Magnetic Stimulation (TMS), Vagus Nerve Stimulation (VNS), or Deep Brain Stimulation (DBS). Check out Chapter 11 for more information.

## CREATIVITY AND MENTAL ILLNESS

Creative people who struggle with a psychological problem almost always have a mood disorder—not schizophrenia or ADHD. Interestingly, people who are creative have more in common with those who are bipolar than they do with "normal" people, but the commonalities lie not necessarily in mood disturbances. Instead, idiosyncratic thinking patterns, enthusiasm and passion for one's art, and one's ability to produce new and strange ideas seem to be the key. It is a myth, therefore, that *mental illness* is a prerequisite for creative genius. In fact, research shows that over time, psychological problems degrade one's capacity for creative output, and obviously suicide cuts short anyone's creative contribution.

Sometimes it takes a while to figure out the best combination of medications and therapy for a particular person's body chemistry, but by working together, the therapist and the client can improve the client's life. Without the barrier of mental illness between the individual and his ideas, his creativity will often flourish.

# ANXIETY DISORDERS

Anxiety disorders affect about 18 percent of people in the United States during any given year, and are diagnosed when people have irrational, unrealistic fears or worries that interfere with day-to-day life. The most common genetic vulnerability is the personality trait "neuroticism," which is a tendency to experience negative emotional states like anxiety, hostility, depression, guilt and self-consciousness.

In those people who have biological problems with anxiety, the limbic system—a series of brain structures that handle emotions and memory—is most likely to be affected. The neurotransmitters or brain chemicals most likely to be off balance are GABA (gamma-aminobutyric acid), norepinephrine, and serotonin.

## SPECIFIC PHOBIAS

By definition, a phobia is a fear of something specific. This fear is almost always classically conditioned, which means that the person has learned to associate fear with something that does not automatically cause it. Maybe the individual was bitten by a dog; maybe his father is afraid of dogs; maybe he just saw a re-run of *Cujo* on TV. Regardless, at some point—usually during childhood or early adolescence—he learned to feel terror around dogs, and he may or may not remember how it happened.

Over time, the person may begin to associate anxiety not only with dogs, but also with objects that remind him of dogs: collars, food dishes, or even caricatures or cartoons of dogs. Obviously, if he avoids these triggers, he doesn't have to feel anxious. This maintains the phobia, because the person attributes the lack of catastrophe to the avoidance behavior. Still, it may be the avoidance behavior that brings the person into therapy. For example, the client might be afraid to turn on the TV lest he see a dog food commercial, or afraid to leave his home because he might see someone out walking a dog.

Once in a while a phobia is symbolic. In other words, the person is so overwhelmed by the thing he's afraid of, he displaces that fear onto something symbolically related to the fear. For example, Lisa is afraid of rats. Unlike some people with phobias, she can say the word, but she's paralyzed by anything that reminds her of rats or their movement: skittering leaves, shifting shadows, even a guy in a commercial dressed up as a big, goofy rat.

Suspecting a symbolic phobia, the therapist asks Lisa why she hates rats. Lisa says that they're dark, dirty, shadowy, even evil. Soon the therapist learns that "doing bad things" makes Lisa feel the same feelings she does about rats. It turns out that what Lisa really fears is not rats, but the concept of "sin" and the possibility that her sins will damn her to hell.

There are four main groups or types of phobias: animal type (animals and insects), natural environment type (things that occur in nature like storms, heights, and water), situational type (things that are due to human technology like airplanes, tunnels, bridges, and math tests), and blood-injection-injury type (invasive medical procedures, general anesthesia, needles, and so on). This fourth phobia subtype, the blood-injection-injury type, seems to run in families. When confronted with the feared object or situation, people with this type of phobia often faint; that isn't the case with other phobias. Finally, if the phobia—a fear of clowns, for example—doesn't fit one of the above four categories, it's dropped into the "other" category.

Many people have more than one type of phobia, though it's most common to have multiple phobias in the same type category. For example, someone who is afraid of airplanes may also be afraid of elevators.

**Misconceptions**

- People often refer to dislike or discomfort with something as a "phobia" when the problem isn't crippling enough to be diagnosable. Indiana Jones, for example, isn't nearly scared enough of snakes to have a phobia. He may hate snakes, but he functions extremely well around them. People with true phobias are often incapacitated by the thing they fear.

## Social Phobias

Social phobias are more common than the average specific phobia, so they get their own category. People with social phobias are unreasonably afraid that they will embarrass themselves in a social situation. They may avoid speaking in a group, eating in public, or even walking down a busy street because they are afraid of being judged inadequate by others. Usually their discomfort is obvious to others. They may blush, have shaky hands or a shaky voice, make poor eye contact, sweat, or seem confused.

Social phobias can be learned, either due to a bad experience one has had, or as a result of seeing someone *else* humiliated in a social setting. People who develop them may be genetically predisposed—research shows that infants who are shy, avoidant, and easily upset are more likely to grow up with social anxiety. Finally people with social phobia operate based on "danger schemas"—models of the world in which they expect others to think poorly of them or reject them. They become so preoccupied with the idea that they will behave the wrong way that they fall prey to a "self-fulfilling prophecy." In other words, because they expect to interact awkwardly with others, that's exactly what they do, which can cause others to respond in a way that reinforces their fears.

**Additional Information**

- Social phobia usually first appears during a person's mid-teens, though it can begin in childhood.
- Often people who develop social phobia have a history of shyness.

## Generalized Anxiety Disorder (GAD)

Generalized Anxiety Disorder is an ongoing problem with "free-floating" anxiety; that is, with anxiety that is not attached to anything, the way it might be "attached" to dogs in someone with a phobia of dogs.

People with GAD are more likely than people with most other anxiety disorders to have had traumatic childhoods. Having learned that life is unpredictable and uncontrollable, they constantly scan the environment for danger. They often startle easily and strike others as "worrywarts."

In the film *Adaptation*, screenwriter Charlie is plagued by generalized anxiety. In addition to struggling with self-doubt, he is overly preoccupied with himself and his worries. The film's voice-overs provide a nice insight into Charlie's self-defeating thought patterns.

**Additional Information**

- People with GAD often have other anxiety disorders and mood disorders as well, such as specific phobias, social phobias, panic attacks, or major depressive disorder.

- Serotonin and GABA, a neurotransmitter that helps keep anxiety at bay, are often low in people with GAD.

- People with GAD often abuse drugs that depress their nervous systems, including alcohol, sleeping pills, and tranquilizers.

## Obsessive-Compulsive Disorder (OCD)

Obsessive-Compulsive Disorder is sometimes called the "doubting disease" because sufferers have trouble differentiating between what is unlikely to happen, what might happen, and what will probably happen. If a terrible thought crosses their minds, they become convinced that that thing will happen. The average person just dismisses the thought and moves on.

Thoughts and feelings of dread, called obsessions, usually involve fears of contamination, fears about hurting or having hurt someone else, embarrassing or aggressive impulses, or sexual thoughts. The discomfort caused by the obsessions can be eased or relieved through ritualistic behaviors called compulsions. If someone with OCD isn't allowed to perform his ritual, his anxiety *will* go down over the next twenty to thirty minutes. The ritual just provides more immediate relief.

OCD often has an existential or symbolic flavor. For example, some people wash compulsively because they feel emotionally soiled, dirty, or contaminated. For others, though, there's little logical connection between the obsession and the compulsion.

The most common compulsions include washing, checking, counting, putting things in order, repeating actions, and needing reassurance from others. Many people with OCD struggle with behaviors from more than one of these categories. Compulsions are always far in excess of what they're supposed to prevent or stop. For example, it's realistic to wash your hands if you've touched something dirty; it's not realistic to scrub your hands until they're raw because you're afraid you *might* have touched something dirty.

There's more to OCD than the psychological, though. Most people with the disorder benefit from medications, suggesting that there is a strong biological component.

The movie *As Good as It Gets* offers a fairly accurate portrayal of OCD. Like many people with the disorder, Melvin has multiple compulsive behaviors, though his obsession with cleanliness is paramount. He not only washes compulsively, he eats at the same restaurant each day, where he must sit at the same table and use his own pre-wrapped utensils. When his routine is disturbed, Melvin becomes anxious and angry. The biggest problem with the movie is that Melvin's symptoms get better ostensibly due to his relationship with an attractive waitress, rather than due to therapy or medication. Love, unfortunately, does not usually act as a magical cure for psychological problems!

**Additional Information**

- The brain's basal ganglia (in the limbic system) and frontal lobes are overactive in OCD. This overactivity contributes to the "broken record" thinking and the ritualistic behaviors. Medications that affect serotonin, like SSRI antidepressants, affect these areas of the brain and can reduce symptoms.

- Obsessions and compulsions may wax and wane with the amount of stress in one's life. If your character just had a fight with his girlfriend, his symptoms may temporarily get worse.

- Some people with OCD are afraid to get therapy because to them it means they would have to give up control. "For me," writes one sufferer, "OCD is my best friend as well as my worst enemy…it has given me control and a sort of stability, and each time I go to therapy I am afraid of losing it."

- In extreme situations, when the OCD has resisted all other treatments and is making a normal life impossible to live, doctors may propose a cingulotomy as a last resort. A bilateral cingulotomy permanently destroys a very precise area in the brain's frontal lobes called the anterior cingulate cortex. Long-term side effects can include problems with attention and executive functioning (e.g. thinking and problem-solving), but over 60 percent of the people who have had cingulotomies report significant benefits.

- OCD can run in families. Experts are also starting to link other disorders that include compulsive behaviors to OCD, including eating disorders (e.g. anorexia and bulimia) and impulse-control disorders (e.g. pyromania, kleptomania, and other compulsive behaviors like compulsive shopping or sex addiction). Family members of your character with OCD could conceivably have any of these problems.

**Misconceptions**
- Most people assume that OCD is easy to see; however, sufferers are usually quite adept at hiding their obsessions and compulsions, especially from strangers. They are aware that they are behaving differently than others, and that can be embarrassing. Those whose compulsions are so overwhelming that they can't hide them often wish they could.

- Not everyone with OCD washes, counts, or is tidy. For example, people who have repeated plastic surgeries to correct imperfections only they can see are believed to have OCD. Other people with OCD are terrified that they may harm someone or have harmed someone. Your character could be obsessed with the idea he ran over someone at an intersection. He might spend hours revisiting the site looking for evidence of the accident.

---

### HOARDING AND OCD

Though less than 1 percent of the general population hoards, between 10 and 40 percent of people with OCD are compulsive hoarders. Over time their living spaces become so cluttered that they can scarcely live there. The objects being collected seem useless to others—gum wrappers, junk mail, catalogs, old TV guides, even the seeds from fruits the person has eaten.

---

Friends and family members who want to intervene can be over-whelmed by how monumental the problem is; worse, some hoarders claim they would kill themselves if someone came in and removed everything.

Brain activity in hoarders is different from the activity in the brains of other people with OCD, which may explain why many of the medications that help people with OCD do little to help hoarders. (The antidepressant Paxil is one exception.) As a result, some experts argue that OCD and hoarding should be separate diagnostic categories.

People who hoard say that they are terrified to throw things away due to one or more of the following reasons:

- Sentimental value

- Inability to make decisions – People who hoard are afraid of mak-ing a mistake or a wrong decision, so they just keep *everything*.

- Hyper-responsibility – People with OCD typically feel overly responsible for the people and events in their environment. With this in mind, objects may be stored "just in case" they are needed in the future.

- Control – By keeping objects in their possession, people who hoard feel in control of them. By contrast, if they throw those things in the trash, the trash will be taken away and they will never be able to find the items again.

- Fear of forgetting – Since people with OCD are stricken with the "doubting disease," many worry they will forget information they need. By keeping stacks of newspapers, magazines, catalogs, and so forth, they can always (in their minds) find and re-learn the infor-mation. Some people with OCD also compulsively write down things they see in everyday life in case they need those things later—license plate numbers, phone numbers, and other informa-tion that seems irrelevant to others.

- Fear of letting go – Some people may hoard because they are afraid to lose pieces of their lives, and therefore—symbolically—parts of themselves.

## Panic Disorders

During a panic attack, the body suddenly goes into full-blown fight-or-flight mode. The person feels exactly the same way he would if he opened his linen closet and a hungry tiger burst out—but there's no tiger in sight. For that reason, panic attacks are often mistaken by the people having them for heart attacks, especially if they begin during middle age.

The very first panic attack a person experiences usually follows an extremely stressful experience like the death of a friend or family member, a mugging, or losing one's job. People who go on to have additional panic attacks usually become anxious about future attacks, which can actually cause future attacks. In other words, they constantly monitor their bodies for any physical indication that they are going to have a panic attack. Because they're so focused on the possibility, they misinterpret normal physiological signs and then work themselves into a panic. For example, someone who always flushes when he has a panic attack will constantly monitor his body for signs that his face is getting warm. If he goes outside on a hot day, eventually his face will get warm, which can trigger a panic attack.

Usually people have poor insight into how their thinking processes lead to panic attacks, so the attacks feel like they come out of the blue. As a result, sufferers worry that the next one could hit at any time. Some people are so afraid they'll have an attack while on the road that they stop driving. Others are so afraid their panic will make them behave strangely in public that they avoid public situations.

### Agoraphobia

Though many people are taught that agoraphobia is a fear of wide-open spaces, this is a misconception. Agoraphobia literally means "fear of the marketplace." The individual worries that he'll be trapped literally or figuratively in a public place from which escape would be embarrassing or difficult—as might be the case in a marketplace. Agoraphobia thus leads people to avoid these types of situations. Sometimes the avoidance behavior is so extreme the person refuses to leave his home.

Agoraphobia is associated with panic attacks about 95 percent of the time, but it can also develop in conjunction with another anxiety disorder like social phobia.

**Additional Information**

- The average panic attack peaks within ten minutes and eases off in twenty to thirty minutes.

- Some people have regular panic attacks—which can lead to agoraphobia—and others go for months or years between attacks.

- Panic disorder runs in families more strongly than most of the other anxiety disorders, which suggests a biochemical component. Therefore, parents or siblings are likely to struggle with the disorder as well.

- Panic disorder usually first appears between one's late teens and mid-thirties, and it may be accompanied by other disorders like social phobia, generalized anxiety disorder, or major depressive disorder.

- In some cultures, panic attacks are associated with fear of magic or witchcraft.

---

**WHAT'S A NERVOUS BREAKDOWN, ANYWAY?**

Fictional characters use the term "nervous breakdown" to refer to everything from panic attacks and hysteria to major depressive disorders and psychotic episodes. So what is a nervous breakdown, really?

The fact is that there is no formal definition, because it's not a clinical or diagnostic term. In other words, "nervous breakdown" is just a vague colloquial phrase that describes an upsetting experience. Your therapist character should always ask a client who uses the term to explain exactly what she means. Then he can identify the condition with a real diagnostic label if doing so is appropriate.

---

**Treatments for Anxiety Disorders**

Anxiety disorders often respond to antidepressants like Paxil and Effexor and anti-anxiety medications like Buspar and Ativan. Cognitive-behavioral therapy is also very effective. In addition to having clients complete thought records to identify and combat irrational thoughts, a cognitive-behavioral therapist is likely to teach relaxation methods. She might also use one or more of the behavioral interventions described below.

Panic disorders and phobias respond best to *exposure-based therapies* that confront the person with the feared thing. One exposure-based treatment, called systematic desensitization, begins with the client learning a variety of relaxation techniques. After he gets good at using them, the therapist exposes him to the anxiety-provoking thing. If the client is afraid of snakes, for example, the therapist might use cartoons, photographs, or snake toys to help simulate a real encounter. In some cases, the client and therapist might agree to work—eventually—with a real snake. Over time, as the client practices relaxing during these systematic encounters, she becomes less sensitive ("desensitized") to the anxiety.

Remember, the therapist and client are working together as a team to defeat the fear. Therefore, the therapist models calm behavior and encourages the client throughout the encounter. Despite some fictional portrayals of exposure-based treatments, this is *not* an antagonistic situation where the therapist is thrusting the snake in a gibbering client's face!

Social phobia also responds well to exposure-based treatments, including systematic desensitization. Group therapy can provide "in vivo exposure," or real-life practice facing the fear in a safe environment. Since some people with social phobia really do lack strong social skills, social skills training can also be helpful.

*Exposure coupled with ritual prevention* is the most effective treatment for obsessive-compulsive disorder. The client is exposed to the feared thing (e.g. germs) but not allowed to perform the ritual (e.g. scrubbing the hands with soap). As noted earlier, if someone prevents the client from engaging in the ritual, the anxiety will soon go away by itself. Eventually, the client realizes that his fear is irrational, and that a catastrophe won't occur if he doesn't perform his ritual.

## PSYCHOTIC DISORDERS

There is some debate about just how inclusive the word *psychotic* should be, but all definitions agree that psychosis includes a loss of contact with reality, as in the case of hallucinations or delusions.

Hallucinations can be associated with any sense—auditory, visual, tactile, gustatory, or olfactory—but the most common hallucinatory experience is hearing voices. In fact, about 75 percent of people with schizophrenia hear voices. The individual hears the voices out loud, typically at a normal spoken level. It's not unusual for some of the voices to "belong to" someone the person knows. Usually, the voices make paranoid remarks or attack the person who hears them, but once in a while they may be helpful or kind. Auditory hallucinations are more common when the person is alone. Research suggests that hallucinations of voices are actually subvocalized speech, because when the part of the brain that processes speech is temporarily incapacitated, the voices get fewer or go away completely.

Some types of auditory hallucinations are especially characteristic of schizophrenia. For example, if the person hears multiple voices holding a conversation or a running commentary on what she does, schizophrenia is automatically diagnosed. Visual hallucinations, while far less common (only about 15 percent of patients have them), usually involve vivid scenes with religious figures, family members, and animals.

*Delusions* are ideas and beliefs that are not based in reality and are unshakable regardless of logic or contradictory proof. Persecutory (aka paranoid) delusions are the type most frequently reported, though referential delusions are also common. Someone who has referential delusions believes that things in the environment like newscasters' words, song lyrics, or passages in a magazine are in direct reference to him.

---

**Don't Let This Happen to You!**

In *New Moon*, the follow-up to Stephenie Meyer's bestselling novel *Twilight*, the author repeatedly confuses hallucinations with delusions, using the two words interchangeably. "I was addicted to the sound of my delusions," the heroine, Bella, says. This is impossible, since delusions are *ideas* or *beliefs*. Hearing voices and seeing things both fall into the category of hallucinations.

Delusions can be broken into two categories: *nonbizarre* and *bizarre*. Nonbizarre delusions are possible in the world as we know it; bizarre delusions are not. For example, let's say someone has a delusion that the CIA is after him and wants to bury him alive. While unlikely, it *could* happen, so it's a nonbizarre delusion. By contrast, imagine someone who says that his next door neighbors are (literally) stealing his thoughts and collecting them in a glass jar. That's impossible in the world as we know it, so it's a bizarre delusion. Likewise, believing that the government is replacing coworkers with exact clones is a bizarre delusion; believing that a coworker is working for the FBI is nonbizarre. Any time someone reports bizarre delusions, schizophrenia is diagnosed (see below).

---

## A FEW BIZARRE DELUSIONS

- **Capgras delusion**—Belief that someone the person knows well has been replaced with an imposter; in some cases, the person believes *he* is the imposter. The fear that someone has been replaced with an imposter has a long history. In Western European folklore, for example, fairies were sometimes thought to steal a human child and replace it with a changeling that looked exactly like it. Parents went so far as to keep a constant watch over their children to prevent their abduction. In the modern world, people with Capgras delusions are more likely to believe that the imposter is a clone or alien.

- **Fregoli delusion**—Belief that several different people are actually one person who is able to shapeshift or otherwise change his appearance. Shapeshifters are also common in folklore and fiction. In the 1998 thriller *Fallen*, the hero is trying to track down and kill a demon that can move from body to body, constantly changing its appearance. If the hero were to explain this belief to a therapist, the therapist would most likely diagnose a Fregoli delusion.

- **Cotard delusion** (aka **nihilistic delusion**)—Belief that one is dead or does not exist. In some cases the person argues that he has no internal organs or believes he is an immortal creature. People who have Cotard delusions are usually upset about having died, and some end up committing suicide trying to prove to others that they are dead. A study by McKay and Cipolotti recounts the story of a twenty-four-year-old secretary who "repeatedly stated that she was dead… She was extremely distressed and tearful as she related these beliefs, and was very anxious to learn whether or not the hospital she was in, was 'Heaven.' When asked how she thought she had died, she replied 'I don't know how. Now I know I had the flu…maybe I died of [the] flu." Therapy included asking her if she had ever seen a dead person and how that dead person had behaved. When the therapist pointed out that she did not behave in the same way, she "acknowledged that the fact that she herself was moving and talking was inconsistent with the typical characteristics of dead people, and she subsequently expressed some uncertainty about her beliefs."

- **Delusional parasitosis**—Belief that one has bugs crawling on or under the skin. (If the person can *feel* the imaginary bugs, he is experiencing a tactile hallucination, not a delusion. A person can experience simultaneous hallucinations and delusions.) One of the best fictional depictions of delusional parasitosis is the Tracy Letts play *Bug*, which was later adapted into a movie. In it, both of the main characters become convinced that their bodies are infested with bugs that transmit information back to the government. Frantic to stop the signals, they first line the apartment with tinfoil. Eventually, convinced that there is no other way to destroy the bugs, they set the place—and themselves—on fire.

- **Thought insertion.** Belief that someone (or something) else's thoughts are being placed in the person's mind.

- **Thought withdrawal**—Belief that someone (or something) else is stealing the person's thoughts.

- **Delusion of control**—Belief that someone (or something) else is controlling the person's body or behaviors. If your character believed that he had no free will, that some power—whether government, alien, or supernatural—were manipulating his every move, making him into a puppet of sorts, he would be diagnosed as suffering from a delusion of control. Thought insertion and thought withdrawal delusions are common with delusions of control.

## SCHIZOPHRENIA

There's usually more to schizophrenia than delusions and hallucinations. Disorganized thoughts and behaviors are characteristic of the disorder; so is catatonia.

Disorganization doesn't mean the person keeps his space messy; it means he has extremely jumbled and strange thoughts and behaviors. To be diagnosable, these symptoms must be so bad they make it nearly impossible for him to communicate effectively.

*Disorganized thoughts* are apparent in the way the person talks. He may answer questions with ideas that are completely unrelated to what the person asked ("tangentiality") or jump rapidly and repeatedly from idea to idea ("loose associations"). In severe cases, words are tossed together into a grammatically correct but nonsensical mess called a "word salad." The person may also create new words ("neologisms"). In many cases, the person does all of this in a normal conversational manner and without any indication that he knows he isn't making sense.

*Disorganized behavior* is a little harder to identify, since people sometimes behave in disorganized ways when they're under the influence of drugs or alcohol, or when they're really upset. A disorganized person may seem extremely agitated or display immature silliness. People who are deteriorating ("decompensating") into schizophrenia may be unable to maintain hygiene. As a result, they might be unkempt, smell bad, or wear layers and layers of clothing in spite of warm weather.

People who are *catatonic* may seem completely unaware of their surroundings, even though their eyes are open ("catatonic stupor"). In some cases they assume bizarre poses ("catatonic posturing"). They may become rigid and resist being moved ("catatonic rigidity"). In other cases, they will allow their limbs to be moved, and keep themselves in the position in which the other person placed them ("waxy flexibility").

Depending on which type of symptom is most prominent, schizophrenia is diagnosed with one of five subtype specifiers: paranoid, disorganized, catatonic, undifferentiated, or residual. People with the undifferentiated type do not meet the criteria for paranoid, disorganized, or catatonic subtypes, either because symptoms from all three appear, or because there are too few symptoms to diagnose any of those categories. Residual type is diagnosed when the person has clearly had schizophrenia, but is not currently having *severe* symptoms. Overall, people with the paranoid type of schizophrenia function better than those with disorganized, catatonic, or undifferentiated types.

Schizophrenia is considered by many experts to be the most crippling mental illness. It is not curable, and few if any sufferers ever recover full functionality. Because most people with schizophrenia don't understand or appreciate that they're sick, they're likely to ignore treatment suggestions, be hospitalized against their will, and overall do worse than people with other types of disorders. As a result, only about a third of people with schizophrenia are able to live independently. Most of the rest live with a family member or in a supervised group home; a few end up in jails, prisons, nursing homes, and hospitals; and around 6 percent end up living in shelters and on the streets.

Most people develop schizophrenia in their late teens or during their twenties. Sometimes the disorder appears suddenly ("acute onset," sometimes colloquially called a "psychotic break") as a result of a crisis or major life change; other times people decline slowly. Someone with acute onset may disappear, holing up in a dorm or apartment and ignoring the phone and the door. In these situations, it may not be until a family member, a landlord, or the police force their way in that someone finds the person. By contrast, the person may publicly display such bizarre behavior that witnesses call the authorities because they don't know how else to deal. Fortunately, in these situations the police know to take the person to a hospital.

The life spans of people with schizophrenia are shorter than those of the average person. Because they can have trouble taking care of themselves and holding a good job, they often struggle under poor living conditions and poverty. Ten percent commit suicide and an additional 10 to 30 percent make at least one suicide attempt.

**Additional information:**

- Eighty to 90 percent of people with schizophrenia smoke, most of them heavily. New research suggests that they are able to think better when they're using nicotine.

- In people with a particular gene type, using cannabis can contribute to the development of schizophrenia. That is, if your character has the genes to develop schizophrenia and he smokes a lot of marijuana, he's likely to trigger the schizophrenia.

- Schizophrenia can run in the family, but it's also more common in people whose brain development was disrupted prenatally because the mother got the flu during the second trimester. In these situations, the mother's antibodies cross the placenta and jumble up the organization of brain cells. Researchers aren't sure why this only happens in *some* people whose mothers got the flu. The most important brain chemical implicated in schizophrenia is dopamine. The "dopamine hypothesis" was derived from two observations. First, scientists noticed that people who take drugs that increase dopamine in the brain often develop temporary psychoses, including hallucinations and delusions. Second, drugs that block dopamine receptors in the brain reduce psychotic symptoms. Rather than there being too much dopamine in the brain, the problem seems to be that the brain cells (particularly the D2 receptors) are overly sensitive to dopamine.

**Misconceptions**

- Most people with schizophrenia are not violent. In those who are, delusions that someone or something is controlling them or persecuting them ("threat/control-override delusions") are usually to blame. However, because the average person with schizophrenia tends to retreat from other people, advocates argue that in most cases people with schizophrenia are *less* likely to be violent than other people.

- Schizophrenia is different from dissociative identity disorder (discussed in Chapter 8) and bipolar disorder. Neither people with schizophrenia nor people with bipolar disorder have "split" or multiple personalities. Only people with dissociative identity disorder (DID) have more than one personality.

---

**Q & A**

**Q:** How would the siblings of a person with schizophrenia function? What are the traits of a schizophrenic family bind that I used to hear about?

**A:** Because schizophrenia is a biological disease, siblings of people with schizophrenia are ten times more likely to develop the disorder than other people; they are also at greater risk for schizophrenic spectrum disorders like schizotypal personality disorder and schizoaffective disorder. So some siblings may have schizophrenic tendencies of their own, even if they don't have the full-blown disorder.

Double-bind theory is Gregory Bateman's 1950s-era proposition that what causes schizophrenia is repeated no-win dilemmas in the child's family life. In other words, the child is repeatedly confronted with statements that contain two contradictory statements (i.e. a double bind). Sometimes double binds are called "no-win situations," though double binds are often psychologically more complex than the average no-win situation. For example, imagine a mother who has a temper and withdraws love when something upsets her. Now imagine that this character insists that she will abandon her child (or otherwise stop loving him) if he doesn't provide her with negative feedback. Suddenly the child is trapped in a double bind. If he doesn't give her the negative feedback, she will withdraw love. If he does give her the negative

---

feedback, she will withdraw love. If he tells her that she's providing him with an unfair situation, she will withdraw love. Several of these messages are nonverbal, but they're there.

Because of the child's attachment to the caregiver, he is eager to do as the caregiver asked. The problem is that by meeting one demand, he would be defying the other. Because he is presented with such double binds on a regular basis, and because he doesn't have the cognitive maturity to know how to choose one statement over the other to escape the double bind, he eventually escapes from the extraordinary stress the double bind causes by retreating from the "real world" into psychosis (i.e. delusions and hallucinations).

Double-bind theory has fallen out of favor with regard to schizophrenia for two reasons. First, we have so much data that demonstrates a biological cause for schizophrenia rather than a wholly environmental one. Second, double-bind theory is nearly impossible to test, so there is little empirical research that can support it.

There is research, however, to support the idea that a problematic family environment can contribute to the relapse of someone who's been treated for schizophrenia. Most notably, people with schizophrenia are likely to relapse when their family is high in expressed emotion. Expressed emotion consists of three parts: criticism, hostility, and emotional over-involvement.

People with schizophrenia are extremely sensitive to stress, and being treated with constant dislike, disapproval, rejection, disrespect, and the assumption that they are not capable human beings is enough to stress anyone out!

So even if the siblings in your story don't have schizophrenic tendencies themselves, you could make them somewhat critical and hostile people who show a lot of expressed emotion toward their brother or sister!

## OTHER PSYCHOTIC DISORDERS

### Schizophreniform Disorder

The symptoms of schizophreniform disorder are the same as for schizophrenia except that the disorder has only lasted between one month and six months. As soon as the individual has had symptoms for six months and one day, the diagnosis becomes schizophrenia. In about a third of people, symptoms will disappear before the initial six months are up and never return, though researchers aren't sure why. The other two-thirds are eventually diagnosed with schizophrenia because the psychosis lasts or recurs.

---

### Don't Let This Happen to You!

Be careful not to make the same mistake Nate Kenyon did in *The Reach*, where a character has had a schizophreniform diagnosis for four years! Schizophreniform disorder is only diagnosed when schizophrenic symptoms have lasted six months or fewer. Kenyon also implies that schizophreniform disorder is a mild form of schizophrenia, which is inaccurate. Symptom severity can be just as bad as with schizophrenia.

---

## Brief Psychotic Disorder

In brief psychotic disorder, psychotic symptoms appear suddenly (i.e. the person has a "psychotic break") and can include hallucinations, delusions, disorganization, and/or catatonic behavior. Symptoms last for at least one day but less than one month, and always disappear before one month is up, leaving the person just like he was before the episode. Brief psychotic disorder is often triggered by a severe stressor or stressors; for example, catching a partner with a lover or being the victim of terrorism. Some women also experience postpartum psychosis; brief psychotic disorder is the official diagnosis in these situations..

## Schizoaffective Disorder

Schizoaffective disorder is diagnosed in people who clearly have *both* schizophrenia and either a major depressive disorder or bipolar I disorder. Though people with schizoaffective disorder may respond a little better to treatment than someone with schizophrenia alone, the coupling of two such crippling disorders can make living independently difficult.

In the movie *Terminator 2*, heroine Sarah Connor is diagnosed with schizoaffective disorder. From the doctor's perspective, her belief that a machine was sent back from the future to kill her and her unborn son looks like a bizarre delusion, and therefore she gets the schizophrenia diagnosis. Since her apparent delusions are coupled with major depressive episodes, a schizoaffective diagnosis makes more sense.

---

**Don't Let This Happen To You!**

In *The 6th Target*, James Patterson's psychiatrist describes schizoaffective disorder as "a kind of bipolar disorder" with "schizoid aspects." The author has jumbled several diagnoses together, misusing both the term "bipolar" and the term "schizoid."

While someone with schizoaffective disorder *may* have bipolar disorder with his schizophrenia, he could alternately have another mood disorder, such as major depressive disorder. Therefore, not all people with schizoaffective disorder display "ups and downs, despair and depression—and hyperactivity or mania," as Patterson's psychiatrist claims.

People with schizoid personality disorder are uninterested in relationships because they perceive them as too "messy." They display so few emotions they can seem robotic to others. In other words, their behavior is in direct contrast to bipolar disorder. Usually when people misuse the term "schizoid," as Patterson has, they mean to refer to "schizophrenic" or psychotic behavior.

Patterson would have been safer if he'd used a simple description like the one under the *schizoaffective disorder* heading above.

---

## Delusional Disorder

People with delusional disorders have had a fixed nonbizarre delusion for at least one month but don't meet the criteria for schizophrenia or a mood disorder. Except with regard to the delusion itself, people with this disorder do not behave strangely.

People with erotomanic type delusions believe that someone of higher status is in love with them; celebrity stalkers often have erotomanic delusions. People with grandiose delusions believe they have special power or knowledge or that they are deities or celebrities. People with jealous delusions believe their sexual partners are being unfaithful. People with persecutory delusions believe someone is out to get them.

## Shared Psychotic Disorder (Folie à Deux)

Sometimes, someone who has a psychotic disorder convinces someone else that his bizarre or nonbizarre delusions are true. If the relationship with the person who had the original delusion (the "primary case") is disrupted, the second person's delusion will usually disappear. Shared psychotic disorders appear most often in relatives or spouses of people with schizophrenia or another psychotic disorder.

---

### IT'S NOT PARANOIA IF THEY'RE REALLY OUT TO GET YOU

In the 1970s, Martha Mitchell, the wife of Nixon administration Attorney-General John Mitchell, told her therapist that White House officials were involved in illegal activities. The therapist diagnosed her with a nonbizarre delusional disorder, but when the Watergate scandal broke, it was obvious to everyone that Martha had been telling the truth!

Psychologist Brendan Maher subsequently coined the term "Martha Mitchell effect" to refer to any time a therapist misdiagnoses someone who's telling the truth with a delusional disorder.

---

## TREATMENT FOR PSYCHOTIC DISORDERS

Medication is the cornerstone for treatment of someone with a psychotic disorder. Antipsychotics are the most obvious medication because they block the brain chemicals that cause the psychosis. Doctors may also prescribe mood stabilizers, antidepressants, and anti-anxiety drugs to help with the range of symptoms. Electroconvulsive therapy is used more often with mood disorders than schizophrenia, though it sometimes can help with acute psychosis.

Psychodynamic therapies (see Chapter 2) are *not* recommended for people with schizophrenia because their capacity for insight is low. Instead, they need practical advice and support. Cognitive-behavioral and supportive therapies are a better fit, because therapists can help clients and their families with problem-solving and management of the illness. This management might include learning to take medication consistently, recognizing signs of an impending relapse, learning how to collaborate with case and social workers, dealing with hallucinations and delusions, and building social skills. As noted earlier, most people with schizophrenia need to live with family or another support system, and if that environment is high-stress—either because the family is critical of or hostile toward the client, or because the family is over-involved—relapse is almost inevitable. Therefore, interventions with family members are also crucial.

**Q & A**

**Q:** Could a person with schizophrenia have such a mild version that to most he appears completely normal? That is, could he just have a few "quirks" that appear during periods of high stress? My villain has murdered a man who gave him bad investment advice; he now threatens the heroine because he's afraid she'll tell what he did.

**A:** Because schizophrenia has such a profound effect on one's thoughts and behavior, it's going to be obvious to anyone who spends much time around the person that something is up. And while many people who have schizophrenia do better on medications or have periods when their symptoms are reduced, the disorder still wouldn't be transient in the way you're describing.

A better fit for your story would be a delusional disorder; persecutory type. People with delusional disorders often seem just like others until the delusional idea is activated, and stress from a situation like the one you described would certainly make your villain's paranoia worse. It is also possible that someone as desperate as your villain might kill as part of his delusional disorder.

# 7
# The Disorders, Part II
## *Childhood Disorders, Dementia, and Eating Disorders*

In this chapter, we'll look at disorders that usually first show up during a particular stage of life, and therefore might be appropriate for your characters in those age groups. For example, ADHD and autistic spectrum disorders are normally diagnosed during childhood, while eating disorders are most often diagnosed in teens and dementia is usually diagnosed in the elderly. Note that disorders that are first diagnosed in children and teens don't usually spontaneously disappear as the person gets older. Sometimes the way the disorder looks changes over time because the person learns to adapt to her symptoms in order to "get by" in the world; however, the disorder itself is still present.

## DISORDERS USUALLY FIRST DIAGNOSED IN INFANCY, CHILDHOOD, OR ADOLESCENCE

### AUTISTIC SPECTRUM DISORDERS

Autistic spectrum disorders (ASD) are neurological conditions. That is, the brains of people with ASD are wired differently than other people's. As a result, people with ASD are confounded by social interactions and have trouble communicating effectively with others. Nonverbals like gestures and vocal tone can feel like a foreign language to them. Since they have trouble understanding their own and others' emotional states, they can also have trouble expressing the "right" emotion for the situation. Because they don't have a good social filter, they sometimes make remarks that seem uncouth to others— "I really like the hair dye you're using," for example. Their attempts to conform to social conventions can also backfire. For example, if they've been taught that they should nod and smile when others are talking, they might continue to do so even as someone talks about a recent death in the family. Finally, routine and sameness is so important to some people with ASD that they may react to changes in the daily schedule with emotional outbursts or other extreme behavior. Though many learn to adapt to changes as they get closer to adulthood, others continue to feel anxious or lost and adrift when something unexpected happens. Routines make the day more predictable and manageable.

Severe ASD is usually diagnosed before the age of three because children with the disorder don't begin speaking at the same time as other children. Sometimes they never learn to speak at all, though they may learn to communicate through sign language. When they do use language, they often do so in an odd way. For example, they may involuntarily repeat what they hear ("echolalia"), have trouble using the correct pronoun (they say "he" when they mean "I"), or say the same thing over and over ("perseveration"). They may avoid interacting or playing with their caregivers or other children, make only limited eye contact, and resist being cuddled. They might also repeat actions like rocking, spinning, or pacing in a pattern for long periods of time, and they are usually preoccupied with objects rather than people. Remember though, symptoms vary with the individual. Many people with autism *can* make eye contact, speak, show affection, and pick up nonverbal cues. Their approaches to these things may just be idiosyncratic.

While about 75 percent of people with severe forms of ASD also have intellectual disabilities, the other 25 percent function at average or above-average levels. Further, only about 10 percent of people with ASD are savants. Like Dustin Hoffman's character in the movie *Rain Man*, savants show extraordinary skills with music, math, or another area.

Children with milder ASD, which is called Asperger's disorder, are less likely to have intellectual or language delays. Instead, their problems revolve around social interactions. As a result, the ASD diagnosis may not be made until they reach grade school. Rather than displaying ritualized behaviors and preoccupation with objects, people with less severe ASD often like to collect information and facts on a particular topic. Irony, humor, and the give-and-take nature of conversation may escape them, but many do want relationships with others.

Children with Asperger's may prefer the company of adults, who better understand why people with ASD are the way they are and behave in a more predictable way than other children. As they get older, high-functioning people with ASD often choose careers that let them work with math, science, or technology, and thus may choose to become engineers, researchers, and programmers.

ASD is four to five times more common in males than in females. According to researchers, this may not be because autism is genetically a sex-linked problem. Instead, girls may be biologically and environmentally primed to be better at navigating the social world. As a result, they are better able to hide or overcome symptoms.

## Additional Information

- People with autistic siblings are more likely to be autistic themselves, or to have other developmental disabilities.

- People often prejudge and discriminate against those with autistic spectrum disorders and their families. Strangers regularly assume that eccentric or annoying behavior is the parents' fault and make rude remarks intended to force the parent to step up and discipline the child. Though the children themselves are often treated poorly by peers because they're "weird," their poor understanding of social language may keep them from realizing they're being mocked or laughed at.

## Misconceptions

- Because autistic spectrum disorders can seem uniformly strange to people unfamiliar with them, there is a tendency to say things like, "All people with autism avoid making eye contact." In fact, many people with ASD can and do make eye contact. Since ASD symptoms tend to be idiosyncratic, be wary of making blanket generalizations in your story about *all* people with autism or Asperger's disorder.

- A stereotype perpetuated by films like *Rain Man* is the idea that someone with autism or Asperger's would be happiest in an institution. In reality, mental health systems around the country have worked hard to get these people *out* of institutions and integrated into the community. Though in many cases this means moving them into group homes, sometimes even people with severe ASD can live in their own homes with housemates they've chosen.

### *Treatments for Autistic Spectrum Disorders*

Though there is no cure for ASD, many do function better in society with treatment.

As with other disorders, psychiatrists prescribe medications based on symptoms. For example, antidepressants like Prozac and Luvox can decrease irritability and reduce repetitive behaviors, antipsychotics like Zyprexa and Seroquel can decrease hyperactivity and stereotypical behaviors, and stimulants like Ritalin and Adderall can decrease hyperactivity and impulsiveness. Some vitamins and supplements like vitamin B, vitamin C, and cod liver oil have also been shown to help with behavioral problems and attention deficits.

Most people with autism respond well to structured behavioral interventions. Applied Behavioral Analysis (ABA) is a rewards-based approach to teaching life skills. Speech therapy, occupational therapy, social skills therapy, and/or physical therapy can help people with ASD to make better eye contact, interpret gestures, and use sarcasm and humor appropriately.

Some people with ASD respond extremely well to trained animal companions (usually cats or dogs) or therapeutic interactions with animals (including horses and dolphins). In many cases, they're able to show the animals the affection they don't know how to show people. Taking care of the animals also teaches them about responsibility, commitment, and problem-solving, and can help them improve social and language skills and confidence. The animals help in other ways, too, since they're trained to respond helpfully when the individual is upset or confused.

## ATTENTION DEFICIT HYPERACTIVITY DISORDER (ADHD)

Some people with attention deficit hyperactivity disorder (ADHD) have trouble paying attention. Their brains aren't able to selectively pay attention to one thing versus another; instead, they tag irrelevant distractions like the ticking of a clock as being as important as, for example, a teacher's voice. A second group of people with ADHD can pay attention, but they have trouble controlling impulses and hyperactive behaviors. Finally, a third group struggles with both inattention and hyperactivity.

School-age children with ADHD typically have difficulties with academics, and children who are particularly hyperactive may also have problems with accidentally hurting themselves as well as peer rejection.

ADHD often persists into adulthood, but people learn to adapt to it, which means that adult symptoms can look different than children's. Adults with ADHD are often disorganized and forgetful, manage their time poorly, miss parts of conversations, jump from one project to another, make careless mistakes, and say and do things without thinking.

To be diagnosable, the problematic behaviors must occur in multiple settings, be extremely uncommon in the person's age group, and be impairing the person's social, occupational, or family life. Since ADHD becomes particularly debilitating once a child begins school, it is usually diagnosed after schooling begins.

**Additional Information**

- ADD (Attention Deficit Disorder) and ADHD (Attention Deficit Hyperactivity Disorder) are the same thing. In 1994, the American Psychiatric Association changed the name from ADD to ADHD. Some health professionals still use the term ADD to refer to ADHD without hyperactivity.

- People with ADHD may also have problems with conduct disorder, mood disorders, anxiety disorders, or learning disorders.

- Abbreviated attention spans and easy distractibility don't always indicate ADHD. Sometimes they're symptoms of mania. (See the information on bipolar disorders in Chapter 6.) Especially in children, mania can be misdiagnosed as ADHD.

- Most people with ADHD have the ability to hyperfocus. They can become completely absorbed by a task they find engaging. Since they can pay attention and sit still while they're hyperfocused, others may mistakenly believe they don't actually have ADHD.

- Writer Thom Hartmann has proposed that ADHD is an evolutionary throwback to when our ancestors were hunters. Hunters had to constantly be on the lookout for danger and prey (which looks like inattention in a modern setting), able to make quick decisions (that is, be impulsive), and focus intently on a task like the hunt (hyperfocusing). Following the agricultural and industrial revolutions, humans needed to become more patient, linear-thinking, and detail-oriented. Schools still stress deliberation, planning, and repetitive techniques, which don't mesh well with the hunter brain. While Hartmann's ideas began as a metaphor designed to reduce the stigma of ADHD, research suggests that this metaphor may be based in reality.

## *Treatment of ADHD*

Psychological and behavioral interventions are the treatments of choice for ADHD because they help clients learn to manage their symptoms. Many people misunderstand the purpose of accommodations for school-children with ADHD, seeing them as "special treatment" when the true goal is to level the playing field and teach the child how to manage his symptoms as he grows into an adult. While some accommodations, like being able to take a test in a quiet room, directly affect the child's ability to perform on the exam, the child is also learning that he performs better without distractions. Not only should this affect how he studies, it should help him figure out how best to get his work done in a future career. For example, he might need to request a quiet conference room to complete important paperwork.

ADHD lasts into adulthood for about 60 percent of people. Therapy for adults may include coaching to help them keep their home and work lives organized, find ways to minimize distractions, control impulsive behavior that causes problems, and find hobbies that provide outlets for hyperactive and nervous energy.

Stimulant medications can also be helpful for both children and adults. Research suggests that the part of the brain that "puts the brakes on" behavior is underactive in people with ADHD. A stimulant increases the activity in this area, making it easier for the individual to pay attention and control impulsive and hyperactive behavior.

## CONDUCT DISORDER

Children or adolescents who persistently violate others' basic rights or flaunt societal norms are diagnosed with conduct disorder. They may be aggressive toward others—tormenting them, using weapons against them, attacking or assaulting them, or forcing them into sexual activity. They may vandalize property or commit arson, break into people's homes, run cons, steal expensive items, forge checks, or use blackmail. They often skip school, stay out despite parental rules, and run away from home.

One of film's best examples of conduct disorder is Christian Slater's character, JD, in the cult hit *Heathers*. After shooting a pair of jocks with blanks, JD starts killing off the popular kids and making each murder look like a suicide. In real life, children and teens who commit aggressive and violent acts like school shootings would also be diagnosed with (at the very least) conduct disorder.

**Additional Information**

- Conduct disorder can appear in preschoolers. Ted Bundy was only three when he threatened his aunt by placing butcher knives in her bed while she was in it.

- Researchers point to several possible causes for conduct disorder, including abnormal brain wave patterns ("neurological dysregulation"), a lack of emphasis on personal responsibility, and extremely stressful family lives. Children with conduct disorder are more likely to come from families with maternal depression, paternal alcoholism or criminality, antisocial parents, divorce, family violence, poverty, or unemployment. Parents are often violent, critical, inconsistent, and overly permissive, and sometimes they even punish pro-social behavior.

- Antisocial Personality Disorder (APD), the adult version of conduct disorder, cannot be diagnosed in people who are younger than eighteen. For someone to be diagnosed with an antisocial personality disorder, he must have shown evidence of a conduct disorder before the age of fifteen. You can read more about APD in Chapter 9.

## *Treatments for Conduct Disorder*

Because children with conduct disorder are often defiant and untrusting of adults, treating them can be difficult. Goals include the development of appropriate problem-solving skills and pro-social behaviors, and therapists often intervene with family members as well as with the child.

Children and teens with conduct disorder often have additional diagnoses that are treated with medication—stimulants for ADHD, for example, or a mood stabilizer for bipolar disorder. Appropriate treatment of these problems can positively impact the conduct disorder symptoms.

---

### DON'T LET THIS HAPPEN TO YOU!

In James Patterson's novel *Jack & Jill*, one character's "doctors couldn't figure out whether he was a bipolar disorder or conduct disorder." The most obvious question here is how any psychological professional could be stymied by the difference between two such different diagnoses. Though people with bipolar disorder can be irritable and difficult, they don't consistently violate other people's rights;

---

meanwhile, people with conduct disorder alone don't have mood symptoms. Of course, the two disorders can be diagnosed simultaneously, but even then two distinct diagnoses exist.

The wording is also a little awkward. If the character who was speaking was indeed a psychological professional, it would be important to refer to the boy as "a *person with* bipolar disorder or conduct disorder." The American Psychological Association discourages the popular convention of calling a person by his diagnosis.

## DISORDERS THAT TYPICALLY OCCUR LATE IN LIFE: DEMENTIA

Dementia is abnormally severe cognitive decline caused by brain damage or disease. Alzheimer's, Parkinson's, Huntington's, Creutzfield-Jakob, and Pick's disease are all types of dementia, and sometimes it's not clear which form an individual had until after he dies and the brain can be autopsied. Dementia appears most often in people who are over sixty-five years old, and especially in people who are eighty-five or older; however, your character could also have dementia as a result of head trauma, AIDS, or substance abuse.

People with dementia have problems with memory and other thinking ("cognitive") processes. Common symptoms include aphasia, apraxia, agnosia, and disturbances in executive functioning:

- *Aphasia* is an impairment in the use of language and speech. *Receptive aphasia* means the person has trouble understanding language and is caused by damage to a section of the brain's left frontal lobe called Wernicke's area. *Expressive aphasia* means the person has trouble producing language and is due to damage to a section of the left temporal lobe called Broca's area. Damage can be caused by things like accidents, stroke, and disease.

- *Agnosia* is an inability to recognize and name something that should be familiar. For example, someone with *tactile agnosia* can't identify a triangle just by touching it. Someone with *color agnosia* can't tell you that a particular color is green. *Mirror agnosia* means the person can't recognize himself in the mirror.

- *Apraxia* is an inability to make one's body do what one wants it to, even though the body works fine. This can make it difficult for someone to cook, eat, write, brush their teeth, or dress themselves.

- *Executive functioning* lets us pay attention, plan, think abstractly, make decisions, react to unexpected events, find creative solutions, and decide which behaviors are appropriate in a given situation.

Disturbances in these four types of cognitive processes can lead to poor judgment and unrealistic plans or decisions, or to inappropriate behaviors. Problems often start slowly, with sufferers occasionally becoming confused and disoriented. Though their symptoms can interfere with their lives, some can hide the problems for a while by avoiding difficult tasks.

As the disease progresses, the problems become more obvious. Sufferers may forget that they are supposed to be taking care of a child or cooking food on the stove, get lost in their own neighborhoods, or forget important facts like their birthdays or even their own names. Over time, family members may also notice personality changes. A few people with dementia become more easygoing and mellow, while others become suspicious, fearful, depressed, anxious, or confused. Because they have trouble communicating and doing tasks that were once easy for them, they can become agitated and even hostile in an attempt to communicate or express frustration. In the late stages of dementia they have trouble with basic tasks like using the bathroom and keeping themselves clean. Apraxia can prevent walking and even swallowing, but these things aren't usually fatal. As with many elderly people, death is usually the result of an infection like pneumonia.

Though physicians and nurses handle many aspects of the treatment of someone with dementia, additional psychological problems are common, necessitating the assistance of a psychological professional. Between 20 and 30 percent of people who have dementia also have depression, about 20 percent struggle with anxiety, and psychosis is common. Up to 25 percent of patients experience hallucinations, and up to a third experience delusions. Both types of psychosis appear gradually over several months, and the most common delusional themes are persecutory: they believe that someone is stealing from them, abusing them, or cheating on them.

The most common hallucinations are visual rather than auditory. They see things like people, animals, light flashes, patterns, objects, distorted faces, and bizarre landscapes. The hallucinations usually only last a few seconds, though in some people they persist.

**Additional Information**

- Alzheimer's disease is the most common form of dementia.

- The neurological hallmarks of Alzheimer's, visible only during an autopsy, are called plaques and tangles. Tangles are the unraveling, bunching together, and knotting of the brain cells. Plaques are abnormal protein buildup. The plaques and tangles interfere with the brain's ability to send and receive messages, resulting in confusion, memory loss, language problems, and personality changes.

**Misconceptions**

- Not all cognitive decline in older people is dementia. For dementia to be diagnosed, the cognitive impairments have to be interfering with the person's ability to function.

- Studies haven't supported the ideas that contact with aluminum, mercury, or aspartame (the sweetener behind NutraSweet and Equal) contribute to Alzheimer's disease.

## Treatments for Dementia

- *Dementia prevention.* Staying mentally, physically, and socially active as one ages can keep the brain healthier and possibly reduce the risk of dementia.

- *Reversible dementia.* If the dementia is caused by drugs or alcohol or nutrition or hormone imbalances, it may be reversible.

- *Vascular dementia.* If dementia is caused by stroke, it's not reversible, but by reducing the risk of additional strokes, the treatment team can reduce the likelihood that the dementia will get worse.

- *Progressive dementia.* Alzheimer's, Parkinson's, and Huntington's dementias are all progressive and cannot be halted or reversed.

Dementia is most often treated with cholinesterase inhibitors, which slow the breakdown of acetylcholine, a substance in the brain that helps people remember and think. Depending on the individual's other symptoms, the physician or nurse practitioner may also prescribe drugs like anticonvulsants, antidepressants, anti-anxiety medications, or antipsychotic drugs. Vitamins like vitamin C, vitamin E, and folic acid can also be helpful.

Rather than arguing with patients who are hallucinating or delusional, psychological professionals use techniques like distraction, redirection, and structured activities. When all else fails, doses of antipsychotic medications for people with dementia typically start at one-quarter to one-half of normal doses due to the patient's age.

To help people in earlier stages of dementia, psychological professionals can recommend memory tricks ("mnemonics") and memory aids like calendars, lists, and written instructions. As the dementia gets worse, families may move the person with dementia into their own homes or enlist the help of elder companions who can assist with housekeeping, cooking, and errands. Eventually, some families choose to place their loved one in an assisted-living facility or a nursing home. At all stages of dementia, caregivers can help by patiently explaining what they are doing, maintaining a set routine, and remembering that, regardless of her problems, the person with dementia still deserves to be treated with dignity and respect.

---

### DON'T LET THIS HAPPEN TO YOU!

Though Nicholas Sparks's novel and subsequent film *The Notebook* provides one of the most famous depictions of dementia, it definitely isn't the most accurate. Alzheimer's affects short-term memory first, not long term memory. Many people with Alzheimer's can recall incidents from decades earlier in vivid detail. In fact, someone who has progressed to the point that she can't recall her family would not be perfectly coiffed and eloquent—she'd be bedridden, unable to remember things from one minute to the next, and unable to perform even simple tasks.

A far more accurate depiction is neuroscientist Lisa Genova's *Still Alice*, which follows the title character through her brutal battle with early-onset Alzheimer's.

# DISORDERS THAT TYPICALLY OCCUR DURING THE TEEN YEARS: EATING DISORDERS

About 90 percent of the people diagnosed with eating disorders are female, and most of them are white. Male eating disorders are most common among gay and bisexual men and athletes whose performance is affected by their weight—for example, wrestlers, jockeys, runners, and gymnasts. As movies and television push the envelope on the "perfect" male body, however, more heterosexual men are becoming preoccupied with attaining unrealistic body ideals and taking more extreme measures to reach those ideals. For these men, the focus is on reducing body fat, increasing athletic performance, and becoming muscular through compulsive over-exercise rather than on being thin. The 2003 film *Seabiscuit*, which shows the main character forcing himself to vomit so he can weigh less and ride faster, was based on Laura Hillenbrand's book by the same name. "The weight maximums were so low [for horse jockeys]," she writes, "that near fasting and water deprivation weren't enough. Even what little water and calories the body had taken in had to be eliminated. Many riders were 'heavers,' poking their fingers down their throats to vomit up their meals."

Research clearly links eating disorders to the consumption of media that promote bodies that are difficult, if not impossible, for the average person to attain. When American, Australian, and British television programs like *Friends*, *Melrose Place*, and *Ally McBeal* reached the Pacific island of Fiji in the late 1990s, the ideal body shape became drastically thinner and disordered eating behavior skyrocketed.

Despite the denials of the fashion industry, models sometimes struggle with eating disorders. For example, '90s supermodel Carré Otis, who appeared in Guess jeans ads and *Sports Illustrated Swimsuit* issues, suffered from anorexia. When doctors discovered three holes in her heart caused by malnutrition, they warned her that she would die if she continued her eating-disordered ways. Otis decided to become a plus-sized model. More recently, in 2006 and 2007, three young models died of anorexia, rocking the fashion industry. The agency that represented one of the girls was encouraging her to "lose a few more pounds" when she collapsed and died during a fashion show. At 5'9", twenty-two-year-old Luisel Ramos weighed a mere ninety-nine pounds.

## ANOREXIA NERVOSA

There are two types of anorexia: restricting type and binge-eating/purging type. Regardless, people with anorexia refuse to maintain 85 percent of what would be considered normal weight for their age, height, and build. That is, what separates anorexia from bulimia is *not* binging and purging—it's the person's typical weight. Someone with anorexia is severely underweight, while someone with bulimia is usually around normal weight.

Despite how tiny they are, people with anorexia are phobic about gaining weight or becoming fat. Women with anorexia often stop having periods ("amenorrhea"), and both men and women develop symptoms like weakness, exhaustion, dizziness, fainting, sensitivity to cold, and kidney and heart problems. Some grow a fine layer of downy hair called lanugo, which is the body's attempt to keep itself warm when it's malnourished.

Between 10 and 20 percent of people with anorexia die of complications related to the disease. Up to half of those deaths are due to suicide.

Eating disorders often have a genetic basis, and anorexia in particular is usually triggered by transitions (e.g. moving to a new city or school, parental divorce, or puberty) and relationship problems. The individual develops the disorder as a way to try to feel in control of a world that feels out of control. Sufferers are typically bright, attractive, conscientious, and perfectionistic young women who feel lonely, defective, and inadequate on the inside. They may come from rigid, enmeshed families who emphasize overachievement or physical fitness.

When asked why they don't try to recover, girls with anorexia say things like "How would I define myself without it?" and "If I parted with it, I'd be alone, and right now I just can't afford to be alone." Possibly the most revealing answer, though, is "Because my eating disorder is the symptom and not the cause."

### Additional Information

- Anorexia often appears around puberty. Sometimes girls are horrified by the natural development of breasts and hips, assuming the changes mean they're getting fat. Others aren't ready to grow up and unconsciously lean on the disorder to try to avoid becoming an adult.

- Major depressive disorder commonly co-occurs with anorexia. In those who have obsessions and compulsions beyond those associated with food, obsessive-compulsive disorder may also be diagnosed. A few people are also diagnosed with obsessive-compulsive personality disorder (OCPD; see Chapter 9).

- People with anorexia who binge and purge are more likely than those with the restricting type to abuse drugs or alcohol, attempt suicide, or meet the diagnostic criteria for borderline personality disorder.

- The official cause of death for someone who's anorexic is usually heart failure or kidney malfunction caused by starvation.

- Because treatment of eating disorders is often not covered by insurance, it gets expensive very quickly. The South Carolina Department of Mental Health estimates that treatment costs between $500 and $2,000 a day, costing families tens and sometimes hundreds of thousands of dollars.

**Misconceptions**
- Though anorexia appears most commonly in white adolescent females, it is not limited to that population. People with anorexia can be, for example, male, black, Latino, pregnant, or a long time out of their teen years.

- Not all people with anorexia are easy to identify; many are good at hiding their disorder. They often wear baggy clothes, eat in front of other people, and deny they have an eating disorder.

## PRO-EATING DISORDER WEBSITES

Thanks to pro-eating disorder websites, anorexia (aka "Ana") and bulimia (aka "Mia") have become a religion to legions of young women. Ana and Mia have been personified into goddesses who expect slavish obedience to their "thin commandments." The popular *Letter from Mia* says, "you might feel [like] a servant, but then you will think of all I do for you and remember that I am your only true friend." And part of the *Letter to Ana* reads, "I offer you my soul, my heart, and my bodily functions….I pledge to obtain the ability to…lower my weight to the single digits…to fear food, and to see obese images in the mirror. I will worship you and be a faithful servant until death does [sic] us part."

The websites are peppered with images of bony models (often referred to as "thinspiration") and girls with their lips sewn shut. Some include sayings like "get thin or die trying" and song lyrics that promote obsession, over-exercise, thinness, and the blurry, disconnected state of mind produced by starvation. Most include tips like "drink ice water to make your body work harder to keep your temperature up" and "only eat soft foods during a binge, they are easier to vomit." Some include links to recipes and "food porn," which is "food for your eyes and not your thighs"—appetizing images that look like they belong on a restaurant menu. Here and there are links to additional information on problems commonly associated with eating disorders, like compulsive over-exercise and self-injury.

Most pro-ana and pro-mia sites masquerade as support sites, some going so far as to say "don't do the things below!" with an implied wink. Many clinicians bemoan the existence of these sites because it's difficult to convince someone to give up her pro-ana or pro-mia ways when the web is packed with sites glorifying the disorder (while claiming they do nothing of the sort).

If you're writing about a character with an eating disorder, be sure to consider the ways the internet might be supporting her disorder or making it worse.

## BULIMIA NERVOSA

People with bulimia binge and then compensate for the food intake in some way. Some purge by using laxatives, diuretics, enemas, or vomiting, while others fast or exercise excessively.

A binge is defined as the consumption of an abnormally huge amount of food in a short period of time—often so much food that the average person has trouble imagining eating so much without being sick. During the binge, the individual feels out of control. After the binge, guilt drives her to compensate in some way for all that she ate.

Vomiting is the most common method of purging, followed by the misuse of laxatives. Some women also abuse thyroid hormones, diet pills, and stimulants like Ritalin to try to control their weight.

Thanks to the binge-purge cycle, people with bulimia often have electrolyte and fluid imbalances. Vomiting causes physical symptoms like cracked lips, acid reflux, swollen salivary glands, broken blood vessels in the face, and tooth damage, while the abuse of laxatives results in rectal bleeding and hemorrhoids. Though fewer people die from bulimia than anorexia, electrolyte imbalances can lead to heart attacks. Gastric or esophageal ruptures can also be deadly.

**Additional Information**

- Experts estimate that between 20 percent and 50 percent of college-aged individuals engage in bulimia-like behaviors without meeting full diagnostic criteria.

- Sometimes people who start out with anorexia develop bulimia later in life. Partly for this reason, bulimia tends to appear in a slightly older population than anorexia.

- Family members of people with bulimia may have disorders like depression, anxiety, personality disorders, substance abuse problems, eating disorders, or physical illness.

# Treatments for Eating Disorders

The first goal of anorexia treatment is to get the individual to gain weight so she won't die. The second goal is to eliminate the problems that cause and maintain the disorder. If someone is below 15 percent of her normal body weight, has associated medical issues, or is in danger of suicide, she's likely to be hospitalized. If she refuses to eat regular meals, she might be force-fed through a tube that's passed through her nose and down into her stomach. With bulimia, there's far less risk of the person dying during treatment, so the primary goal is to change eating patterns.

Though there are no medications specifically for eating disorders, doctors may use antidepressants to treat the underlying depression. Anti-anxiety medications are also common, as are estrogen supplements, which help with the osteoporosis that can accompany anorexia.

Studies show that cognitive-behavioral therapy is the most effective intervention for eating disorders because it attacks the irrational thinking and behavior patterns. The second most effective treatment is interpersonal psychotherapy, which has a more psychodynamic feel and focuses on relationships. Some clinicians recommend family or group therapies, while others discourage parental involvement, believing that the sufferer learned the unhealthy messages she uses to maintain her disorder from the family. Finally, some therapists employ feminist therapy techniques. Feminist therapies are systems-based treatments that seek to empower women and free them from the social and cultural messages that suggest that a woman's worth should be based on how thin or beautiful she is.

# 8
# The Disorders, Part III
*Posttraumatic Stress Disorder and Dissociation*

## ACUTE STRESS DISORDER AND POSTTRAUMATIC STRESS DISORDER (PTSD)

In the psychological sense, trauma is a brutal attack on an individual's sense of self, ability to cope, and feelings of competence. Acute stress disorder and posttraumatic stress disorder (PTSD) are the psychological fallout from an experience so terrifying that it completely overloaded all of the person's mental resources and defenses, leaving him utterly degraded and helpless. The trauma is so intense that it can change the body's biochemistry, leaving the person stuck in a hyper-alert mode. This causes problems with thinking clearly, sleeping normally, regulating emotions, maintaining self-esteem, relating to other people, and finding hope for the future.

Though most people exhibit some PTSD-like symptoms following a trauma, acute stress disorder and PTSD are *only* diagnosed when the symptoms are persistent and extreme. For the first four weeks following the trauma, acute stress disorder is the diagnosis; after four weeks, it's PTSD. In about half of the people who are diagnosed with acute stress, the symptoms diminish and a diagnosis of PTSD is never made. Understanding and support from others can make an enormous difference in whether the symptoms resolve themselves without therapy.

People with PTSD have three types of symptoms:

1. *Intrusive symptoms.* Reminders, called "triggers," cause the person to re-experience the trauma through flashbacks, nightmares, and vivid, intrusive memories. The person may react to the trigger with a fight

reaction, a flight reaction, or freeze reaction. Fight or flight reactions are caused by a burst of adrenaline. Freeze reactions are caused by a burst of the stress hormone and neurotransmitter noradrenaline. There's no telling which reaction someone's body will have, so just pick the one that fits your story's needs best.

2. *Avoidant symptoms.* Consciously or unconsciously, the person tries to avoid reminders of the trauma. For example, someone whose child was viciously attacked by a dog in a garden might not only avoid flowers but also large patches of grass. He might withdraw from other people, stop pursuing hobbies, or become convinced that he isn't going to live very long. Dissociative symptoms—feelings of detachment, numbness, or amnesia for parts of the trauma—are also common.

3. *Hyperarousal.* The person is easy to startle, feels irritable, has trouble sleeping, and is constantly on the lookout for danger. He might tell you he feels like his skin is crawling or like he's "on the ceiling" with anxiety.

Though war veterans and rape survivors often develop PTSD, they're not the only ones. Serious plane and car crashes, explosions, fires, muggings and robberies, terrorist attacks, kidnappings and hostage situations,

## CHANGES IN THE BRAIN WITH PTSD

Trauma can affect both brain chemistry and brain structures. People with PTSD tend to experience atrophy of the hippocampus thanks to high cortisol levels. Cortisol is a stress hormone, and over time it can damage neurons, especially the ones in the hippocampus, the brain's learning and memory center. As a result, survivors often have trouble learning new material. Meanwhile, the amygdala, which deals with emotional responses, is often enlarged, contributing to extremely strong emotional reactions.

Severe stress also leads to depletion of neurotransmitters like norepinephrine, dopamine, serotonin, and endogenous opioids. Sufficient quantities of these neurotransmitters buffer us against further stressors and help us deal with our emotions. In people who have PTSD, however, reduced neurotransmitter levels can lead to depression, mood swings, outbursts, an exaggerated startle response, and overreactions to subsequent stress.

domestic violence, natural disasters, and being diagnosed with a terminal illness can also cause PTSD.

In general, human sadism is the most common cause of PTSD. Something about knowing that another human being has *chosen* to harm you or someone you care about overwhelms the psyche. In the film *Shutter Island*, the main character, Teddy, is one of the soldiers who freed the prisoners from the Dachau concentration camp in 1945. Over and over he relives the nightmare of finding so many innocent women and children discarded and frozen like so much garbage. Because he also lost his own family to traumatic events, he often sees their faces superimposed on the remembered bodies. In both situations—finding the murdered prisoners and losing his own family—he felt so overwhelmingly powerless to deal with the horrific acts of others that he developed PTSD.

Some people also experience secondary wounding when people and institutions to which they have turned for help react in ways that harm them all over again. PTSD expert Aphrodite Matsakis recounts the experience of a concert violinist who survived a hurricane, only to be told that three of her fingers needed to be amputated. When she began to cry, the nurse called her a "big crybaby," adding, "Look around you. Bed number one has lost his arm, and bed two has to have both legs removed. Count your blessings and don't upset the others."

People often minimize how enormously the trauma has or will impact the survivor. They may also disbelieve him; blame him; argue that he just wants money, attention, or sympathy he doesn't deserve; treat him like he's crazy; or ridicule him. Rape and incest survivors, for example, are often treated as though they "asked for" or "deserved" to be assaulted. Victims of domestic violence who gather the courage to leave are often blamed for "breaking up a happy home" or "taking the children away from [the other parent]." In some cases, it's not the actual trauma that causes the PTSD, it's the secondary wounding experience.

The people who cause secondary wounding usually don't want to accept that something so horrible can happen to another person because that would damage their own sense of security. They may be ignorant or unable to comprehend the other person's experience. If they're rescue workers, they may be burned out or numb to all the things they see on a daily basis.

PTSD frequently appears with major depressive disorder, bipolar disorder, and anxiety disorders including OCD and panic disorder. Sometimes compulsive behaviors like self-injury, eating disorders, or gambling develop after the trauma. Substance abuse is another common problem for trauma survivors as they attempt to self-medicate and escape the pain.

Vulnerability to these disorders may make someone more likely to develop PTSD, but they can also develop in reaction to the PTSD. People may also blame themselves for the trauma, even if there's no logical way they could have been responsible. Self-blame typically leads to survivor guilt, which is expressed by phrases like "It should have been me" or "If I had died, my friend would have lived."

PTSD often has profound effects on loved ones who are confused by the changes in the survivor, frustrated by his unwillingness to talk about what happened, or stymied by emotional symptoms like numbness, anger, or withdrawal.

**Additional Information:**

- Children don't usually experience visual flashbacks or amnesia the way adults do. Also, unlike adults, they may believe they have the ability to foresee future disasters, a tendency called "omen formation."

- Because they don't have the verbal skills to talk through what they experienced, children often "relive" trauma through repetitive play. For example, after 9/11, children from a daycare near the Twin Towers continually built and destroyed tall buildings. This was their way of working through the trauma.

- People with PTSD are sometimes treated as invalids, as if they are no longer capable of working a job, raising a family, or contributing to society. If your character has PTSD, you can make your story more authentic by including secondary wounding experiences.

- Most people don't realize how powerfully language can impact our psychological states. Constantly referring to oneself or someone else as a "victim" keeps the person trapped in the thinking and behavioral patterns of someone who is still vulnerable and helpless. For that reason, have your therapist character refer to any client who has experienced a trauma as a "survivor," not a "victim."

- People with PTSD have "triggers," which are unique to them. Triggers can be people, places, pictures, objects, or words that are somehow reminiscent of the trauma and therefore cause flashbacks, nightmares, overwhelming fear or anger, and fight-or-flight reactions. In online forums where people share their traumas, "trigger warnings" are common. These warnings let readers know that the material in a story, post, or piece of art might be triggering if it reminds them of their own trauma.

- Because they deal with horrific situations on a regular basis, police, paramedics, firefighters, and other rescue workers are at a higher risk than the average person for developing PTSD. Even therapists can develop "secondary PTSD" from listening to the graphic stories of trauma survivors.

## Misconceptions

- PTSD is not a sign of weakness, so your hero is just as susceptible to it as anyone else. The intensity, severity, and duration of the trauma all contribute to the likelihood that someone will develop PTSD.

- Not everyone develops PTSD right away. A few people develop symptoms weeks, months, years, or even decades after the trauma. This is most common in people who were abused as children.

### DON'T LET THIS HAPPEN TO YOU!

Fictional therapists hypnotize clients they don't know well to force them to remember and deal with the memories they've lost all at once (a technique called "flooding" or "in vivo exposure therapy"). Though the approach provides the hero with oodles of important information he needs to save the day, in real life the approach would be an almost guaranteed disaster (and probably a lawsuit) because without suitable groundwork and follow-up, the only thing the therapist is really going to do is re-traumatize the client.

Hypnosis and flooding are both controversial approaches to trauma, and many experts argue that they should be used as an absolute last resort by an extremely well-trained practitioner if they are used at all. Further, neither of these techniques cures the client the way it does in fiction. Once a memory is recalled, the client must still process it.

You can use hypnosis and flooding as a magic bullet in your story, but also consider the possibilities for conflict if the supposed magic bullet fails. For example, what if your hero needs this information *now*...and doesn't get it? Or what if the hero trusts an unscrupulous therapist and is re-traumatized by the flood of memories? That's going to make it awfully difficult to deal with the villain!

## TREATMENT OF PTSD

Therapy can help people with PTSD in many powerful ways. It can help them understand why they're having the symptoms they are, begin to feel safe and in control of their lives again, grieve psychological and other losses, and reconnect to other people. It can help them bolster their ability to cope with seemingly overwhelming anger, stress, and relationship issues. Cognitive-behavioral therapy helps the client identify and dispute distorted and irrational thoughts. The therapist is also likely to use graded exposure-based procedures, which means she systematically exposes the client to the feared thing while he's in a relaxed state. Over time, the simulations can be made more intense. One way to do this is through Virtual Reality (VR), which is an immersive computer-simulated situation similar to the client's trauma. VR systems typically include a display, which the client wears over his eyes, a high-performance computer that can generate high-fidelity three-dimensional interactive environments, and input devices that track body movements and translate them into the VR world. Some programs even include smells—burning rubber and cordite for example. The therapist slowly, carefully, and systematically exposes the client to the simulation environments to avoid flooding him. Over time, repetition helps clients integrate what happened to them and overcome their fears. Examples of simulation environments used in the treatment of PTSD include *Iraq World* and *Middle East World* for soldiers and *Bus Bomb Survivor* for civilian victims of terrorism.

Eye Movement Desensitization and Reprocessing (EMDR) is controversial, but supporters say it's one of the most effective treatments for PTSD. According to the theory behind it, trauma interferes with the way the brain normally deals with, encodes, and stores information. The trauma is thus stored in a raw, unprocessed form. EMDR helps clients work through the memories, beliefs, sensations, and feelings associated with the trauma. As the memories become less upsetting, clients are able to move on with their lives.

EMDR treatment includes eight phases. In the first, the therapist and client identify a target memory that needs to be processed. Second, the therapist teaches the client the self-care techniques he will need to handle any strong emotions that come up during or after the sessions. During phases three through six, the client focuses on an image of the trauma and any associated bodily sensations, a negative belief related to the memory, and a preferred positive belief. Then, while the client recalls the trauma, the therapist guides his eyes back and forth in a pattern, often by waving one or two fingers back and forth. Alternately, especially with people who are visually impaired, therapists can use tapping or auditory tones. The client's job is to notice any reactions that come up and associate them appropriately with the traumatic memory, and then to focus on a positive belief to replace the negative one. Doing two things at once— moving the eyes in the therapist-guided pattern and thinking about the trauma—is called "dual processing," and it reprograms the brain to resume normal functioning. Over the next week, during phase seven, the client keeps a journal, both to track any additional reactions and to practice his coping skills. During phase eight, the client and therapist evaluate the client's progress and, if necessary, start the process with a new target concern.

Education is also important. Clients are often relieved to learn that their symptoms are due to biochemical changes caused by the trauma, not because they're going crazy. They also benefit from the therapist's confidence that PTSD can be treated, and that their symptoms *will* get better.

Medications for PTSD can include antidepressants (to treat depression and anxiety), anti-anxiety medications (to reduce anxiety, improve sleep, and decrease nightmares), mood stabilizers (to help with depression, mood swings, and impulsivity), and anti-psychotics (to help with flashbacks and nightmares).

## REPRESSED MEMORIES AND FALSE MEMORY SYNDROME

If you put a DVD in a player, you can be confident that the story will play out exactly the same way each time. Memories are not so trustworthy. Each time we remember something, we rebuild the memory from lots of little pieces. Over time, the memory is affected by the things other people tell us, new knowledge about the way the world works, and changes in our values or beliefs. This is why lawyers are discouraged from "leading the witness": they're verbally guiding the memory in the direction they want it to go. Though a leading statement can be struck from the court record, it may have been enough to affect the witness or the jury—which is partly why lawyers insist on leading witnesses even though they're not supposed to.

Because memory can be pliable, it's possible for an unscrupulous therapist to create a false memory of, for example, incest, if she repeatedly *insists* that depression symptoms or an ambiguous memory *must* be due to incest. A false memory of abuse is just as upsetting as a real one, which means that these therapists are actually traumatizing their clients. People who have been encouraged to create false memories by a therapist or other "professional" are said to be suffering from false memory syndrome. Unfortunately, some political groups insist that *all* recovered memories are false memories, which is both inaccurate and invalidating to the abuse survivor.

Sometimes people do hide or repress part or all of a trauma from themselves because it's too painful to think about what happened. The memories aren't gone; the psyche just buries them and then does its best to pretend they're gone. Over the course of therapy, as the client begins to feel safe and *without the therapist nudging*, memories will often bob to the surface. Remembering can help the client better understand what happened to him and why he has the symptoms he does. Rather than pushing hard for more memories (as therapists often do in fiction), the therapist may need to remind the client to take it slow. Some clients may never remember pieces of the trauma, and sometimes that's okay.

# DISSOCIATIVE DISORDERS

Dissociation is an alteration or split in one's consciousness, perceptions, or sense of identity that leaves the person feeling disconnected from what is actually happening or has happened. If you've ever realized that you don't remember your drive home because you were thinking about something else, you know what mild (and normal) dissociation feels like.

More extreme dissociation is a common response to trauma, and dissociative disorders are diagnosed when the dissociation doesn't resolve after the traumatic event has passed.

## DEPERSONALIZATION AND DEREALIZATION

Depersonalization is the feeling that one has disconnected from one's body and is watching what's happening from the outside. The person may feel like he's lost control over his actions or speech or like he's living inside a dream. If you've ever taken strong cold medicine and felt "out of it," like your head isn't connected to your body, or like you're watching yourself without having a lot of control over what you're saying, you know what depersonalization feels like. During derealization, the world feels surreal or unreal. For example, if you've ever been in a car accident, time sometimes seems to slow down while the accident is happening, and objects such as other cars or telephone poles may seem oddly shaped or sized as they move toward or past you. This is derealization. Passing depersonalization and derealization are common (even normal!) responses to alcohol and drug intoxication or withdrawal, and to traumas like car accidents.

Depersonalization and derealization can occur as part of other disorders, especially anxiety disorders like panic disorder and PTSD. Drugs like PCP, ketamine, and nitrous oxide are especially notorious for creating feelings of dissociation; sleep deprivation, migraines, and epileptic seizures can also be culprits.

Depersonalization and derealization are only diagnosed when they happen *after* a trauma, are recurrent or persistent, and aren't due to another disorder or drug or alcohol use. In other words, if the person has a diagnosis like PTSD or another anxiety disorder, neither depersonalization nor derealization is diagnosed, even if the person is having symptoms of one or both.

### Additional Information
- Episodes of depersonalization or derealization can last from a few seconds to years. Usually the person who gets one of these diagnoses feels depersonalized or derealized most of the time, with symptoms getting worse when he is feeling particularly stressed.

- Depersonalization and derealization are rarely the presenting problem; instead, sufferers are likely to come into therapy for problems with anxiety or depression.

### Misconceptions
- Be careful not to confuse the dissociative experience of depersonalization with the discriminatory act of depersonalizing another individual.

If you depersonalize someone else, you are choosing to see her as less than a person; that is, as someone who doesn't deserve the same rights as you. This is not a dissociative experience. If you are experiencing depersonalization as a dissociative experience, you feel split off *from yourself*, as if you are watching yourself from the outside.

- During depersonalization or derealization experiences, the person doesn't literally see himself from the outside; instead, he's likely to tell you he feels disconnected, out of it, spacey, or like everything is a dream rather than reality.

### Treatment

Since depersonalization and derealization are almost always symptoms of another disorder, in most situations the therapist or physician treats the underlying disorder. In cases of true depersonalization disorder, where the individual has felt detached from himself, often for years, a psychiatrist might try medications such as SSRI antidepressants and lamotrigine. Lamotrigine is an anti-seizure medication that is also used as a mood stabilizer and antidepressant.

## DISSOCIATIVE AMNESIA AND DISSOCIATIVE FUGUE

Someone with dissociative amnesia can't remember important information about himself or his experience, usually because something traumatic happened and he can't bear to remember. If the amnesia is due to a physical injury or a substance, dissociative amnesia is *not* diagnosed.

In *The Bourne Identity*, hero Jason Bourne does experience a physical injury, but his amnesia is really due to his inability to face the fact that he is an assassin. Therefore, a diagnosis of dissociative amnesia is appropriate.

Once in a while, someone is confronted by something so stressful that he suddenly forgets who he is and flees his home or workplace in an attempt to escape the stressful thing. Dissociative amnesia coupled in this way with sudden, unexpected travel is called a dissociative fugue.

Sometimes, people experiencing a fugue will assume a new identity. Trips are often short, lasting only a few hours or days, but some people travel thousands of miles over extended periods of time. When the person comes out of the fugue, he may have no memory of what happened during it. Although fugues can occur more than once, this is rare, and people who experience multiple fugues usually have dissociative identity disorder.

Writer Agatha Christie and actress Anne Heche famously experienced fugues. In fiction, the titular character in *Nurse Betty*, a diner waitress, watches her husband tortured, scalped, and murdered. During her fugue, believing she is a nurse, she leaves her home town and heads off to Los Angeles in search of a hospital job.

**Additional Information**

- If dissociative amnesia is a symptom of another disorder like PTSD, it is *not* diagnosed separately.

- If someone develops a second personality in adulthood, it is typically part of a fugue. People with dissociative identity disorder develop additional personalities during childhood.

- Someone having a fugue may seem completely normal to those he encounters.

- Dissociative amnesia and dissociative fugue are often associated with wartimes and natural disasters, though they can also happen following a motor vehicle accident, sexual assault, or a personal trauma like finding out one's partner is cheating.

---

**Q & A**

**Q:** How realistic is it for a man in his early twenties to have few conscious memories of his childhood? What could account for this volume of lost information?

My protagonist was put up for adoption at age two because his mother died and his father couldn't support him. He was soon adopted and raised by an older couple. He's convinced that a) his childhood doesn't "count" because of his father's absence and b) he can restore a traditional father/son relationship. He values his life with his adoptive parents very little and is looking for his father obsessively.

**A:** What you're talking about are "repressed memories," or memories that have been pushed away from conscious awareness because they're too painful to recall. Painful can mean a lot of things: humiliating, scary, devastatingly sad, confusing, and so on. Repression is a defense mechanism.

I suggest that you put the protagonist up for adoption just a bit later in life. I think you need to give him more time to attach to his dad and

---

make some memories to repress. Most people's first memories are from age three, four, or even five years old in the first place. This is arguably either because the brain physically hasn't developed enough to retain memories well or because the child hasn't yet acquired enough language to store the memories in a way that can later be retrieved by the adult brain.

If your protagonist is put up for adoption at age five or six and then has few memories of his childhood, perhaps including after he got adopted, you've got something pretty realistic as far as repressed memories go. It would also help if the couple who adopts your protagonist is not an ideal family. They can be good people, but perhaps they don't really know how to relate to a child and are distant or extremely busy with their own lives. Or maybe they're not great people. Not abusive, per se, but cold and critical, causing your protagonist to unconsciously put his father on a pedestal. I could see someone discounting his life with his adoptive parents if they were never really "there" for him emotionally, and yearning for a connection with this father he's built up in his head.

## DISSOCIATIVE IDENTITY DISORDER (DID)

When the *DSM-IV* was released in 1994, Multiple Personality Disorder (MPD) was renamed Dissociative Identity Disorder (DID). The change was intended to convey the psychological community's belief that rather than housing multiple "people" (personalities) in one body, people with DID have one single personality or identity that has been splintered by trauma.

DID is usually caused by severe, recurrent, and sadistic childhood trauma. Over 70 percent of people with DID report that they were sexually abused, and close to 100 percent report sexual and/or physical abuse. A few people who have watched family members massacred during wartimes have also developed DID. What sets the accounts of people with DID apart from those of people who did not develop DID is how sadistically, creatively, and sometimes bizarrely they were tortured.

Because children haven't yet developed adequate coping skills and defense mechanisms, when they are overwhelmed by sadistic trauma, they may psychologically wall off the part of the personality that experienced the trauma. Therefore, the more unique types of trauma the person experiences, the more personalities he is likely to have.

Because a part of the person's identity is walled off with the trauma, an "alter," which is another personality, is created. Each of these alters has a job in the system of personalities. One's job might be to do schoolwork, another to endure rape, another to be present during physical beatings. The more a particular personality is "out," the more it will develop its own interests, ideas, and idiosyncrasies, because more of life's experiences are being stored in that splinter of the personality.

The walls between personalities are called "amnestic barriers," and blocks of amnesia are the hallmark symptom of DID. Though some of the alters may be aware of each other, before treatment the core or birth personality is probably not aware of them. Instead, he has amnesia whenever an alter was out. At first the therapist may encourage the core and the alters to write notes to each other in a notebook, but eventually alters are usually able to talk directly.

In an old video of the real "Eve" (of *The Three Faces of Eve*), the interviewer asks one of the personalities, Eve Black, where she went when the others, Eve White and Jane, were out. She thinks about it and then says, "I don't know. Just somewhere."

If the core personality is only "out" in the evenings, it may have no memory of going to school. This is how different alters can sometimes speak different languages. One alter was paying attention in German class and the rest weren't! In the same interview mentioned above, the interviewer notes that Eve Black doesn't seem as well educated as the other two personalities. "I guess I just wasn't interested in getting an education," says Eve Black. "You have to study!" The interviewer argues that *somebody* had to study. "Not really. [Eve White] didn't *have* to. [But] she wanted [an education] and I didn't."

Eve Black's quotes provide a good example of how personalities usually talk about themselves and each other: they refer to themselves as "I," to other personalities as "he" or "she," and—once they've had enough therapy to recognize that they're all part of the same person—to the entire system as "we."

Most people with DID hear voices and see things (for example, disembodied faces floating in front of them), but because these experiences are the other personalities' means of communicating with the host personality, the individual is not considered psychotic. Unlike in schizophrenia, the person with DID usually hides that he is hearing and seeing things. Remember, DID develops to protect the person from other people's cruelty, and the alters will try to resist acting in ways that can put the person in harm's way. Since people often treat individuals with DID as curiosities and freaks, the system of alters learns to defensively hide the disorder from others.

Also unlike schizophrenia, when the voices are heard "out loud" and often indistinctly, people with DID report that the voices of the other alters speak clearly and distinctly and sound like loud thoughts.

Since the different alters were created to deal with different types of stressors, the personality most suited to deal with whatever's going on will immediately and automatically "come out" when needed. However, one personality, called the host, is out most often. Usually the host is the core personality, but not always.

If all of the alters are simultaneously overwhelmed, the person with DID may experience a "revolving door crisis": the personalities begin switching so quickly that the person may cycle extremely fast through a variety of emotions, produce jumbled speech, and behave erratically. Sometimes different alters are fighting for control; other times, the main personalities have simply surrendered control, forcing out alters that don't want to be out.

If splintering happens often enough, the psyche may begin to create alters for every function, even the ones that have nothing to do with abuse. For example, the person may create a personality that's responsible for doing homework or going to school, and another for doing unpleasant chores around the house. In some cases, he will also incorporate qualities of people he admires into new personalities that can take care of the more damaged personalities.

---

### Don't Let This Happen to You!

If your detective or psychiatrist character is arguing against multiple personalities (or any other diagnosis), be careful not to make up "typical" symptoms the way Jeffery Deaver did in *The Bone Collector*: "The classic multiple personality is young and has a lower IQ." In fact, there is no "typical" IQ in people with DID, and while the disorder sometimes becomes less obvious around middle age because the person has learned to adapt to it, it does not spontaneously disappear as one gets older.

Except when revolving door crises occur or when young alters pop out due to a trigger of some kind—both of which are rare occurrences around strangers; remember, DID is a defense to protect the person, not make her stand out—the person with DID doesn't obviously have DID. She may seem moody and inconsistent to people, but most people just assume she's flighty and erratic. In most cases, another disorder, such as the ones listed in the next paragraph, is what brings the person into therapy.

Though amnesia *may* bring people with DID into therapy, more often their presenting problems are things like depression, suicide attempts, anxiety, panic attacks, phobias, PTSD, or substance abuse. Because therapists must often ask about amnesia and dissociation to uncover DID, some therapists argue that DID is *iatrogenic*. They believe that therapists create *all* cases of DID by suggesting the diagnosis to extremely suggestible people. (See the sidebar on false memories above for more information on how a therapist might do this).

One of the most famous cases of DID, that of "Sybil"—whose real name was Shirley Mason—may have been iatrogenic. The therapist, Dr. Cornelia Wilbur, gave Mason sodium pentothal, which is sometimes used as a "truth serum," although all it really does is reduce higher thinking processes and make someone more susceptible to talking under pressure. Wilbur then hypnotized Mason and gave names to her different emotional states. In other words, she chose Mason's strongest personality characteristics and gave them names. This is equivalent to naming the assertive part of yourself that stands up to difficult customers at work, and then naming the part of you that feels romantic toward your significant other something else, and so on. As Wilbur explained it to Flora Rheta Schreiber, author of the book *Sybil*: "And I said, 'Well, there's a personality who calls herself Peggy…she is pretty assertive…she can do things you can't,' and [Mason] was…obviously perturbed by this…and I said… 'She wouldn't do anything you wouldn't approve of. She might do something you wouldn't think of doing.'" In reality, though some personalities in a person with DID may stand out because they behave differently than the others (for example, by being extremely assertive), a distinct personality will have multiple characteristics, enough to function as its own entity. What Wilbur seems to be doing is naming the personality characteristics of a person *without* DID and treating those as separate personalities, rather than recognizing pre-existing distinct personalities that developed due to traumatic splintering.

Later, both Mason herself and Dr. Herbert Spiegel, who met with Mason when Dr. Wilbur was out of town, told Schreiber that Mason didn't have multiple personalities. According to a 1997 interview with Spiegel, Schreiber's response was, "If we don't call it multiple personality, we don't have a book! The publishers want it to be that, otherwise it won't sell."

While some cases of DID probably are iatrogenic, most therapists who have worked with DID insist that it is a real phenomenon. Further, in some people, different alters have different EEG patterns. Other brain imaging studies have shown that the blood flow in the brain changes with different alters. People with DID often say that some personalities need glasses, have asthma, or are allergic to particular substances, while others are not.

Most people expect different alters to behave like completely different people, when really they have more in common than not. After all, they do share a genetic background and have had similar experiences! Alters may have different speech patterns, accents, and vocabularies, but most people either don't notice or attribute the behavior to an affectation.

### Additional Information

- During childhood, people with DID are often accused of pathological lying, especially because they swear they didn't do things another person saw them do.

- Someone with DID may not realize until he reaches college or begins a career that other people don't experience these periods of amnesia.

- DID is more common in adult females than adult males. Females also average more personalities—usually fifteen or more—while males average only eight. Despite these numbers, some people have as few as two personalities and others have over one hundred.

- People with DID often have alters that are the "opposite sex" from the body. They also commonly have *child alters* who are developmentally stuck at a younger age than the body because they hold raw, unprocessed memories of abuse. In other words, they're emotionally trapped in the past. *Persecutory alters* are internalizations of the abuser(s); they treat other alters the same way the abuser did. In some cases, these alters may try to hurt or kill another alter, not realizing that they share a body.

- Self-injury (sometimes called self-mutilation) appears in at least a third of people with DID. You can read more about self-injury in Chapter 9.

- People with DID often marry people who have problems of their own, such as depression, alcoholism, and personality disorders. Sometimes they are abusive toward the person with DID and actually enjoy making the person switch personalities. Along the same lines, some men find it sexually gratifying to be with a woman who has DID—they argue that it's like having multiple sexual partners—but the way they encourage their spouses to switch is by creating situations reminiscent of the original sexual abuse.

- Children whose parents have DID are very aware of the changes in their parent, and are aware that they have several "mommies," for example. Just as spouses can learn to manipulate the disorder to their own ends, so can children. Children may figure out how to trigger more permissive personalities or claim the parent allowed something and just doesn't remember doing so.

- Though DID does appear in other cultures, it is diagnosed much more often in North America, leading some to argue that it is a culture-bound disorder.

### Misconceptions

- Though a number of serial killers have tried to convince juries that they have DID, few actually do. In most cases, they are faking the disorder for personal gain, just like the character played by Edward Norton in the film adapted from William Diehl's book, *Primal Fear*.

---

**DON'T LET THIS HAPPEN TO YOU!**

In Robert K. Tanenbaum's novel *Malice*, the villain "spoke with the voice of a young boy that she recognized as Andy, one of the personalities of the schizophrenic Kane." Though this is a common mistake, by now you know that people with schizophrenia do not have more than one personality—only people with dissociative identity disorder do.

In Barbara Michaels's novel *Annie, Come Home*, one character describes how "the alternate personalities in this type of psychosis regard each other as different entities." As noted above, DID is *not* a

---

psychotic disorder. People with DID have *not* lost contact with reality as other people experience it, nor is their thinking generally jumbled and confused.

In films like *Fight Club* and *Secret Window*, adults dissatisfied with their lives develop new personalities who infuriate and challenge them. Based on what you now know about sadistic *childhood* abuse, you now understand why this is unrealistic. In both stories, a history of DID would have solved the problem; alternatively, the characters could have experienced dissociative fugues.

## *Treatments for DID*

Once a therapist recognizes DID, she must find out who the different alters are, why they were created, and what their jobs are within the system. The best way to get to know alters is simply to invite them to come forward and talk with the therapist. They may not do so right away, but eventually, if the therapist has truly created a safe place, they will. Once the therapist has learned an alter's name, she can call that alter at any time by asking to speak with him or her. Alters often respond the same way you might if you heard someone say your name in a crowded room—they start paying attention.

The therapist who works with DID must remember that many alters are probably listening in on therapy. Therefore, it is unwise to talk about alters as if they aren't there. At the same time, the therapist can trust that the system of alters will protect any personalities that shouldn't hear something particular.

Though hypnosis is the classic treatment for identifying DID and the alters, it will almost always result in suggestions from others that the disorder is iatrogenic; therefore, it should be used very, very carefully, if at all.

The therapist's goal is to establish a relationship with the different alters and help them begin to work together effectively. For small groups or systems of alters the ultimate goal is re-integration into a single personality. Larger systems may prefer to work cooperatively without integrating.

## Hypnosis

Hypnosis is a practice riddled with even more myths than the ones we looked at in this chapter, so before you decide to use it in your story, be sure you know what a real hypnotist can and cannot do.

Hypnosis is a natural, relaxed, dissociative state, and most people fall into a hypnotic "trance" within several minutes of settling down to watch a good television show or movie. Some people argue that they can't be hypnotized, but this is only because you do have a choice over whether to allow someone to hypnotize you or not. Some people find it easier to reach a hypnotic state than others, but everyone is capable of it!

During hypnosis in a therapist's office, the client is awake and aware and can easily come out of the trance. In fact, many people wonder if they were hypnotized at all because the experience is so different from what they expect. Usually the only "symptoms" of being in a hypnotic trance are deep relaxation and sometimes a "floaty" feeling.

Because the individual is awake and aware, a hypnotist can't force him to reveal his deepest secrets or do something he wouldn't normally do. How then, you might wonder, does a stage hypnotist convince someone to behave foolishly? He chooses the most suggestible people in the audience and those most willing to behave foolishly. He identifies them through a series of tests and then makes them act progressively sillier. That's why it takes a while to get to the part of the act where someone behaves in a truly ridiculous way.

A therapeutic hypnotist would never make a client act silly. The purpose of hypnosis is to help the person absorb ideas that the therapist and client have agreed are important.

Though people who are hypnotized *are* in a more suggestible state during hypnosis, and may give more weight to what they're being told, hypnosis is not a magical cure. Those who go through hypnosis for smoking cessation still crave cigarettes; the hypnosis is just intended to reduce that craving a bit and help the person focus on why he is quitting—for example, because he wants to have a healthier body. In other words, hypnosis alone probably won't be very effective—additional efforts must be made to achieve and maintain the desired results.

# 9
# The Disorders, Part IV
## *Personality Disorders*

Personality disorders—a general term for disorders in which people take an extremely narrow, inflexible, and dysfunctional approach to life—are unique (and uniquely difficult to treat) because they're "ego-syntonic." That means the person doesn't think there's anything wrong with her, regardless of how many problems her disorder is causing. Personality disorders are diagnosed on Axis II (see Chapter 5) rather than Axis I, though someone with an Axis II diagnosis who ends up in therapy usually has a problem on Axis I as well.

People with personality disorders behave in ways that frustrate and alienate others. They blame everyone else for their problems, and they can be self-centered, manipulative, and difficult to please. They have a characteristic approach to everything. For example, someone with a paranoid personality disorder views everyone and everything with mistrust. A person with a histrionic personality disorder approaches everything with emotionality and drama. When someone has a personality disorder, the characteristic approach dominates every interaction, every behavior, every emotion. If you removed the disorder, the individual would be a totally different person. That's not the case with most disorders.

Though personality disorders may be influenced by biochemistry, the child's experiences while her personality was still developing are key. As we discussed in Chapter 2, many therapists believe that children form a psychological blueprint of the way the world works and then rely on it for the rest of their lives. Rather than realizing that a blueprint is not an accurate representation of reality, most people behave in ways that cause it to seem true. In other words, they live as though the blueprint is accurate, which causes other people to respond in ways that reinforce that belief. For example, if their blueprint says other people will be rude to them, they approach the world with anger and defensiveness, which then *causes* people to be rude to them. People with personality disorders manipulate their environments to fit their beliefs.

The trick in portraying a character with a personality disorder is to have the disorder affect *all* of her thoughts, emotions, behaviors, and interactions with others. People with personality disorders are stuck, like a broken record, on one characteristic maladaptive pattern. Therefore, if your character has a paranoid *personality* disorder, she must be paranoid *all the time*. If she has a paranoid *delusion*, by contrast, she will only seem paranoid if the topic of the delusion comes up.

While many people possess quirks or even traits like the ones listed in the descriptions below, they're not diagnosable. A disorder is diagnosed only when a person has a narrow, long-term, inflexible personality style that causes serious problems.

The *DSM-IV* groups the ten personality disorders into three "clusters." Many people with personality disorders show characteristics of more than one disorder, usually within the same cluster.

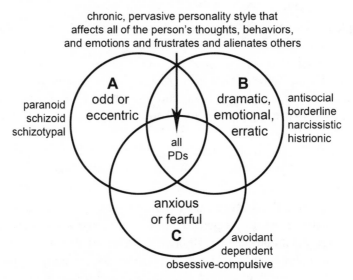

Fig 9.1. Cluster A, B, and C personality disorders.

# CLUSTER A PERSONALITY DISORDERS: PARANOID, SCHIZOID, AND SCHIZOTYPAL

People with cluster A personality disorders are odd or eccentric. These disorders appear most often in families with schizophrenia, leading some theorists to suggest they are low-grade manifestations of schizophrenia. However, people with personality disorders do not have full-blown psychotic symptoms.

## PARANOID PERSONALITY DISORDER (PPD)

People with paranoid personality disorders approach the world with suspicion and mistrust.

When someone's thoughts, traits, and/or emotions are unacceptable to him, he unconsciously uses a defense mechanism called projection to blame them on someone else. Most people project from time to time, but people with paranoid personality disorder are constantly blaming their feelings of impotence, inadequacy, and self-hatred on others. They see others as demanding, intrusive, and controlling, and live in fear that others are out to get them. They're likely to see innocuous remarks as demeaning or threatening, and to react with anger that may or may not be expressed outwardly. Their behavior can *cause* others to treat them poorly, which only justifies their beliefs and makes them even angrier, more fearful, and more paranoid.

People with PPD were often subject to parental criticism, ridicule, and suspiciousness. As children, they felt demeaned, humiliated, and overpowered. As adults, they continue to fight authority, often in passive-aggressive and self-defeating ways. Sometimes they get involved in conspiracy theories and fanatical groups.

People with PPD are most often male.

In C. S. Forester's 1952 novel *Lieutenant Hornblower*, the main character, Horatio, finds himself under the command of Captain Sawyer, who first appears on the quarterdeck "looking suspiciously around him." Invariably thereafter Sawyer casts "sidelong, shifty glances" and finds guilt on innocent faces. In the A&E television adaptation of the novel, Sawyer goes so far as to have a boy whipped for trying to fix a flaw in the sail because Sawyer is convinced the boy was trying to sabotage the ship.

## Schizoid Personality Disorder

People with schizoid personality disorder are reclusive, detached, and indifferent to others. They see themselves as self-sufficient loners and others as intrusive. As a result, they feel relationships are messy and unrewarding. Though they may care about other people, they are afraid of connecting in even small ways because they believe they might somehow lose themselves if they do. Because they tend to be emotionally unresponsive, other people experience them as cold, aloof, boring, robotic, odd, or humorless.

Some theorists have suggested that schizoid personality disorder develops thanks to smothering, over-involved parental figures who caused the child to defensively withdraw—a pattern she carries into adulthood.

### Additional Information

- People with this disorder find relationships with others so uncomfortable that they may choose masturbation over sex with another person.

- On the outside, schizoid personalities have a lot in common with people who have Asperger's disorder. As we discussed in Chapter 7, people with Asperger's have brains that function differently than others', but they do feel plenty of emotions and they often want relationships with others. They just don't understand how. By contrast, people with schizoid tendencies neither want nor enjoy relationships, nor do they experience strong emotions. The gaucheness of their social interactions stems from a lack of interest rather than a biological impairment.

- Be careful not to confuse schizoid personality disorder with antisocial personality disorder, which is discussed later in this chapter. Though people with schizoid personality disorder can seem (or be) unfeeling, they're not parasitic, cocky, or prone to exploit people for personal gain the way someone with antisocial personality disorder is. If you want to create a character with both sets of traits, that's easy enough. People often have more than one personality disorder.

## Schizotypal Personality Disorder

People with schizotypal personality disorders are so peculiar that others might describe them as flaky, eccentric, or just plain weird. They have strange ideas, and they look, act, and sound strange. For example, they might be disheveled, talk to themselves, or insist that they're in contact with dead relatives. They read special meaning into events that have nothing to do with them and are likely to be superstitious and believe in magic, curses, omens, hexes, and ghosts. They often believe they have psychic powers or magical control over others. For example, they might believe they can influence the weather just by thinking about it. Their speech may wander and include excessive, meaningless, or irrelevant details, and their emotional reactions are sometimes inappropriate to the situation. For example, they might laugh at a funeral or cry during a joke, if they show emotion at all. Finally, they experience illusions; for example, they might believe they see people in the patterns in the wallpaper. Though they know there aren't *really* people in the wallpaper, they believe it's meaningful that they perceive people in the pattern. Couple their odd behavior with their tendency to be anxious around or suspicious of other people, and you can see why they rarely have close friends.

Many psychological professionals believe schizotypal personality disorder is a mild form of schizophrenia, and some argue that it should be diagnosed that way (i.e. on Axis I), rather than as a personality disorder (on Axis II).

# CLUSTER B PERSONALITY DISORDERS: ANTISOCIAL, NARCISSISTIC, HISTRIONIC, AND BORDERLINE

People with cluster B personality disorders are dramatic, erratic, or emotional. They can be manipulative, volatile, and uncaring in relationships, and sometimes they display impulsive, even violent behavior that shows little regard for their safety or the safety of others. Others may refer to people with cluster B personality disorders as "exhausting," "draining," or even as "emotional vampires."

## ANTISOCIAL PERSONALITY DISORDER (APD)

Antisocial personality disorder is diagnosed in people who constantly disregard and violate other people's rights, sometimes without any remorse. Opinionated, cocky, and superficially charming, they may also be promiscuous, impulsive, parasitic, irresponsible about jobs and money, and many get in trouble with the law. They see other people as weak and vulnerable or otherwise deserving of exploitation, and themselves as superior and therefore entitled to break the rules. In the *Pirates of the Caribbean* movies, Johnny Depp's character, Captain Jack Sparrow, fits these criteria. He defies rules right and left, is constantly in trouble with the law (and women), and manipulates everyone he can.

APD is never diagnosed before the age of eighteen, but symptoms must have begun in childhood or early adolescence (during which time the individual should have been diagnosed with conduct disorder—see Chapter 7).

People with APD usually grow up in families without love, and in many cases they were severely neglected or abused. As a result, they learned to associate the emotional need for relationships or warmth with weakness and vulnerability.

In addition to the characteristics listed earlier, some people with APD also fall into the category of "psychopath." Characters like Hannibal Lecter, Thomas Harris's cannibalistic serial killer in *The Silence of the Lambs*, and Jigsaw, the creatively sadistic torturer in the *Saw* films, fall into this category. "Psychopathy" isn't an official diagnosis, therefore, APD is what your fictional psychological professional should write on the diagnostic chart for your thriller's cold-blooded serial killer, or for the womanizing freeloader who doesn't feel an ounce of guilt for bilking girlfriends of their entire life savings before he disappears. We'll look more at psychopathy in Chapter 10.

**Additional Information**

- Though APD does appear in women, it's more common in men.

- Three quarters of convicted felons meet the *DSM* criteria for APD. One criticism of the APD diagnosis is that it's essentially synonymous with criminality.

- The trick to getting someone with APD—especially more extreme versions of APD—to confess is not by pressuring or scaring him. Instead, your interrogator should casually remark that she doesn't believe the accused is smart enough or smooth enough to pull off the crime. Insulted, the antisocial character is likely to explain just what he did and how he did it. He might even throw in a few other crimes he's committed just to show how clever he is.

- Both biological and adopted children of parents with APD are at risk for developing antisocial characteristics.

- People with antisocial tendencies may be easily-bored thrill-seekers. Those without criminal leanings may still be attracted to dangerous and exhilarating jobs like a racecar driver or test pilot, or to hobbies like skydiving.

**Misconceptions**
- People sometimes misunderstand "antisocial" to mean "not wanting to be around other people." Instead, the term is meant to imply that the person is recalcitrant and contemptuous of societal rules. If your character is an extreme recluse, consider the schizoid personality disorder diagnosis instead.

- Antisocial personality disorder is *not* a synonym for sociopathy or psychopathy. Sociopaths and psychopaths are always diagnosable with APD; however, many people with APD are *not* cold, ruthless, or remorseless enough to qualify as sociopaths, let alone psychopaths. Also, there are no biological markers for APD, whereas psychopaths' brains are different from other people's.

# NARCISSISTIC PERSONALITY DISORDER (NPD)

People with narcissistic personality disorder are arrogant and self-aggrandizing, and they expect to receive special treatment and privileges. Should someone fail to provide them with that special treatment, they treat him like an insubordinate servant. Rather than being contemptuous of society's rules, the way someone who is antisocial is, they simply see themselves as exempt.

A somewhat facetious example of the narcissist appears in William Goldman's *The Princess Bride*. The Sicilian Vizzini confronts the man in black in a battle of wits. Whoever picks the wrong goblet—the one with poison hidden in it—dies; the other man gets the Princess. After a long demonstration of his brilliant reasoning, Vizzini declares he knows where the poison is. The man in black says, "Only a genius could have deduced as much." "How fortunate for me that I happen to be one," Vizzini replies. He waits until they have both drunk from their goblets before launching into an explanation of how brilliant he is…only to fall over dead.

151

A less humorous (and probably less intentional) portrayal of narcissism appears in the *Blade* films. Like other narcissists, Blade is self-centered, self-important, pretentious, and a show off. He sneers at the idea that anyone could have power over him, always believes he's right, and sees everyone else as beneath him.

Narcissism can develop thanks either to repeated messages that one is better than others, or in reaction to feelings of inadequacy, weakness, and shame. Psychodynamic theorists argue that people with NPD were used as "narcissistic appendages" by caregivers, which damaged their sense of genuine self-worth. In other words, the caregiver pushed the child into meeting *her* needs, as if the child had no needs or feelings of his own. Further, the caregiver saw each of the child's successes and failures as reflections of *her* worth and therefore insisted on perfection. If the child fell short of these expectations as sooner or later he must, he was treated with scorn or disgust. The child was important to the caregiver only insofar as he fulfilled the parent's narcissistic needs.

As a child like this grows up, he needs others to act as admirers and narcissistic appendages so he can feel less empty and inadequate. In this way he *needs* people, but he doesn't really love them or appreciate how they feel. As a result, he often leaves others feeling ignored, devalued, or used.

Writers like Jean Twenge and W. Keith Campbell, authors of the 2009 book *The Narcissism Epidemic*, have argued that America is teeming with narcissists, both male and female. Many reference the 2006 study that found that 25 percent of college students agreed with most of the items on a diagnostic narcissistic inventory. They point to t-shirts and bumper stickers like the one that says "I'm the Princess, we'll do it *my* way;" swaggering song lyrics; reality TV exhibitionism; and the cultural emphasis on physical appearance, material wealth, and creating a "personal brand." They argue that all this narcissism is at the root of everything from huge debts (as people strive to materially outdo everyone else) to the sexy pictures young teens post on social networking sites (in search of flattery, status, and "friends") to the aggressive self-righteousness that characterizes road rage. These writers' viewpoint may be extreme, and they're being a little unfair by pathologizing an entire generation, but they do make good points about how selfish and shallow American values have become.

Narcissistic people usually show up in therapy because they're having relationship problems and were given an ultimatum or because they're struggling with a problem like depression. Depression in narcissists is typically caused by some kind of discouragement or humiliation that damages their lofty view of themselves.

**Additional Information**

- According to the *DSM*, the majority of people with NPD are male.

- While not a diagnostic term endorsed by the *DSM*, "malignant narcissism" is sometimes used to refer to people who display not only narcissistic personality disorder but also antisocial behavior, paranoia, and aggression that they feel is justified. Malignant narcissism is considered a more severe problem than NPD alone but not as severe as antisocial personality disorder.

# HISTRIONIC PERSONALITY DISORDER (HPD)

People with histrionic personality disorder are so eager for the attention of others that they'll do nearly anything to get it. They're inordinately dramatic, enthusiastic, flirtatious, and demonstrative, and they're not above making a scene to keep the spotlight on them. They rely on physical appearance to draw others' attention, usually by dressing and behaving in ways that are inappropriately seductive. Though their emotions can shift rapidly, each one is played up to its fullest: rather than being sad, they're utterly devastated; rather than being happy, they're over the moon. They're conspicuous for their histrionics and hyperbole.

At first they strike others as engaging and lively, but over time their insistence on attention embarrasses others, wears them out, or leaves them resentful. People with HPD are thus described as shallow, vain, immature, and cloying. They're likely to have tempestuous romantic relationships, and if a significant other disagrees with them or tries to leave them, they may make superficial suicidal threats for attention.

Histrionic personalities like jobs that make them center stage, so they're drawn to professions like acting, dancing, politics, and preaching. Someone with this diagnosis might sob loudly over a minor point, going through an absurd number of tissues. She might dress in inappropriately sexy clothes for a job interview or court appearance. She might wear sunglasses inside or dramatically wave a scarf to emphasize a point. In many ways, people with HPD are living caricatures of sex roles. Females and some gay men diagnosed with HPD are hyper-feminine. Men with

HPD are usually hyper-masculine, flaunting machismo and virility in the absence of real competence.

People with HPD are terrified of rejection and desperate for approval; most of them were rewarded at a young age for superficial things like physical attractiveness, sexiness, and their ability to entertain. As a result, they put all of their energy into their outsides and none into developing themselves as people. A child regularly entered in beauty contests, for example, might soon learn that her value as a person is based on her appearance and her ability to charm others.

In the film *American Beauty*, Annette Bening's shallow, melodramatic Realtor character is obsessed with her appearance and the way things look. Her laughter is loud, her anger violent, her sadness devastating. When she can't sell a house by exaggerating the wonderful things about it, she throws a loud, dramatic temper tantrum, wailing, hitting herself, and calling herself names.

**Additional Information**

- HPD is diagnosed more often in women, and some argue that the diagnosis unfairly pathologizes the very qualities society encourages in females: dependency, emotionality, sexiness, focus on appearance, and so on. Just remember—for the tendency to be diagnosable, it has to be causing significant problems for the person or for others.

- To portray HPD, think "over the top." Show your character exaggerating every gesture as if she were on a stage, and have her spew purple prose in a way that makes other characters look twice and wonder if she's for real. If you're thinking that HPD sounds like a typical teenager, you have a point. What's abnormal is when the behavior is still rampant when the person is thirty-five instead of fifteen.

---

### DON'T LET THIS HAPPEN TO YOU!

Some writers get the description of a personality disorder right but give it the wrong name. For example, a psychologist in Joy Fielding's novel *Charley's Web* says, "Borderline personality disorder...[means] that she's intensely narcissistic and lacks the basic human emotions, including empathy." As you know from the sections above, the psychologist is actually describing an antisocial personality disorder, probably with narcissistic traits.

Likewise, one of Janet Dailey's characters in the novel *Mistletoe and Molly* says that "narcissistic personality disorder [means] she'll do

---

anything to be the center of attention. Including lie." In fact, the need to be center stage isn't indicative of narcissistic personality disorder. The character is describing histrionic personality disorder. Of course, non-therapist characters could reasonably make these kinds of mistakes if those mistakes serve some purpose in your story.

## BORDERLINE PERSONALITY DISORDER (BPD)

People with borderline personality disorder are unable to manage their emotional "volume" the way other people do. This makes them incredibly intense, volatile, and frantic to have help from someone they've decided they need.

Neuroticism, or the tendency to experience strong negative emotional states, can leave someone vulnerable to developing BPD, especially when the person is also hyper-sensitive and raised in an environment that is invalidating, confusing, and abusive. In such situations, the child never learns how to deal with and inhibit her overwhelming emotions. This then leads to inappropriate emotional behavior and an inability to work toward personal goals or self-soothe when things go wrong.

Because they feel so empty inside and because they have no ability to regulate their emotions, everything comes out full blast, leaving recipients feeling like they stepped on an emotional landmine. Inside, people with BPD feel depressed, angry, or anxious, so these are the emotions most likely to explode outward. Rather than quietly feeling down because something bad happened, they might wail and sob. Rather than telling someone they're disappointed over a misunderstanding, they might scream and throw things. While the emotional displays and manipulative ploys of people with histrionic personality disorder are shallow ploys for attention, the interactions of people with BPD have a painful, desperate, life-or-death quality that both pulls in and repels those who deal with them.

The relationships of someone with BPD are always intense and unstable. The sufferer swings back and forth between idealization and devaluation, sometimes very quickly. Idealization means the individual worships the ground "important" people walk on and believe they can do no wrong. Devaluation means the individual hates and despises the important person. So someone with BPD who is angry may beg a significant other not to leave her, insisting she will die without him, only to spew venomous declarations of hatred seconds later. Attempts by the significant other to set boundaries or break up with her may lead her to do something dangerous like deeply slitting her wrists or wrecking the car.

In the HBO film *Gia*, the adult main character, played by Angelina Jolie, is devastated when her mother, who is visiting, says she needs to go back home. Gia clings to her mother, sobbing, "I need you, I need you!" When her mother explains that she has stayed too long and must go, Gia flips from idealization to devaluation and starts screaming at her to "Get out!" She opens the apartment door and, still sobbing, flings her mother's suitcases down the hall, shouting profanities the whole time.

BPD is diagnosed far more often in females than males. Because people with BPD are so demanding, needy, and unstable, they are one of the most difficult groups to work with. They often call the therapist's emergency number in crisis, and they are in constant danger of harming themselves. As a result, they tend to burn out their therapists, and new therapists may be reluctant to take them on. This makes a BPD diagnosis so stigmatizing that many feminist therapists refuse to use it at all. They argue that because the childhoods of people with BPD are littered with sexual abuse, neglect, and hostility, the proper diagnosis is actually PTSD (see Chapter 8). Others believe that BPD is an ugly wastebasket diagnosis for female clients perceived as difficult. Researcher T. A. Aronson goes so far as to call BPD "an institutional epithet in the guise of pseudoscientific jargon." While it is unlikely the disorder will disappear from the *DSM*, a name change seems likely in the near future.

**Additional Information**

- Characters like the one Glenn Close played in *Fatal Attraction* have BPD. They will go to astonishing extremes to keep someone they believe they need attached to them in some way. In their view, even hatred is better than being ignored.

- People with BPD often undermine themselves, especially when a goal is within reach. If a job, relationship, or therapy is going well, they do something to ruin it. For example, they might pick a fight with the boss when the job has been going well or drop out of school during their last semester.

- EMDR, a controversial treatment for PTSD, is helpful to some people with BPD. (See Chapter 8 for more information on EMDR.)

- Because people with BPD genuinely suffer with this disorder, they do end up in therapy more than people with other personality disorders. Their unhappiness may, in some cases, also make them more treatable. Dialectical behavioral therapy (DBT) has proven helpful for many people with BPD.

- Psychologist Marsha Linehan developed dialectical behavioral therapy (DBT) to help people with borderline personality disorder. DBT combines behavioral therapy with the principles of Zen Buddhism and includes weekly individual therapy, a year-long skills training group, and individual phone coaching. Problems are tackled in a strict hierarchy. First, the client and therapist work to reduce and eventually eliminate the desperate behaviors that burn out caregivers. Second, the client begins cognitive-behavioral work to address PTSD symptoms. Third, she works on day-to-day problems like career choices and disagreements with partners. Clients who are able to advance to this point may then address spiritual and existential needs.

## SELF-INJURY

People who intentionally harm themselves are referred to as self-injurers or self-mutilators. Cutting is just one form of self-injury (SI)—others include branding or burning oneself with cigarettes, erasers, or chemicals; stabbing oneself with pins, needles, or nails; constantly picking at or re-opening wounds; and banging one's head against the wall or punching or biting oneself. People who have a lot of piercings or tattoos may be self-injuring in a culturally sanctioned way, especially if they experience a release of tension during the process.

Repeated SI leaves scars, usually in places that are somehow connected to the original hurt or trauma. For example, if someone was held down by her upper arms while she was sexually abused, she is more likely to self-injure there. She might also self-injure her breasts or genitals. SI is common in people with borderline personality disorder, though it is also found in conjunction with disorders like OCD, PTSD, dissociative disorders, mood disorders, and eating disorders. Based on the above definition of SI, far more females than males engage in self-harm.

SI is not usually a suicidal gesture; in fact, people who self-injure do so to try to relieve emotional pain that they don't know how to express any other way. They report a variety of reasons for SI, including:

- Attempts to express psychological pain (author Marilee Strong calls SI "a bright red scream").

- Attempts to regulate overwhelming emotions. Some people mildly dissociate during SI, which lets them get away from the pain a bit. SI can also release endorphins.

- Self-hatred and self-punishment following a history of abuse.

Self-injury is usually a secret, shameful act. Because the person feels better after she self-injures, it can become addictive. She is likely to get good at covering the evidence with, for example, long sleeves.

Because SI is a coping mechanism, a good therapist doesn't try to force the client to stop immediately. Instead, he makes sure she isn't going to accidentally kill herself. Then he helps her identify what triggers the behavior and works with her on healthier ways to express anger, guilt, and shame. Cognitive behavioral approaches can help her change distorted thinking patterns, group therapy can help reduce her shame and learn healthier ways to share emotions, and Eye Movement and Desensitization Reprocessing (EMDR; see Chapter 8) may be used to reduce post-traumatic symptoms.

# Cluster C Personality Disorders: Avoidant, Dependent, and Obsessive-Compulsive

Cluster C personality disorders look a lot like anxiety disorders, but they dominate the personality and are ego-syntonic.

## Avoidant Personality Disorder

People with avoidant personality disorder are so afraid of being criticized or rejected that they avoid being around other people. Inside, they feel incompetent and inferior, and they're usually reluctant to try new things because they fear they might embarrass themselves. Social phobia (see Chapter 6) is so similar to avoidant personality disorder that even the *DSM* admits they may be the same thing.

## DEPENDENT PERSONALITY DISORDER

People with dependent personality disorder are childlike in their passivity, clinginess, and neediness. They're subservient and sycophantic with other people they deem important, refusing to disagree and bending over backwards to make them happy. They hate being alone because they're afraid they won't be able to take care of themselves, and they're so sure they can't function independently that they don't even try. Because they won't try, they may *not* be capable of regular adult tasks. If the relationship on which they depend ends, they'll quickly find someone else to care for them.

Dependent personalities seem to result from overbearing and overprotective parenting. People with the disorder never developed an autonomous sense of self or feelings of competence.

In the 2003 remake of the movie *Freaky Friday*, Jamie Lee Curtis plays a busy psychologist with a dependent client named Evan. When she arrives at the office a few minutes late, she finds him in the hall, rocking himself. "I thought you forgot about me!" he cries. When she reminds him that she'll be out of town the following week but that he can reach her on his cell phone, he worries that there isn't good cell phone reception in certain parts of the city and that he won't be able to get along without her.

Bill Murray's fussy, clingy, and sometimes desperate character in the 1991 movie *What About Bob?* also has a dependent personality disorder.

## OBSESSIVE-COMPULSIVE PERSONALITY DISORDER (OCPD)

People with obsessive-compulsive personality disorder are stubborn, controlling, and perfectionistic. The individual is so focused on the way things "should" be that he alienates others with all of his details, rules, schedules, and demands that things be "just right." Not only is the point of the activity lost, but it takes much longer than it should. People with OCPD work so much that they don't have any hobbies or friends, and they may be stingy with time, money, and gifts. Usually they strike others as dogmatic, abrasively stubborn and controlling, passive-aggressive, stilted, stiff, and miserly. In other words, OCPD is the diagnostic label for someone who is extremely and abnormally "anal-retentive."

OCPD is different from obsessive-compulsive disorder (OCD, see Chapter 6) because it involves obsessive and compulsive personality *traits*, not specific, repetitive thoughts and ritualized behaviors.

| OCD | OCPD |
|---|---|
| Diagnosed on: Axis I | Diagnosed on: Axis II |
| Ego-dystonic | Ego-syntonic |
| Behavior involves rituals | No rituals: perfectionism |
| Interferes with both social and work environments | Does well at work, has trouble socially |
| Constant doubting (e.g. Did I lock the door?) | Interpersonally stubborn and controlling |
| Appears equally in both sexes | Diagnosed twice as often in males |

Fig 9.2. Differences between OCD and OCPD.

**Additional Information**
- The families of people with OCPD are often moralistic. Productivity, self-control, and the delay of gratification are esteemed as virtues.
- People with OCPD often have trouble making decisions. Some insist on keeping worthless and worn-out objects just in case they need them. In extreme situations, they become compulsive hoarders. (See Chapter 6 for more information on hoarding.)

# TREATMENT OF PERSONALITY DISORDERS

Because of their ego-syntonic nature, personality disorders are difficult to treat. People who have them rarely come to therapy unless they're forced to or are having trouble with Axis I symptoms, and even then they often terminate treatment prematurely. In addition, because these disorders affect relationships so profoundly, the therapist may find himself reacting to the client with uncommonly strong—and often unpleasant—

emotions. Psychodynamic therapists refer to these unusually powerful therapist reactions as "countertransference."

Each of the different forms of psychotherapy is used with personality disorders, usually without a great deal of success. Cognitive-behavioral therapy, for example, focuses on identifying beliefs and attitudes common to each personality disorder (e.g. the paranoid belief that "people are potential adversaries," or the histrionic belief "I must impress others and be the center of attention") and then changing those beliefs by methodically testing and disputing them. Psychodynamic therapists attempt to identify what went wrong during development, and then try to repair— or at least patch—the massive resulting damage. Again, however, when people don't believe there's anything wrong with them, and their entire personalities are structured around one belief and approach to life, asking them to change can be like asking a giraffe to become a palm tree. Antisocial and narcissistic personality disorders are especially impervious to treatment. When treatment does yield change, the changes may be small, and they can take years. Drug therapy may be used to deal with Axis I symptoms, but medications don't affect the personality traits themselves.

# 10
# Psychopaths and Villains
## *Crossing the Line*

A villain is someone who indulges the dark side of his personality. He breaks the rules. He pursues what he wants even when he knows someone else wants or needs that same thing. Some villains are worse than others, though. Some revel in their wickedness.

Writers are often interested in what drives people to extraordinary and monstrous acts. They're familiar with stereotypes that assume a history of abuse or a genetic predisposition toward antisocial behavior, but the details are fuzzy. This chapter looks at the situations, upbringings, and genetics that contribute to people crossing the line into committing evil acts. Once you're properly grounded in the underlying factors that can cause malicious behavior, your nefarious antagonists will be that much more realistic—and sinister.

## PROFILE OF A PSYCHOPATHIC VILLAIN

In his book *Evil*, social psychologist Roy Baumeister profiles common assumptions about the most wicked of villains. They:

- Intentionally hurt other people.
- Are sadists; they *enjoy* harming others.
- Enjoy creating chaos for the sake of chaos.
- Are fundamentally different—that is, less human—than other, "normal" people.
- Are egotistical.
- Have trouble controlling their urges and emotions.
- Can't be changed or rehabilitated.

Characters like Hannibal Lecter and Batman's nemesis the Joker are prototypical villains: they smile and laugh their way through arbitrary, gratuitous violence that shreds other characters' lives. They're monsters in human disguise.

As we discussed in Chapter 9, people who consistently take advantage of others and violate their rights through lies, cons, aggression, and irresponsibility are diagnosed with antisocial personality disorder (APD). In extreme cases, someone with APD may also be a psychopath. Renowned criminal psychologist Robert Hare defines psychopaths as "remorseless predators who use charm, intimidation and, if necessary, impulsive and cold-blooded violence to attain their ends."

Hare discovered as he worked with psychopaths that they could fool most of the standard personality tests, including one of psychology's favorite objective personality tests: the Minnesota Multiphasic Personality Inventory (MMPI). Hare spent years developing a new instrument he calls the Psychopathy Checklist, which is now in a revised format (PCL-R). The PCL-R is the tool used most often to identify psychopathy, contrasting it in particular with simple criminality, social deviance, and garden-variety antisocial personality disorder. In other words, though more than 80 percent of incarcerated criminals can be diagnosed with antisocial personality disorder, a mere 20 percent meet the criteria Hare has identified for psychopathy.

According to Hare, psychopaths are:

- Glib and superficial. Smooth-talking psychopaths are persuasive and even charming, but underneath their avowed sincerity is an utter lack of caring. They don't experience emotions the way other people do, and can describe the details of their gruesome deeds in the easy, even cavalier manner of someone sharing the details of a picnic with friends.

- Egocentric and grandiose. All psychopaths might be antisocial, but they're also narcissistic. They're cocky, opinionated braggarts who love power over others above all else. Some people experience their outrageous confidence as charisma; others find them too snake-oil slick. Regardless, if they're caught for a crime, trying to spook them into sharing information won't work. If your detective can get a psychopath to start bragging, however, she may find out about crimes she never suspected him of committing.

- Utterly lacking in remorse, guilt, or empathy. Not only do psychopaths not feel bad for destroying other people's lives—they sometimes argue that they did the victim a favor. If they simply tortured and mutilated someone, at least they didn't kill him—they were giving him a break. If they killed him, at least they didn't leave him all cut up—they were giving him a break. And if they didn't give him a break—well, he didn't deserve one in the first place. And psychopaths don't just ignore the rights, needs, and feelings of strangers; they also care nothing for family and friends.

- Deceitful and manipulative. Psychopaths have a special talent for excuses, and according to Hare, "memory loss, amnesia, blackouts, multiple personality, and temporary insanity crop up constantly in interrogations of psychopaths." Given their grandiosity, many of their lies are outrageous, and yet even people trained to work with criminals sometimes fall prey to their silver-tongued fictions.

- Emotionally impoverished. Though psychopaths can seem cold and unemotional, they sometimes also display emotions that smell of histrionics—theatrical and shallow. They literally do not display any physiological indicators of fear, even on sensitive laboratory equipment, and they don't understand the shades of emotion most people take for granted. Hare tells the story of one psychopath who read self-help books so he could regurgitate emotional language and better fool his victims.

- Impulsive, even whimsical. Psychopaths do things because they feel like it at the moment. If it's more convenient to lie, take something, hurt someone, or kill, then that's what they'll do. At no point, however, is their behavior out of control. They know exactly what they're doing; in fact, they're so focused that things like heart rate and breathing may go *down* rather than up, the way they do in other people. Though Hollywood loves to portray cold-blooded heroes with secret hearts of gold *á la* movies like *Cobra* and *The Dirty Dozen*, the truth is that psychopaths are callous and capricious, and have loyalty to no one but themselves. If they even show up for something, they'll goof off, screw around, and make trouble…just because they can.

- Easily offended. Extreme outbursts are likely to follow even small provocations, and psychopaths believe their aggression and violence is completely justified. Rather than staying upset once they've "taken care of" the problem, they behave as though nothing happened.

- Eager for excitement. A psychopath will do anything for a thrill, regardless of the consequences to himself and especially to others.

- Irresponsible. Psychopaths think nothing of leaving young children at home alone, running up debts (especially if they're on someone else's dime), breaking promises, shirking obligations, and abandoning commitments. Yet they always know what to say to talk themselves out of trouble and get "one more chance."

- Different from other children. Family members of psychopaths often remark that they knew very early that a child was "off" or "not right." It's not unusual for even young psychopaths to torture animals and display the remains, torture or kill other children, and get in trouble thanks to vandalism, arson, theft, extortion, lying, and promiscuity. As they get older, this behavior only continues, often leading to criminal convictions.

- Without conscience. Because they do not experience normal fear or anxiety, and because they do not feel bad or worry about what others will think or do, the psychopath has no internal controls to keep him from doing anything and everything that occurs to him. Don't forget, though, that a psychopath is always in control: he may weigh the costs against the "benefits" of a particular action and choose not to do something because it's not worth the potential payoff.

Increasingly, research shows that psychopaths' brains are structurally different from those of other people, making it easy for them to do things others would find unthinkable. Be aware, however, that not all psychopaths kill, and not all of them are caught and branded as criminals. "Successful psychopaths," as they are sometimes called, seem to function well enough in society. Authors like Hare and Paul Babiak have detailed ways in which clever psychopaths successfully navigate and manipulate the corporate world.

### THE CORPORATE PSYCHOPATH

Corporate psychopaths are Machiavellians attracted by positions of power; they're very good at working the system and manipulating their way up the corporate ladder. They tend to do well in interviews because they're polished and decisive, think well on their feet, and know how to get others to like them. They're happy to fire or blackball people they see as inferior or in their way, and they aren't above bullying, manipulating numbers, or getting ahead in other immoral, unethical, or illegal ways. Like Patrick Bateman in Bret Easton Ellis's *American Psycho*, they are persuasive, charismatic, and intelligent, and their friends and partners may not realize that the psychopath sees them as completely expendable until they're no longer of use to him.

## SADISM

What makes many psychopaths so frightening is their sadism: they seem to *enjoy* controlling and harming others and having godlike power over them. The psychological community acknowledges a sadistic personality type; in fact, the revised third edition of the *DSM*, which was in use from 1987 to 1994, included a "sadistic personality disorder," a diagnosis that has since been removed for political reasons. Researchers worried that putting a diagnostic label on nonsexual sadism might give lawyers a way to excuse their clients' evil deeds, i.e. by suggesting to juries that they were due to a "mental illness." As you might imagine, this is already a problem with the antisocial personality disorder diagnosis, which is *not* considered a mental illness, but rather a problematic behavioral pattern.

According to the *DSM-III-R*, people with sadistic personalities:

- Use physical cruelty or violence to establish dominance over others.

- Humiliate or demean people in front of others.

- Treat or discipline others with extreme harshness.

- Enjoy or are entertained by the psychological or physical suffering of others.

- Lie with the explicit goal of hurting others.

- Intimidate or terrorize others to get what they want.

- Control people they're close with by restricting their freedom and independence.

- Are fascinated by violence, weapons, injury, or torture.

Sadists come to realize that they enjoy hurting others gradually. In other words, early instances of violence aren't caused by sadism, but if someone realizes he enjoys hurting others, sadism can give him a reason to *keep* committing violence. Some sadists even describe the enjoyment as addictive. One rapist told researcher Diana Scully, "Rape is like smoking. You can't stop once you start."

According to social psychologist Erich Fromm, sadists are uninterested in a fight between equals—they enjoy controlling and torturing those they see as weaker than themselves. When confronted by someone he sees as truly more powerful than him, some sadists may become submissive.

## CHILDHOOD

When one sees how neglectful and traumatic some criminals' childhoods were, APD and even psychopathy can seem inevitable. While that doesn't excuse monstrous behavior, it does make it more predictable to those who argue for an environmental cause for psychopathy.

As children, we are biologically pre-programmed to want to form special emotional bonds with our caregivers. We instinctively "attach" to the people who love us, and we learn to love in return. We then develop a conscience by internalizing the values and rules of the people we love. If no one treats a child with love, he doesn't attach securely, if he attaches at all. Unattached children do not learn to care about others or their feelings, nor do they develop a conscience.

Serial killers in particular often have strange, sexualized, and sadistic relationships with their mothers. They also tend to display a triad of symptoms in childhood: bedwetting, fire setting, and animal torture. Bedwetting sometimes results from abuse, and it's humiliating when the abuser mocks the child for it. Because the child has no recourse against the abuser, he tortures and kills animals, which are weaker and more vulnerable than he is. Since this makes him feel better, he escalates the behavior over time until he is selecting and killing human victims, often those who resemble whoever initially humiliated or hurt him. For example, Ted Bundy killed women who resembled an ex-girlfriend who dumped him. Gary Ridgeway, who said his mother "dressed like a whore," killed women he described as "whores and sluts."

Don't assume that all psychopaths come from abusive backgrounds, though. Some children are simply, in the words of writer William March, "bad seeds." According to Robert Hare, someone with psychopathic personality traits or brain abnormalities "who grows up in a stable family and has access to positive social and educational resources might become a con artist or white-collar criminal, or perhaps a somewhat shady entrepreneur, politician, or professional." Someone from a darker background, however, "might become a drifter, mercenary, or violent criminal."

## HEROES VS. VILLAINS

According to psychologist Roy Baumeister, most violence doesn't start with a wicked person attacking a hapless victim. Instead, it's the result of "reciprocal, mutual grievances and provocation" that escalate until one party hurts or kills the other. Nonetheless, each party sees itself as wholly innocent and the other as utterly evil. In reality, most people who do evil things are not actually evil people, nor are most victims completely innocent. But we still have a tendency to want to see things that way.

What this means is that your bad guy may be bad simply because you have chosen to take the hero's point of view. Consider, for example, the way Gregory Maguire turned *The Wizard of Oz*'s Wicked Witch of the West into a sympathetic character by making her the protagonist of his book *Wicked*.

Well-written heroes and villains represent opposite sides of the same proverbial coin. A truly great villain represents the hero's dark side: his weaknesses, foibles, and dark desires. Conflict escalates because the hero is responding to the villain's last move, and the villain to the hero's last move.

In the science fiction television series *Farscape*, the villainous Scorpius wants exactly the same thing hero John Crichton does: to harness the energy created by wormholes. Both want the power for reasons so selfish that they're willing to inconvenience and even endanger those around them to get it. What makes Crichton the hero is not that he is incapable of evil, but that he is able to overcome the evil in himself—the evil that is represented by his nemesis, Scorpius. His eventual defeat of Scorpius is the symbolic defeat of his own dark tendencies.

## THE PSYCHOPATHIC BRAIN

Psychopaths' brains can be different from the average person's in several ways. In particular, the orbitofrontal cortex (OFC) and anterior cingulate cortex (ACC) do not seem to work properly. The amygdala, hippocampus, and/or the MAO-A gene may also be affected.

- *Impaired orbitofrontal cortex.* The orbitofrontal cortex (OFC) is in the frontal lobes of the brain, right above the eye sockets. It regulates mood, affects the person's sense of social responsibility, and modulates aggression. It also affects his ability to learn from his mistakes and behave in socially appropriate ways to get his needs met.

The movie *Saw* implies that cancer damaged the villain's OFC and caused his savage tendencies. In reality, while damage to the OFC due to head trauma or disease can cause relatively permanent "acquired sociopathy," acquired sociopathy is never as creative or ferocious as Jigsaw's. While damage to the OFC later in life can affect one's morality and aggressive impulses, that doesn't unravel the person's existing personality or make him have monstrous urges that were never there before.

- *Impaired anterior cingulate cortex.* The anterior cingulate cortex (ACC) helps us understand how our behavior affects others and how they might feel as a result. In psychopaths in particular, the ACC shows reduced activity. Researchers are uncertain whether the ACC itself is structurally damaged, or whether other structures are contributing to the reduced activity. In either case, the problem seems to be due to "faulty wiring" rather than later damage.

- *Smaller amygdala and/or hippocampus due to abuse.* Many people with antisocial and psychopathic tendencies were abused. Long-term abuse can make the amygdala (which helps produce and modulate emotions) and the hippocampus (which helps us make new memories) smaller than normal. This seems to be due to the fact that high levels of stress hormones like cortisol can actually damage the neurons that make up structures like the hippocampus. A smaller amygdala is associated with problems like depression, irritability, and hostility. A smaller hippocampus is associated with aggression and difficulties learning from experience.

- *Gene for low MAO-A activity.* In "normal" people, an enzyme called monoamine oxidase A (MAO-A) helps break down brain chemicals like serotonin, norepinephrine, and dopamine after the body is done using them. A mutation in the gene that handles MAO-A can keep these chemicals from breaking down and lead to abnormally high levels, which are in turn associated with aggression and criminality.

## DON'T LET THIS HAPPEN TO YOU!

"Would it be fair to say," inquired one character in William Diehl's *Primal Fear*, "that Aaron suffers from dissociative multiple personality syndrome and Roy is the psychotic schizophrenic?" Another character answers, "Yes, that is my analysis. Roy has all of the classic symptoms of the psychopath. He feels no guilt or remorse, recognizes no laws."

There are several problems with this passage. First, as you know from Chapter 6, schizophrenia is, by definition, a psychotic disorder, which makes the term "psychotic schizophrenic" redundant. Likewise, as we saw in Chapter 8, multiple personality disorder is, by definition, a dissociative disorder.

Next, Diehl is confusing the term "psychosis" with "psychopathy"—two totally different conditions. He does it again elsewhere in the book with his therapist saying, "Psychotics—psychopaths—[have] a personal history of chronic and continuous...criminality, sexual promiscuity, aggressive sexual behavior." As we discussed in Chapter 6, psychosis is a loss of contact with reality as other people experience it. Psychopathy means someone has antisocial personality disorder and feels no guilt or remorse. The problem in the passage above is that one character proposes that Roy is psychotic, and the other character agrees that he's a psychopath. The two terms are not synonymous at all!

## CAN YOU CURE A PSYCHOPATH?

Psychopaths don't believe they have a problem, nor do they take responsibility for their actions. Add to that their inability to genuinely care about other people and their tendency to see therapy as a joke and an opportunity to manipulate someone else, and you can see why psychopathy is notoriously difficult to treat. Many researchers argue that psychotherapy is flat-out useless in these populations; the research that deals with the treatment of psychopathy is much more likely to talk about what doesn't work than what does. What this means is that with the most severe cases of APD—cases in which true psychopathy are involved—clinicians focus on sequestering dangerous psychopaths from the rest of the population and keeping them as manageable as possible.

# PARAPHILIAS AND IMPULSE-CONTROL DISORDERS

"Paraphilia" is the politically correct term for "perversion." Paraphilias are sometimes part of the psychopathic profile. Meanwhile, people with impulse-control disorders feel gratification after acting on an impulse that is harmful to them or others. Though impulse-control disorders are only diagnosed in the absence of APD, understanding them can help you better understand characters who engage in acts like pyromania and kleptomania.

## PARAPHILIAS

According to the *DSM*, paraphilias are sexual urges or behaviors that cause problems because they involve "1) nonhuman objects, 2) the suffering or humiliation of oneself or one's partner, or 3) children or other non-consenting persons." These criteria do leave room for interpretation. That means that some therapists find "kinky" behavior like light bondage and S&M pathological; more often, though, therapists respect that it's perfectly fine for consenting adults to experiment. Most also encourage the use of "safety words" and other protections during such play.

People with paraphilias usually have trouble engaging in affectionate, mutually satisfying sexual relationships. Because they may have trouble finding a consenting partner to indulge their unusual desires, they may turn to prostitutes or unwilling victims. They may also seek work that will keep them close to the things that turn them on—for example, someone with a shoe fetish might work in a shoe store, and someone with necrophilia might work in a mortuary. Paraphilias are diagnosed more often in males than females.

Paraphilias include:

- *Fetishism*. Though many people joke about having a fetish for some object, in true, diagnosable fetishism, the object is so arousing that the person can't function well sexually without it. Thus, if someone has a high-heel fetish and his partner removes the high heels, he might experience erectile dysfunction. In some cases, a partner is not required. The person is aroused just by handling, rubbing, or smelling the object in question.

- *Sexual sadism*. In sexual sadism, the individual is aroused by real (not simulated), extreme psychological and physical suffering of another person. Sadistic fantasies usually start during childhood, and once the person begins to act on them, he is unlikely to stop. In the movie *The Cell*, serial killer Stargher slowly drowns women in glass cells. He records every harrowing moment so he can watch the tapes over and over—especially the actual deaths, which he finds most exciting.

- *Sexual masochism*. In sexual masochism, the individual is aroused by real (not simulated) torture and humiliation. Masochists tend to replay the same masochistic acts again and again, but some increase the dangerousness over time, which can lead to serious injuries or death.

Though sadism and masochism are technically separate diagnoses, research suggests that many sadists are also masochists and vice versa. These people are often masochistic with people they perceive as dominant and sadistic with people they perceive as inferior.

Also in *The Cell*, Stargher has metal rings embedded into his back. In his basement are a series of hooks that lift him painfully off the ground and position him over the bleached body of one of his victims, where he masturbates.

- *Necrophilia*. Some people who are sexually aroused by corpses have a fetishistic attraction. Others cite reasons like wanting a partner who can neither resist nor reject them, or wanting to show power over someone.

Cognitive-behavioral individual therapy is the treatment of choice for paraphilias. One behavioral technique, aversive conditioning, requires the therapist to do something unpleasant to the client when the client becomes inappropriately aroused. Anthony Burgess vividly portrayed aversive conditioning in the novel *A Clockwork Orange*: the therapist gives the main character, a rapist, a drug that makes him violently ill while he watches brutal acts, until the sight of violence alone makes him sick. Backlash from Stanley Kubrick's film adaptation of the novel made aversive conditioning less popular in the psychiatric community, though it is still used.

Assisted covert sensitization is more subtle: it requires the client to imagine an embarrassing or painful reaction to his arousal while the therapist introduces a foul odor of some kind to induce nausea. Other treatments include social skills training and empathy training to help the person get his needs met in healthier ways and appreciate how badly he's hurting others, respectively. Finally, drugs, including Depo-Provera and Prozac, can be administered to temporarily reduce sex drive and aggression.

## IMPULSE-CONTROL DISORDERS

Some people experience tension or arousal that can be relieved only by performing an act that is hurtful to them or others. In *pyromania*, for example, the individual is fascinated by or attracted to fire and all the things related to it, including fire alarms and fire equipment. Setting and/or watching a fire and its aftermath is pleasurable to the person, and afterwards he may feel little if any guilt or regret.

Though some people describe the tension relief following an act like fire setting as sexual, the behavior is not done for sexual gratification per se. If it were, it would be considered a paraphilia rather than an impulse-control disorder. Someone who is sexually aroused by setting, watching, or talking about fires is said to have *pyrophilia*, not pyromania.

*Kleptomania*, another impulse-control disorder, is different from mere shoplifting because it involves an overwhelming increase in tension that's relieved by stealing. Usually the person doesn't need or even want the object he takes, and he may give it away or even throw it in the garbage. Unlike many shoplifters, people with kleptomania always act alone. Because they know that what they are doing is wrong, they often feel bad about the thefts. People with kleptomania seem to have more obsessive-compulsive disorder in their families than others, which may help explain why they can't seem to stop stealing, even when the behavior causes legal and personal problems.

Since impulse control disorders are related to obsessive-compulsive behavior, they are treated as if they were OCD.

As noted above, impulse control disorders are not diagnosed if the behavior is part of a conduct disorder, mania, or antisocial personality disorder. In these cases, the behavior is considered a *symptom* of another disorder rather than its own disorder. Impulse-control disorders are also not diagnosed if the person is acting out of the desire for profit or revenge, to hide a crime, to make a political statement, or to get attention.

# 11

# Physical and Biological Interventions

*Medications, Electroshock, and One Really Horrible Idea*

In HBO's drama *The Sopranos*, Tony Soprano's psychiatrist prescribes Prozac for his depression and panic attacks...and it actually helps. Movies and television usually emphasize talk therapy over medication, and when they do show medication, they tend to minimize the positives and exaggerate the negatives, often suggesting that psychiatric drugs are used as a form of social control. In reality, medications are used because they reduce symptoms, and a good psychiatrist always weighs the potential benefits of using a drug against the potential for negative side effects.

Further, few writers realize that electroconvulsive therapy is different from the portrayals in most movies and books, or that lobotomies are no longer performed. This chapter reviews historical and modern treatments, including the good, the controversial, and the downright stupid.

## ANTIDEPRESSANTS

Depression seems to be caused by an imbalance in several brain chemicals, which are called neurotransmitters. The three most commonly implicated neurotransmitters are serotonin, norepinephrine, and dopamine.

Antidepressants are medications that alleviate or counteract clinical depressions, probably at least in part by increasing levels of serotonin, norepinephrine, and sometimes dopamine. The first two classes of antidepressants were introduced in the 1950s: tricyclic antidepressants (TCAs) and monoamine oxidase inhibitors (MAOIs). The antidepressants most people are familiar with, the serotonin reuptake inhibitors (SSRIs), weren't developed until the late 1980s.

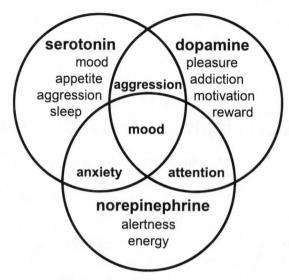

**Fig 11.1. Imbalances in serotonin, norepinephrine, or dopamine contribute to problems like depression and anxiety.**

## TRICYCLICS (TCAs)

While tricyclics help many people with major depressive disorder, they also have a lot of side effects, which makes them less appealing than the newer SSRIs, which work in a similar way. In addition to drowsiness, some people experience confusion, disorientation, tremors, vivid dreams or nightmares, difficulty reaching orgasm, weight gain, and dry mouth and eyes.

Tricyclics take between a week and a month to start working. Brand names include Elavil, Norpramin, Tofranil, Anafranil, Pamelor, and Vivactil. Some of these drugs are also used with obsessive-compulsive disorder (Anafranil), panic disorder (Norpramin), generalized anxiety disorder (Tofranil), and non-psychiatric conditions like chronic pain and migraine headaches.

Tricyclics are very easy to overdose on, making them somewhat dangerous to prescribe to someone who is suicidal. If someone does overdose, she is given a drug like ipecac to induce vomiting. Medical personnel might alternately use activated charcoal, which absorbs the overdosed drug and then causes vomiting.

# MONOAMINE OXIDASE INHIBITORS (MAOIs)

Monoamine oxidase inhibitors (MAOIs) are sometimes used for "treatment-resistant depression," which is depression that hasn't responded to more common treatments, including antidepressants like SSRIs and tricyclics. MAOIs usually begin to work within a few days and brand names include Marplan, Nardil, and Parnate.

MAOIs have side effects like insomnia, inability to have an orgasm, weight loss or weight gain, and low blood pressure, which can cause nausea, dizziness or lightheadedness, and headache. They also have the potential to cause two dangerous syndromes: a hypertensive crisis or serotonin syndrome.

## *Hypertensive Crisis*

Within hours of eating foods or taking drugs that have large amounts of tyramine in them, someone taking an MAOI can experience a hypertensive crisis. A severe elevation in blood pressure causes headaches, nausea, vomiting, confusion, chest pain, and in extreme cases death due to a heart attack or stroke.

Foods that contain lots of tyramine include aged or smoked meats, aged cheeses, packet soup, and fermented foods and drinks, like sour cream, sauerkraut, yogurt, tofu, soy sauce, wines like Chianti, and draft beer.

Drugs and medications that can be deadly in combinations with MAOIs include cocaine, amphetamines, cold remedies, pain medications like Demerol, decongestants, and sleep aids. Patients must also avoid taking SSRIs or tricyclic antidepressants with MAOIs. Therefore, the prescribing physician always has patients take a two-week break from *all* antidepressants before he switches to or from MAOIs.

## *Serotonin Syndrome*

If someone takes an MAOI in combination with substances like tryptophan, appetite suppressants, or St. John's wort, she can develop serotonin syndrome, which is a toxic buildup of serotonin within the body. Symptoms usually develop quickly and include nausea, chills, sweating, dizziness, high blood pressure, twitching, disorientation, confusion, and in extreme cases, eventually coma and death. What all of this means is that if your character is on MAOIs, something as simple as having a glass of Chianti or taking a diet pill can kill her.

Finally, it's easy to overdose on a mere week or two's worth of MAOIs. The individual may not show any symptoms of overdose for up to six hours, but after that she can quickly become restless, fall into a coma, and die.

## Selective Reuptake Inhibitors (SSRIs)

The first SSRIs (selective serotonin reuptake inhibitors), Luvox and Prozac, were introduced in the late 1980s. They were soon followed by Zoloft, Paxil, Celexa, and Lexapro. Next came the SNRIs (selective norepinephrine reuptake inhibitors), which affect both serotonin and norepinephrine; they include Effexor, Cymbalta, and Pristiq. Wellbutrin is unique because it affects norepinephrine and dopamine, making it an NDRI (norepinephrine dopamine reuptake inhibitor). As if that all weren't confusing enough, most people collectively refer to all three types of drugs—SSRIs, SNRIs, and SDRIs—as SSRIs.

Because there is no blood test or brain scan that can determine which brain chemicals are imbalanced, psychiatrists decide which medication to prescribe based on a patient's reported symptoms. If the patient is complaining about things that suggest a serotonin deficit (e.g. insomnia, appetite changes, sadness), the doctor chooses an SSRI. If her symptoms suggest that norepinephrine or dopamine levels are also low (e.g. poor concentration, low energy, lack of motivation), the psychiatrist might choose an SNRI or SDRI instead of or in addition to an SSRI.

Selective reuptake inhibitors are used to treat major depressive disorder, obsessive compulsive disorder (OCD), panic disorder, social anxiety disorder, generalized anxiety disorder (GAD), dysthymia, premenstrual dysphoric disorder (PMDD, colloquially called PMS), and sometimes self-injury and borderline personality disorder. Zoloft is sometimes used for posttraumatic stress disorder (PTSD) or bulimia. Symbyax, which is a combination of Prozac and the antipsychotic Zyprexa, can be used for treatment-resistant depression and acute bipolar I depression.

Finally, selective reuptake inhibitors have few side effects and are extremely hard to overdose on in comparison with tricyclics or MAOIs. The most common side effects include headache, nausea, insomnia, fatigue, weight gain, and sexual dysfunction. Some people also have dreams or nightmares so intensely vivid that they swear the dream really happened. It's not unusual, for example, for someone to say she brought up a conversation she knows she had with someone only to have that person insist the conversation never happened. Eventually the person comes to understand that whenever this happens, she's just had a vivid dream. Though a lot of people think this is a pretty cool side effect (especially because some of them compare it to tripping on LSD), people who have nightmares usually want to stop taking the medication immediately.

If your character were a witness in an important court case, how might symptoms like these impair the likelihood that she'd be believed?

---

### DON'T LET THIS HAPPEN TO YOU!

"SSRI stands for selective serotonin reuptake inhibitor," a character in April Christofferson's *Alpha Female* says. "It's a type of antidepressant. It's *the* antidepressant of the day. Or perhaps I should say the decade. Doctors prescribe it now for everything from depression to headaches to having a couple bad days."

Though the character is exaggerating, misconceptions like this have crept into popular consciousness. People joke that Prozac is a "happy pill" one can take for a "quick fix," when neither of these things is true. First, antidepressants only improve mood if one's brain isn't producing or using neurotransmitters properly, so you can't get high on them. Second, antidepressants typically take between a week and a month to work, so there would be little point to taking an SSRI for a headache or a bad day!

Tricyclic antidepressants *are* sometimes used to prevent migraines, but there's little evidence that SSRIs help them unless the headache is part of the person's depression.

---

## HOW ANTIDEPRESSANTS WORK: ONE POPULAR THEORY

Your brain and spinal cord are made up of millions of special nerve cells called neurons. Neurons have tiny gaps between them called synaptic spaces. Chemicals called neurotransmitters are responsible for carrying messages across these spaces from the sending neuron to the receiving neuron.

When the neurotransmitters reach the receiving neuron, they plug into receptor sites, which are like receiving docks. Whatever message is associated with each neurotransmitter is passed into the receiving neuron. For example, serotonin neurotransmitters send messages about sleep, appetite, and mood, while norepinephrine neurotransmitters send messages about concentration, alertness, and energy.

Once the message has been sent, the neurotransmitter pops out of the receptor site and is sucked back up into the sending neuron by a reuptake pump so it can be recycled. The recycling factory inside the neuron uses a chemical known as monoamine oxidase, or MAO, to break down used neurotransmitters.

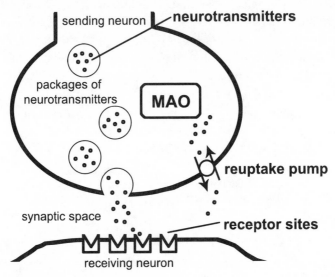

**Fig 11.2. Neuron communication: the delivery, use, and reuptake of neurotransmitters in the synapse.**

Tricyclics and SSRIs block the reuptake pump so the neurotransmitters that make people feel "normal" build up in the synaptic space and return to the receptor sites to send their messages over and over.

MAOIs stop monoamine oxidase from breaking down neurotransmitters, which means the sending neuron sends out more of the neurotransmitter than usual. Again, this helps the person feel better because it restores neurotransmitter levels to normal.

In either case, antidepressants help the brain use its own chemicals more effectively. Over time, they can usually teach the brain to work properly again. Still, stopping antidepressants cold can cause withdrawal ("discontinuation syndrome"). Discontinuation syndrome can include an exacerbation of the symptoms the medication was originally prescribed to treat, such as depression or anxiety, or physical symptoms like headache, dizziness, or the uncomfortable sensation of electrical jolts.

Because their brain chemistry doesn't work properly, some people will need to take antidepressants for the rest of their lives. This is especially true of people with bipolar disorder or recurrent depression. Other people may be able to stop taking antidepressants after six months to a year, but they may need an additional course of medication should their symptoms recur.

## ANTIDEPRESSANTS AND SUICIDE RISK

SSRIs in particular have gotten a lot of press because the U.S. Food and Drug Administration has placed its strongest warning—the "black box"—on them. The black box states that people who take these medications—particularly children, adolescents, and young adults—may have about a 4 percent "increased risk of suicidal thinking and behavior… during the first few months of treatment" when compared to people not taking antidepressants. The warning therefore advises that clients "should be observed closely for clinical worsening, suicidality, or unusual changes in behavior." Note that the risk of suicide goes *down* in older individuals, especially the elderly.

Keep in mind that severe depression is really at the root of most suicidal thoughts; however, people who are extremely depressed may not have the energy or motivation to harm themselves. When they begin taking antidepressants, they start to feel more energetic before they start to feel happier. The suicide risk goes up during that time, and then comes back down when the person starts to get the full effect of the drug and feels happier, too. As noted above, psychiatrists are aware of this and warn their patients to call if they are having problems with suicidal feelings, a worsening of their symptoms, or unusual behavior.

## Mood Stabilizers

Mood stabilizers are used most often to treat bipolar disorder, though they can also be used as an "augmenting agent"—that is, they can be added to antidepressants to make the antidepressants work better. They can also help with the aggression and irritability that accompanies some other psychiatric disorders.

The mood stabilizer *lithium carbonate* is the gold standard treatment for mania, with more than 80 percent of people with "classic" mania (as opposed to a mixed state or mania with psychosis) responding well to it. According to psychiatrist Jenifer M. Takats, "Lithium has a narrow therapeutic range between effective and toxic levels; therefore, blood levels need to be monitored closely during the course of treatment. One of the advantages of using lithium is that clinical effectiveness can be [determined] with blood tests. If after two weeks at therapeutic levels there is no improvement, the prescriber can consider alternative treatments." Because it takes between a week and two weeks for the individual to get the full effects of the drug, if she's extremely manic the doctor can also prescribe an antipsychotic, which works more quickly to get symptoms under control.

Lithium's side effects can include weakness, tiredness, memory problems, hand tremors, headaches, extreme weight gain, or a lack of productivity or creativity. Long-term use of lithium can also cause kidney toxicity or thyroid problems. Taking ibuprofen, naproxen, or diuretics can be lethal in combination with lithium, even if the person has taken no more than the recommended doses. That means that something as simple as combining Midol or Aleve with lithium can be deadly.

If someone overdoses on lithium, she may develop disorientation, hallucinations, or a catatonic stupor. As noted above, severe poisoning can cause coma or death. Finally, lithium can cause cardiac abnormalities in infants who are exposed to it during the first trimester of pregnancy.

*Anticonvulsants* like Tegretol, Depakote, Lamictal, Trileptal, and Neurontin are also used as mood stabilizers for mania and bipolar disorder. Some research suggests that Neurontin can help with posttraumatic stress disorder (PTSD), severe panic disorder, social phobia, and generalized anxiety disorder (GAD). Anticonvulsant side effects can include sedation or agitation, headache, tremors, dizziness, blurred vision, nausea, menstrual disturbances (Tegretol, Depakote, Lamictal), and significant weight gain (Tegretol, Depakote, Neurontin). Depakote and Tegertol can also cause birth defects like neural tube defects and cleft palate.

Stevens-Johnson syndrome (SJS) occurs very rarely with Tegretol and Lamictal. With SJS, the skin swells and then easily sloughs off; if the person is not given immediate emergency medical treatment, the symptoms can occur internally. For example, the lining of the esophagus can slough off ("esophageal stricture") and become septic, which is deadly.

---

### POLYPHARMACY AND PILL PARSIMONY

You may be tempted to have your psychiatrist character prescribe a cocktail of medications for your character, but polypharmacy—as excessive drug prescription is called—is always a bad idea. In addition to multiple side effects and unexpected drug interactions, polypharmacy can be cost-prohibitive for the patient. There also comes a point at which people will simply refuse to take more medication.

Polypharmacy *does* happen, but to avoid accidentally creating an unrealistic combination of drugs, you'll want to pick one—*maybe two*—for your character's problems based on what you're learning in this chapter. Since SSRIs are often prescribed for both depression and anxiety, for example, your character may not need an antidepressant *and* an anxiolytic. Be parsimonious to protect accurate storytelling—that one SSRI may be plenty.

# ANXIOLYTICS (ANTI-ANXIETY MEDICATIONS)

*SSRI antidepressants*, most notably Paxil, Zoloft, Lexapro, and the SNRI Effexor are used as anti-anxiety medications because they work, the side effects are tolerable, and it's difficult to overdose on them.

*Benzodiazepines* like Xanax, Librium, Klonopin, Valium, and Ativan can also be used to treat disorders like generalized anxiety disorder (GAD) and panic disorder, though they're not recommended for long-term treatment due to the risk of abuse and addiction. Benzodiazepines can cause tiredness or fatigue and interfere with thinking processes. However, an overdose is not usually fatal as long as other drugs or alcohol are not mixed in.

Benzodiazepines work quickly, but stopping them after regular use leads to withdrawal that can include symptoms like agitation, sadness, headache, twitching and muscle aches, and in extreme cases psychosis, seizures, and coma.

*Buspar* is a newer drug in its own class. It's useful for chronic anxiety and in people for whom the sedation of benzodiazepines might be dangerous. It has minimal effects on thinking and a low potential for abuse or addiction. It must be prescribed on an ongoing basis to be effective, and it has an antidepressant effect at some doses. Patients taking Buspar don't report withdrawal effects, and overdose doesn't appear to be a concern.

# ANTIPSYCHOTICS (NEUROLEPTICS)

With schizophrenia, antipsychotic medications reduce symptoms like hallucinations, delusions, and thought disorganization. With bipolar mania, antipsychotics also reduce euphoria and irritability. As with other medications, the prescribing physician must weigh the potential benefits of antipsychotics against the side effects.

While side effects are a concern with any medication, they can be particularly problematic with antipsychotics. Noncompliance estimates due to side effects range from 10 percent to 15 percent in people who are hospitalized and up to 65 percent in people who are not hospitalized.

In addition to wanting to avoid side effects, some people stop taking their medications because they like feeling hypomanic or manic (bipolar disorder) or because they feel like the medications are being used to force them to conform to societal expectations (schizophrenia).

Antipsychotics can be broken down into two classes:

1. *Typical or conventional antipsychotics* include Haldol and Thorazine. While effective, at high doses or with long-term use, they're notorious for causing sedation, considerable weight gain, and extrapyramidal effects like tardive dyskinesia and akathisia.

   *Extrapyramidal* side effects include muscular spasms or rigidity, tremors, and other involuntary movements of the body. *Tardive dyskinesia* refers to involuntary, repetitive motions of the lips, tongue, and facial muscles. *Akathisia* refers to an uncomfortable, internal restlessness that can goad the person into pacing or fidgeting. Sometimes these side effects don't go away, even if the medication is stopped.

2. *Atypical antipsychotics* include Risperdal, Zyprexa, Seroquel, Geodon, and Abilify. They are used much more often than the conventional antipsychotics because they're less likely to cause extrapyramidal side effects, particularly tardive dyskinesia. However, most still cause significant weight gain and some sedation and put people at risk for diabetes. Sometimes they're used to help with depression that isn't responding to antidepressants, with self-injury, and for psychotic PTSD symptoms.

Antipsychotics usually begin to help with agitation and sleep within a week, with hallucinations over two to eight weeks, and with thought disorganization in six to eight weeks, though thought disorganization is the hardest thing to treat and may persist in spite of the antipsychotic. A particular antipsychotic is used for at least two consecutive months before the physician gives up on it and tries something new.

Zyprexa is used in hospital emergencies, and it's available in both an injectable form and—for patients who try to hide the pills in their cheeks so they can spit them out later—as a dissolving tablet. Risperdal is available in a Depo form, which means patients only need an injection every two weeks.

## How Antipsychotics Work

In the antidepressants section earlier, we talked about how not having enough of neurotransmitters like serotonin can cause depression. But having *too much* of a particular neurotransmitter can be problematic, too.

In fact, excess serotonin and especially excess dopamine are thought to be responsible for psychotic symptoms.

Antipsychotics block certain dopamine and serotonin receptors so the dopamine and serotonin can't send their psychotic messages.

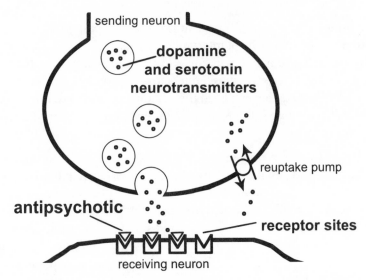

Fig 11.3. Antipsychotics work by blocking the neurotransmitter dopamine in the receiving neuron.

## DON'T LET THIS HAPPEN TO YOU!

On a season eight episode of *Smallville*, a show that chronicles Clark Kent's life before he becomes Superman, EMT Davis Bloome is unable to control his dark side, Doomsday. Desperate to stop turning into a monster, Davis steals packages of "antipsychotics used for multiple personalities."

In reality, as we discussed in Chapter 8, multiple personality disorder (aka dissociative identity disorder or DID) is *not* a psychotic disorder. Therefore, there is no such thing as an antipsychotic (or any other medication) that suppresses personality changes in DID. Sorry, Davis!

# ELECTROCONVULSIVE THERAPY

The most controversial modern psychiatric treatment is electroconvulsive therapy (ECT). The biggest reason for this controversy is that the media perpetuates misconceptions about the treatment, making it look scary, painful, and barbaric when it's really not. In fact, ECT can literally be a lifesaver for people with whom other treatments have failed.

ECT is typically used as a last resort, either because other approaches (e.g. medications) have failed or because the person is so incredibly depressed, psychotic, manic, or suicidal that something has to be done *now*. ECT can make an enormous difference in as little as one treatment session. About 80 percent of people who have had ECT say they would do it again if they needed it.

In 1934, Ladislas Meduna noticed that people with epilepsy rarely have schizophrenia and decided to try inducing seizures in people with schizophrenia. The earliest method, shown in the film *A Beautiful Mind*, involved administering an overdose of insulin to induce seizures and then a temporary coma.

In 1937, a pair of researchers replaced the insulin treatment with actual electrical shocks, and since the new approach was cheaper, less dangerous, and faster, doctors around the world made the switch.

Because it helped people who were severely depressed, manic, or psychotic, ECT became popular in the 1940s and 1950s, especially in the U.S. and the UK. However, the treatments were "unmodified" until 1951, which means that patients weren't given the medications they receive today to keep them from having full-blown convulsions. Some convulsed so badly that they fractured bones.

Ken Kesey's novel *One Flew Over the Cuckoo's Nest*—and the movie by the same name—showed people what unmodified ECT looked like and portrayed it as something used to hurt and terrorize innocent patients. Horror movies still mimic this depiction, which is now inaccurate. In fact, most modern ECT trainees find the actual procedure anticlimactic. Some are still waiting for the excitement to begin when they're told it's already over!

Modern "modified" ECT is always administered by a well-trained treatment team that consists of a psychiatrist, an anesthesiologist, and one or more treatment nurses. First, the patient is given a general anesthetic so she'll go to sleep. Methohexital is usually used because it works quickly and doesn't last very long. If for some reason methohexital is unsuitable for the patient, the anesthesiologist can use etomidate, ketamine, thiopental, or propofol. Next, the patient receives a muscle relaxant, usually succinylcholine, which also works quickly and lasts for a short time. The muscle relaxant keeps the person's body from convulsing, and the anesthesia keeps her from panicking because she can't move.

Electrodes are placed either on the right side of the head ("unilateral ECT") or on both sides of the head ("bilateral ECT"). Bilateral ECT is more effective, but it also produces more memory problems. The team is more likely to use bilateral ECT when someone is in immediate danger of killing herself; is severely agitated or psychotic, catatonic, or manic; or when the patient asks for the most effective form of ECT.

The team always monitors the patient using electroencephalography (EEG) and an electrocardiogram (ECG). A cuff is placed on one of the patient's wrists or ankles to act like a tourniquet and keep the muscle relaxant from reaching it. That part of the body will then convulse, which gives the treatment team a way besides the EEG to monitor the seizure.

The team uses "stimulus dose titration," which means that the nurse always begins with a minimal charge (usually about 10 percent) and slowly works his way upward, doubling the dose each time. Most people respond at or before 80 percent of the dose. Adolescents and people below the age of thirty are started at even lower doses (5 percent), while the elderly may need higher doses. The treatment team will try up to three times to cause a seizure of at least fifteen to twenty seconds. If the seizure lasts more than two minutes, the patient is given Ativan via IV to stop it.

As is true any time patients have been given general anesthesia, confusion and disorientation are common, but improve within ten or twenty minutes. Children and adolescents may complain of a mild headache. Some patients also report general muscle soreness after the first session, but the problem is less frequent following subsequent sessions. In either case, over-the-counter medications like aspirin or acetaminophen help.

The biggest modern problem with ECT is the way it affects memory. In the days following ECT, many people have *anterograde amnesia*, or trouble retaining new information. They forget things they've done or what other people have said to them. The amnesia diminishes over the next few days or—at most—a few weeks.

More troubling is *retrograde amnesia,* or the loss of memories from the last three to six months before treatment—and sometimes even more distant memories. Normally the amnesia is not complete; the person is just aware of gaps in her memory. Over time, the memories almost always come back, but once in a great while the loss is permanent. Permanent loss can be devastating, especially if it involves large blocks of the person's history. Rarely, someone will lose all memory of a spouse or child or will no longer be able to work at a job that requires specialized knowledge. A few people say that their ability to process information has been permanently affected.

So why use ECT at all? Remember, it's used when someone is literally ready to kill herself or when she's been psychotic or catatonic for so long that doctors have run out of options. ECT literally becomes the alternative to death, or to being trapped in a frighteningly disorganized state.

If a patient complains about unusually bad amnesia after a treatment or treatments, the ECT team can adjust the procedure to reduce memory loss. For example, they might switch from bilateral to unilateral treatments, decrease the electrical dose, or do the treatments once or twice a week rather than three times a week. Typically a patient receives a total of six to twelve treatments.

Especially because the treatment is controversial, the attending physician discusses the pros and cons of ECT in depth with the patient. He takes the time to answer questions and address concerns, including those of family members. As long as the patient is capable of understanding and acting reasonably on that information, she has the right to refuse treatment. If she's so sick that she can't give her consent, doctors must respect any wishes she expressed while lucid. Treatment centers also have rules to make sure her rights aren't violated. For example, a treatment center can bring in an independent psychiatric consultant not involved with the patient's care to give an objective opinion about whether ECT is *really* necessary. Because everyone is so careful about getting *informed consent,* there's very little malpractice litigation associated with ECT.

# New Treatments

## Transcranial Magnetic Stimulation (TMS)

During transcranial magnetic stimulation (TMS), the patient sits in what looks like a dentist's chair, and an electromagnetic coil is placed against the left front part of the scalp, near the forehead. The coil is turned on and off rapidly, directing a magnetic field into the brain. Inside the skull, this magnetic field creates very small electrical impulses that stimulate neurons and prompt the release of serotonin, norepinephrine, and dopamine. The TMS machine produces clicking sounds comparable to loud clapping, so both the doctor and the patient must wear earplugs. The clicking lasts for several seconds, followed by a pause. This is repeated multiple times over a thirty or forty minute session. Though the procedure isn't painful, patients often say they experience a prickling or tingling sensation along their scalps and spasms or twitching of facial muscles. Afterward, they may complain of headache or lightheadedness.

Some research suggests TMS may be a noninvasive way of improving the moods of people whose depression has not responded to antidepressants, and many insurance companies have begun to cover the treatment. Other research is less compelling. Even when TMS does work, the results seem to wear off within a few days or weeks, making repeated treatments necessary.

## Vagus Nerve Stimulation (VNS)

In 2005, Vagus Nerve Stimulation (VNS) was approved by the American FDA for depression that resists more standard treatments like therapy and antidepressants. A pacemaker-like device is implanted below the collarbone in the left upper chest. From there, wires called leads run up into the neck and wrap around the vagus nerve, which extends down the spinal cord and up into the brain.

Two weeks after surgery, the device is turned on. Every five minutes thereafter, the device stimulates the nerve for thirty seconds. Though stimulation can be uncomfortable and "prickly" at first, the body quickly adapts, and most patients are eventually unaware of it, except sometimes for vocal hoarseness while the unit is sending out its signal. Vocal hoarseness is caused by the stimulator's vibration against one vocal cord. Patients can turn off the stimulation by holding a flat magnet (provided by the manufacturer) against the device when it turns on. The device will resume normally during the next cycle.

Some people begin to see results within weeks, but it often takes a year or more to see the full effects. Though doctors aren't completely sure how it works, the company that manufactures the device claims that about 80 percent of patients experience some relief from depressive symptoms, while 30 percent feel dramatically better.

Though early on insurance companies covered the implant and procedure, when Medicare and Medicaid expressed doubts and withdrew their coverage, so did most other insurers. The implant under the collarbone, which controls the pulses and contains the battery, costs about $20,000 alone; the surgery to put it in can cost $15,000 or more in larger metropolises.

Finally, because most of the implant is plastic, the device does not set off airport metal detectors.

## Deep Brain Stimulation (DBS)

Deep brain stimulation (DBS) targets the "subgenual cingulate cortex," which is overactive in people who are extremely depressed. As with VNS, a pacemaker-like device is implanted beneath the collarbone. The leads run up the back of the neck, over the top of the skull, and then down into the frontal lobe where the subgenual cingulate cortex is located.

When the hype began to gain steam in 2009, only about sixty patients had been implanted, but 60 percent of that group saw a dramatic improvement in their symptoms. Unlike VNS implantation, DBS is major surgery because it involves inserting an electrode directly into the brain. Researchers aren't exactly sure how it works, but they believe the treatment changes the way different parts of the brain communicate with each other.

Side effects can include thinking problems, apathy, hallucinations, and compulsive behaviors. They often result from misplacement or shifting of the electrode, which can be corrected.

Like the VNS device, DBS implants should not set off metal detectors.

# THE REALLY HORRIBLE IDEA: LOBOTOMIES

Characterized by many modern thinkers as a barbaric mistake, the lobotomy is a destructive, permanent surgical procedure that is no longer practiced. Gottlieb Burckhardt performed the first lobotomies on six schizophrenic patients in a Swiss hospital in 1890. This involved removing both of the frontal lobes, which house "executive functions" such as planning, decision making, and troubleshooting. Damage to the frontal lobes also impairs or destroys the capacity for love, empathy, initiative, and creativity, and destroys the individual's personality.

One patient died following Burchkardt's surgery and another was found dead in a river ten days later, but Burckhardt's goal wasn't to help the patients. He wanted to make them easier for the hospital staff to deal with, and he had accomplished this with the remaining patients. He wrote, "Doctors are different by nature. One kind adheres to the old principle: first, do no harm; the other one says: it is better to do something than do nothing. I certainly belong to the second category." However, criticism from the medical community kept him from performing additional lobotomies.

In 1910, Portuguese neurologist Egas Moniz developed a new version of the procedure, which he called a "pre-frontal leucotomy." He drilled a pair of holes in the top frontal area of the person's head and injected alcohol to destroy the brain tissue there. Later he used a wire loop he called a leucotome to scoop out brain tissue instead. In 1949, he won the Nobel Prize for medicine for this work.

In 1936, Walter Freeman began performing lobotomies in the United States. By 1945, he'd come up with a "more efficient" and less invasive approach than Moniz's: he inserted an "orbitoclast," which was essentially an ice pick, under each of the patient's eyelids and over the top of each eyeball. He used a mallet to break through the bone there and into the brain, where he wiggled the ice pick around to destroy the brain tissue.

Freeman drove around the country in his "lobotomobile" throughout the 1950s and 1960s. He prided himself on how quickly he could perform each lobotomy, and he was as happy to lobotomize an unruly child as he was someone who was moody or depressed. He personally performed over 3,500 lobotomies, arguing that the procedure was a "mercy killing of the psyche."

Patients were typically awake during these "transorbital" (or "ice pick") lobotomies, and sometimes they didn't even get local anesthetic. They were encouraged to talk or sing during the procedure. If they became incoherent, as happened to John F. Kennedy's sister, Rosemary Kennedy, the doctor knew he'd done too much.

Criticism of lobotomies continued, and some physicians who watched the procedure were so sickened they had to leave the room. In 1948, Norbert Wiener sarcastically remarked that the popularity of lobotomies, was "probably not unconnected with the fact that it makes the custodial care of many patients easier…let me remark in passing that killing them makes their custodial care still easier."

Starting in 1953, the number of lobotomies fell dramatically thanks to the discovery of antipsychotics and antidepressants. Soon thereafter, lobotomies were banned in countries like the USSR, Japan, Germany, and in a number of U.S. states. Still, the procedure continued in many hospitals until Ken Kesey's 1962 novel *One Flew Over the Cuckoo's Nest* hit the silver screen in 1975. Lobotomies were finally stopped completely by the early 1980s. Over 100,000 people worldwide were lobotomized, 40,000 of them in the United States.

# 12

# Emergencies in Psychotherapy

*Suicidality, Homicidality, and Hospitalization*

Treating people who have problems means that sometimes there are going to be emergencies. In this chapter we'll look at some of the most common emergencies and how they're handled.

## EMERGENCIES AND CONFIDENTIALITY

Because people enter therapy when they don't know how else to handle a problem, many clinicians check for suicidal or homicidal thoughts in each new client. Thereafter, the therapist continues to listen for any indication of such thoughts or urges and asks about them if she detects them.

As we discussed in Chapter 3, a therapist shouldn't talk about her client with anyone outside the office unless she has the client's written permission (for example, because she's consulting with another of the client's doctors) or the client is in immediate danger to himself or someone else. *Only* if the client or someone else is in *immediate* danger may a therapist break confidentiality.

## SUICIDE ASSESSMENTS

Suicidal clients usually make comments that give away their state of mind. The ideas behind the comments can be classified as either "passive" or "active."

*Passive ideation* is a wish to die without naming an explicit action. For example:

- I wish I'd never been born.

- I can't stand how bad I feel anymore.

- I wish I could just go to sleep and never wake up.

- Sometimes I think the world would be better off without me.

- I feel like such a burden to my family that I wish I were dead.

*Active ideation* is more direct; the person states that he'd like to engage in a self-destructive act. For example:

- I feel like slitting my wrists.

- I think a lot about how easy it would be to overdose on pills.

- I want to put a gun in my mouth and blow my head off.

Many people worry that asking someone if he's thinking about harming himself will give him the idea to do so, but that's just not the case. For the client who's having suicidal thoughts, it's often a relief to be asked, especially by someone who stays calm and knows what to do if he says "yes."

So go ahead and have your therapist character ask the client directly if he's thinking about hurting or killing himself. Most clients say, "No, I would never do that because _____" or "Yes, I've thought about it, but I would never do it because _____". They usually list things like their religious beliefs, their children, or other family members as reasons not to do it.

Once in a while someone says he's thinking about killing himself but doesn't follow up with a reason that's keeping him from taking action. The therapist will then assess how immediate the risk is. Clients are usually very honest when they answer these questions, because they don't really want to die. They want the pain caused by their psychological problem to stop, and they're desperate for an alternative to death. Someone who feels otherwise doesn't usually end up in the therapist's office—he just kills himself.

The therapist continues her assessment by asking the following questions:

1. *Does the client have a plan?* If the client has been vague about what he might do, the therapist can ask "Have you thought about how you would do it?" or "Do you have a plan?" Many clients will say no, they don't have a plan. Others will say things like "I've thought about taking a bunch of pills."

   If the client does have a plan, the therapist must go on to the next question.

2.  *Does the client have the means?* The next step is to ask whether the client has what he needs to commit suicide. If he's thinking about overdosing on pills, for example, has he bought the pills? If he's talking about shooting himself, does he have access to a gun?

3.  *Does the client have a time set?* If the client has both a plan and the means, the therapist asks whether he's planned a time to commit suicide. Some people make elaborate arrangements for when and where. They might commit suicide in a hotel room or call the police just before they shoot themselves so friends and family members don't have to be the ones to find them.

Many clients don't have a time set like an appointment, but will tell the therapist that they "just can't stand it anymore" or that they will kill themselves after they leave the office. At that point the therapist knows she needs to hospitalize the client, but she still doesn't leap to her feet and run to the phone.

Though keeping your therapist character in her seat may be less dramatic than having her make a frantic phone call, you can reveal interesting things about your client character by showing how he deals with the idea of being hospitalized. And involuntary hospitalization, if it's necessary, can be plenty dramatic!

## Q & A

**Q:** What would it take to push a character into suicide? Would there have to be a precipitating event, or would someone be more likely to ruminate on his life and eventually decide that killing himself is simply the right thing to do?

**A:** There's always a reason the person decides he wants to die *now* as opposed to last week or last month, so in that way there's always a precipitating event. That event may be tiny, though. Perhaps the person is exhausted with feeling bad and has come to the conclusion that he's never going to feel better. Then something very small can be the proverbial last straw.

Sometimes a person tries to reach out to others to let them know he's considering suicide, but the hints are too subtle. Feeling like nobody cares is then the final straw. Let's say for example that someone worked in a retail store that used rope to hang advertising signs. He might ask each of the people he works with—including those who have no authority to tell him yes or no—whether he can take some of that rope home. If nobody thinks to ask why he wants it, he might assume no one cares whether he lives or dies and hang himself that night.

In retrospect, it can seem obvious to everyone he asked that he was going to kill himself, but a little strange behavior beforehand doesn't usually get the attention the person believes it should. The suicidal person is so upset he thinks his intentions will be obvious when they're not.

## WHEN HOSPITALIZATION IS NECESSARY

First, the therapist explains why she thinks hospitalization is a good idea and assuages any fears about what hospitalization will be like. Her goal is to get the client to say he will go voluntarily, and the majority of clients do. If a friend or family member is available to transport the client, that person comes to the office and picks him up. Otherwise, an ambulance can take him.

A lot of people say they can't go to the hospital because of other obligations: they need to go into work; they're responsible for making dinner that night; they have a paper due the next morning. That might seem strange, since the client was just talking about killing himself, but when someone is suicidal, he's not thinking logically.

In most cases, people who worry about other obligations just need to be told that going to the hospital is more important. After all, if the client had broken his leg, he would need to go in spite of other obligations; going for psychiatric reasons is no different. Having the therapist insist can be a relief because it takes the responsibility off the client.

Involuntary hospitalizations are rarer than most people think. Clients who feel this bad really just want to feel better, and if going to the hospital means feeling better, they're ready to go! You also have to remember that people who really want to die don't tell anyone. They just do it. If someone realizes your character is suicidal, it's because he's struggling to keep himself going. People who commit suicide do so because they've reached the point where they see no other solution.

In the rare situation that a client *really* doesn't want to go to the hospital and is *really* in danger of killing himself, the therapist can explain that she's legally and ethically obligated to do everything she can to keep him safe, up to and including involuntary hospitalization. Then she explains that the police are the ones responsible for taking him to the hospital if he refuses to go, which means he's likely to end up in the back of a squad car. In the end, most people agree that it's a lot easier to just go voluntarily.

## SAFETY PLANS

If at any point along the way the client says he won't kill himself, the therapist can ask "Can you stay safe if you go home?" Someone who is really in trouble will say, "No," "I don't know," or "I don't think so." Many clients, however, will agree that they can be safe for a given period of time—say, a week.

If the client says he won't kill himself and the therapist believes him, her next job is to put a safety plan (which sometimes includes a "no-harm contract") in place should the client's intentions change.

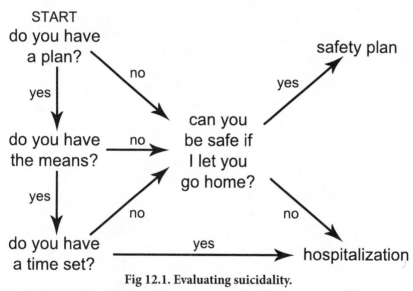

**Fig 12.1. Evaluating suicidality.**

Though safety plans and no-harm contracts can be verbal, clients may have a hard time thinking straight if the suicidal feelings get worse, so having something written can be helpful. Also, clients who have tried to fool the therapist into thinking they'll be all right if they go home may balk at signing a no-harm contract in which they swear not to harm themselves.

199

Some therapists advocate against using no-harm contracts because they don't believe they're effective, especially when the therapist uses a pre-printed form rather than having the client handwrite the contract. Also, no-harm contracts do not provide legal protection for the therapist if the client does kill himself.

Whether or not the therapist asks the client to agree in writing not to harm himself, the creation of a safety plan is always a good idea. Together, the client and therapist make an ordered list of things the client should do if he begins to feel worse. For example, the first thing on his list might be calling a trusted friend. If that doesn't help, the second thing might be asking someone to come over and stay. Most lists also include the options of calling the therapist and going to the emergency room.

---

### DON'T LET THIS HAPPEN TO YOU!

In fiction, therapists often respond to suicidal ideation like lay-people: they panic. In the film *Stay*, Dr. Sam Foster is a perfectly competent therapist until his new client makes it clear he's thinking about shooting himself. Then Foster tenses up and makes a run for the phone, belatedly telling his client that he has to take "certain actions if you tell me you're going to kill yourself." Later, Foster visits a friend who works in a psychiatric ward to "check the protocol on involuntary committal."

This is unrealistic on a number of levels. First, because therapists are always well-trained to deal with suicidal ideation and behavior, they certainly aren't flustered by it. Likewise, all therapists know the protocols for involuntary commitment. Second, they must assess dangerousness before calling the hospital, partly because it can be difficult to get someone admitted to the hospital, and partly because the hospital (and especially the insurance company!) will insist the therapist is sure the person is an immediate risk. Finally, calling someone without being really sure there's an emergency violates confidentiality.

---

## HOMICIDE ASSESSMENTS

Assessments of homicidal intent are similar to assessments of suicidal intent. The therapist establishes intent first, and then asks whether the client has a plan, the means, and a set time to act. If the therapist believes there is a reasonable chance the client will act on his homicidal thoughts, she has two duties. First, to see the client hospitalized voluntarily or, if necessary, involuntarily, and second, to warn the potential victim and notify the police. This "duty to warn" (sometimes called a "duty to protect") is one of the few situations that overrides client confidentiality; still, the therapist must be careful not to share any information besides that which is strictly necessary.

The therapist must also document her actions for recordkeeping and legal purposes. If a therapist has truly done everything in her power to warn and protect a potential victim, this documentation can help protect her if someone tries to sue her.

## USING THE INFORMATION IN YOUR STORY

Though it can feel stilted to include a suicidality or homicidality assessment in your story when you're not quite sure how one would go in real life, you can reveal lots of important and interesting information about your character that way. Knowing that your character not only plans to shoot himself but also has a gun in the car and intends to drive out to a field after the session and do it, for example, forces the therapist to take immediate action.

The approach someone takes to suicide also tells you things about that person, as does where he plans to do it and when. For example, if someone intends to use a gun and he has the means, where did the gun come from? To whom does it belong? Why was it purchased in the first place? Men are more likely to use violent means like guns, while women are more likely to do things they can change their minds on, like taking pills or slitting their wrists. In the U.S., women attempt suicide more often, but men are more likely to complete suicide.

Most suicidal people have thought a lot about how their deaths will affect others. Some lay out plastic to try to make any cleanup easier; some use methods they believe will be "cleaner." (For the record, there is no "clean" method; even carbon monoxide poisoning suffocates the cells in the body, making them rupture, which leaves a bruised and bloated body.) Sometimes people fly or drive a long way to commit suicide in a hotel so their families won't have to find them. People who write notes (and many don't) often tell loved ones not to feel bad or that they simply couldn't go on anymore, which is kind of like telling someone whose house burned down that it's not a big deal. It always is.

# Hospitalization

## Historical Snapshot

In 1357, London's Bethlem hospital (eventually nicknamed "Bedlam") first admitted patients with psychiatric problems. However, they were treated horribly and badly neglected, often chained in dark cells with an iron collar and another hoop around the waist that held them pinned to the wall. Because they were seen as little more than animals, they weren't given enough food or a blanket for warmth, and nobody ever cleaned the cells, which contained only straw. In the 1700s and 1800s, visitors could pay a penny to walk through the hospital and taunt the patients or poke them with sticks.

In 1756, the Pennsylvania Hospital in Philadelphia provided the first U.S. wards for mental patients; the first dedicated mental hospital was the Public Hospital in Williamsburg, Virginia, built in 1773. Treatments amounted to torture and included bleeding and blistering, blasting patients with freezing water, electric shocks, and drugs.

It wasn't until 1792 that Philippe Pinel got grudging permission from administrators at the Parisian hospital La Bicêtre to test his hypothesis that mental patients should be treated as sick people who deserved kindness and respect rather than as criminals or beasts. For the first time, patients were treated well and given sunny rooms, fresh air, and opportunities to exercise. Suddenly violent patients became cooperative, and asylums became far more pleasant places. The approach was so successful that other reformers, including Englishman William Tuke (around the same time) and American Dorothea Dix (in the 1840s), were able to push similar agendas.

Dix advocated self-sufficient communities that gave patients opportunities to craft and build things, garden and farm, tend domestic animals, and enjoy social events like musicals. Patients and staff often developed friendships that helped patients get better. The model lasted in many places in the U.S. until the mid-1950s when antipsychotic and antidepressant medications contributed to deinstitutionalization.

The deinstitutionalization movement, which has spread across the globe, closed mental hospitals and released people back into the community, where they would supposedly be less isolated than in hospitals.

Unfortunately, many of these people have not been able to care adequately for themselves, leaving more than a few of them living on the streets.

Most modern psychiatric facilities continue to operate on a short-term model. Patients are hospitalized only so long as they are a clear and imminent danger to themselves or someone else.

## MODERN HOSPITALIZATION

Short-term psychiatric hospitalization is like any other hospitalization. The physicians, therapists, and nurses work hard to provide symptom relief as fast as possible and keep the person in a safe environment while they do so.

Because the typical commitment time is seventy-two hours, workers on psychiatric units strive to get patients stabilized within that time. During the first day, the patient's problems are assessed by several healthcare professionals, often including a nurse or mental health associate, a psychiatrist, and a social worker or psychologist. If the professionals are all available at the same time, they may work together; more often, each does his or her intake separately.

After the assessments, someone shows the patient around the psychiatric unit and introduces any additional therapists. Therapist specialties vary from unit to unit, but they might include recreational therapy, music therapy, or art therapy. In all cases, therapists and nurses provide both group and individualized care.

Treatment plans are created on the second day. On the third, the psychiatrist evaluates the effects of the medications. Ideally, the patient is able to stay safe and is ready to leave on the fourth day.

If a patient stays longer, the length of that stay is usually dictated by the insurance company. Even then, the hospital staff works to get the patient out before the few days that insurance has allotted are up.

In the U.S., people can't be forced into treatment just because they don't want to go; one must be an immediate danger to himself or someone else, or he must be unable to provide for basic personal needs like food, clothing, shelter, or personal safety due to psychiatric illness.

Parents can commit their children against their will without these things necessarily being true only if the children are still minors. Adults legally have the right to refuse treatment. Because individuals with serious disorders like schizophrenia and bipolar disorder may lack insight into how sick they are, many go untreated despite relatives' best efforts.

## A TYPICAL DAY IN THE HOSPITAL

Though hospitals vary in their routines, a typical day for your story might look something like this:

**8:00 a.m.** Breakfast

**9:00 a.m.** Community Meeting. Patients learn each other's names and then everyone discusses issues from the previous day like conflicts over sharing, requests for increased smoking privileges, and so on. At the end of this meeting, the therapist announces the formal day activities.

**9:30 a.m.** Group Therapy. Examples of topics addressed by groups might include coping, problem-solving, or communication skills; group members might also participate in activities like art or recreational therapy.

**10:00 a.m.** Free Time. Patients might read, watch television, work on puzzles, or play games.

**11:00 a.m.** Group Therapy

**12:30 p.m.** Lunch

**1:00 p.m.** Group Therapy

**3:00 p.m.** Shift Change

**4:00 p.m.** Group Therapy

**5:30 p.m.** Dinner

**7:00 p.m.–9:00 p.m.** Visiting Hours. Visiting hours can turn into organized mayhem, and staff must make sure friends and family don't smuggle in things like cigarettes and drugs or wander off to have sex in one of the rooms. All visitors are required to stay in public areas.

**9:30 p.m.** Relaxation Group

## KEEPING THE WARD SAFE AND SECURE

When a person is committed to a private, short-term psychiatric unit, the accommodations look like they do in the rest of the hospital, with a few exceptions. Most notably, the unit has been carefully suicide-proofed so patients can't cut or hang themselves from anything...including the pipes inside the toilet tank. Why the pipes in the toilet tank? Because patients can be extremely creative, and some have tried tying sheets or clothing to the pipes, wrapping that fabric around their necks, and leaning forward until they pass out. Obviously, once someone passes out he just becomes dead weight against whatever's around his neck, and that can kill him.

Here are some of the other ways a hospital may suicide-proof its wards:

- Make all glass and mirrors on the unit unbreakable.

- Block any real glass, like that of outside windows, with bars or a thick, heavy metal screen that someone can't punch through. (It's not unusual for a screen to be dented from people trying. The screen may also be a good six to eight inches away from the window itself.)

- Use closet clothing hooks that break off or snap downward if too much weight is placed on them.

- Remove clothes bars from the closet and towel bars from the bathroom.

- Use flat, rounded shower spigots that are impossible to hang from.

- Use piano hinges on the doors. Regular hinges—especially on big, heavy institutional doors—stick out. They also leave a gap between the door and the jamb when the door is open. Piano hinges run from floor to ceiling and are closely fitted together, making it impossible for someone to loop a sheet over a hinge or door to hang himself.

- Be sure things like sprinkler heads are impossible to hang from.

Empty rooms are likely to be closed and locked from the outside, and measures will have been taken to keep patients from locking or barricading themselves in a room. None of the doors patients have access to locks from the *inside*—including the ones on the showers. Fire code requires that doors swing *into* a room, but if it's possible for patients to use objects like beds to barricade the door shut, a second, locked door that swings *out* into the hall can be set into the normal door.

Staff members also make frequent rounds to check on everyone—for example, in irregular fifteen-minute intervals.

---

### DON'T LET THIS HAPPEN TO YOU!

In the film *The Devil's Advocate*, Charlize Theron's character, who's desperate to get away from what seem to be demonic hallucinations, easily barricades herself behind her breakable glass door and slashes her throat with a broken mirror. Despite all the screaming, yelling, and smashing of glass, it's only after she's bled to death that a staff member appears, apparently from another part of the hospital.

This is unrealistic on a number of levels. First, staff is readily available at all times in a psychiatric unit. Second, because patients can be extremely creative in finding ways to lock staff out or harm themselves, the hospital will already have taken extensive measures to prevent this. Third, most hospitals only allow visitors in common areas where the staff can keep an eye on things. Granted, staff members are sometimes reading magazines, chatting with each other, or dealing with a patient who's acting out, but they're also conscientious about the potential dangers of glass in patients' hands. Therefore, it's unlikely that a patient would be allowed to hold onto a large, breakable mirror someone had brought her.

---

## NURSES' STATIONS

To get onto a psychological ward, one must be buzzed in or let in by someone with a key. Security cameras are always placed above the outer door and may also be present in hallways but never in the unit itself out of respect for patients' privacy. To get back out of the ward, you also need a key.

In a private or civil setting, the nurses' station is likely to have doors that can stand open, and it may also have sliding (unbreakable) glass windows that can be left open. In a forensic setting, patients with psychological problems are usually either awaiting trial for violent crimes or have been declared not guilty by reason of insanity. Therefore, the nurses' station is much more secure, with heavy, locked doors and only small openings in the windows to pass objects back and forth.

Inside the nurses' station are work areas that include computers. In some wards, a hidden whiteboard lists information on each patient, such as patient name and doctor, movement privileges, group activities in which the patient should participate, notes on medication, and shorthand like U (Unpredictable), W (going through Withdrawal from drugs or alcohol), S (Suicide risk), or E (made Escape attempt). In a forensic unit, there may also be a column to note whether the person was ruled Not Guilty by Reason of Insanity (NGRI) or declared incompetent to stand trial temporarily ("restorable") or long term ("unrestorable"). Many hospitals have stopped using whiteboards due to patient privacy concerns. Instead, they use computers to track relevant information.

---

### DON'T LET THIS HAPPEN TO YOU!

It's not unusual to find characters complaining that a killer "got off" thanks to a not guilty by reason of insanity (NGRI) plea. In *The Stalking Man*, one of novelist William J. Coughlin's characters chafes at the way a killer gets to "enjoy the relatively easy world of a hospital" because a lawyer "got him off." "Not guilty by reason of insanity, that was the jury's verdict," complains the character. "The law is all screwed up on the question of insanity… We break our asses to bring in a psychotic monster and…the bastard either goes free or sits around some ward goosing the nurses."

The first problem here is that NGRI is not a common plea, and even when it's used, it's very, very rarely successful. The M'Naghten Rule, which many states follow, says that to be declared NGRI, the defendant must be so mentally ill that he didn't understand what he was doing, or didn't understand that it was wrong. Usually that means that the individual was so incredibly psychotic when he committed the crime, so immersed in the hallucinations and delusions of that psychosis, that he had no concept that what he was doing was wrong. As you can imagine, that doesn't happen very often. In addition, since most defendants are in a more rational frame of mind by the time they stand trial, juries find it hard to believe the individual was so irrational *during* the crime.

The second problem is that people who *are* declared not guilty by reason of insanity do not go home, nor are they shipped off to palatial estates where they do art and music therapy and talk about their feelings all day. They're secured in facilities that are, in effect, prisons, with

---

heavy steel doors, barbed wire, bulletproof glass, and strict rules. Finally, the typical stay in a psychiatric institution following a NGRI is *longer* than the individual would have spent if he had just gone to prison.

One last problem with Coughlin's passage above. The character is complaining about "psychotic monsters" when he actually means "psychopathic monsters." Interestingly, it's not unusual for psychopaths to fire their lawyers so they can defend themselves, and then to enter a NGRI plea. Which of course fails, because psychopaths, as we discussed in Chapter 10, always know exactly what they're doing during a crime, and just how wrong their behavior is.

## SECLUSION, RESTRAINTS, AND FORCED MEDICATION

The American Psychiatric Nurses' Association makes the rules about seclusion and restraint, which are used only when "the emergency poses serious and imminent danger to the person, staff, or others" and "only after all other less restrictive, nonphysical methods have failed." Further, the "staff involved [must] have been adequately trained and deemed competent to initiate these measures."

Except in a case where someone feels overwhelmed and just needs a quiet place, use of seclusion is seen as a "treatment failure." Use of restraints, whether physical or chemical, is always considered a treatment failure. Therefore, staff members make every effort to avoid using seclusion and restraints. They do things like:

- Ask if the person wants to sit down and talk about what's upsetting him.

- Ask if the person wants something to eat. Because blood sugar levels are low before mealtimes, a lot of seclusion and restraint situations occur just before mealtimes. If the patient eats something, he may feel better.

- Offer a PRN ("as needed") medication such as Ativan to help the person calm down.

If these sorts of efforts fail, the staff explains that if the patient can't gain control, he will need to be secluded and/or restrained. Security is called to help if those measures become necessary.

A physician or Licensed Independent Practitioner (LIP) must then evaluate the patient face-to-face within an hour. The seclusion and/or restraints must be re-ordered every four hours for as long as they're needed. Only a very small percentage of patients are secluded or restrained.

## Seclusion

Seclusion is not intended as punishment; its purpose is to reduce stimulation. The seclusion room is empty except for a gurney. If someone is placed in the seclusion room, assuming they aren't in restraints, the gurney is removed and only the mattress and sheet left behind on the floor. An unbreakable window in the door allows a staff member to observe the person for the first hour. If the person is doing all right after that time, the staff can switch to monitoring the person through a security camera.

## Physical and Chemical Restraints

As noted above, early mental institutions often used chains to restrain patients; later, sometime between the late 1700s and early 1800s, the straitjacket was invented as a more "humane" form of restraint. In reality, mental institutions during this time were often overcrowded and under-staffed, and difficult patients might be left in straitjackets for hours if not days. Over time, stiffness and swelling of the limbs makes such restraint extremely painful.

Though straitjackets are no longer used in American psychiatric facilities, other physical and chemical restraints may be used in emergency situations…but only for as long as the emergency lasts. Physical restraints can include a manual hold (staff members physically grab hold of a patient), ambulatory restraint (immobilization of one or more limbs), or four-point restraints (full immobilization with straps around the wrists and ankles). For as long as the patient is in restraints, the staff must monitor vital signs and circulation and release a limb to exercise it every hour. For safety reasons, security is always in the room during these exercise periods.

Though in fiction seclusion and restraints are often used abusively, in reality there are dozens of procedural and legal edicts in place to prevent abuse. Of course, that doesn't mean seclusion and restraints are never abused, but most hospital staff feel that it's more trouble than it's worth to use them except when absolutely necessary.

According to the American Psychiatric Nurses' Association, chemical restraints include any drug or medication that "is not a standard treatment or dosage for the person's condition" and is used "to manage the person's behavior or restrict the person's freedom of movement." The antipsychotic Haldol and the anti-anxiety drug Ativan are often used in such emergency situations. Both are strong sedatives.

Forced medications cannot be used in the absence of an immediate threat. In other words, staff members cannot give a patient a shot because they think he'll become violent—they have to wait for the person to become dangerous.

## Forced Medication

Medications can be forced on a patient under one other circumstance. Staff can submit a report to the Court describing why the medication is absolutely necessary and demonstrating how the patient lacks the capacity to make informed decisions. If the Court authorizes the order, the hospital can force the patient to take medications even when he isn't on the verge of violence. Such a court order will even allow the staff to use physical restraints to administer the medications, though most patients usually just start taking them once they learn of the Court's decision. As psychologist John Tilley puts it, "It's a little more dignified to just take some pills as opposed to having a bunch of staff manhandle you and strap you to a bed to give you a shot in your buttocks."

# Conclusion

Congratulations, you now have the tools to write accurately about everything from nervous breakdowns to psychopathic killers! You know all about the mistakes so many writers make and how to avoid them. You know how to make your therapist character think and sound like a real shrink. You know the difference between psychologists and psychiatrists, and how some ethical slips can land a therapist in jail. You know how to get reticent characters to open up, and what kinds of impressions they're making on others…whether they intend to or not. You know how to create a truly psychopathic villain…or just a situation that's gone too far. You know the difference between schizophrenia and bipolar disorder, psychosis and psychopathy, and ADD and ADHD. You also know how modern electroconvulsive therapy and medications work, and what your character's hospital stay will be like. Though sometimes it may seem easier or more dramatic to lapse into an inaccurate cliché, you know that taking the time to flesh out your stories with authentic details will increase tension, make your characters more interesting, and give you credibility with your viewers/readers!

If you find yourself wishing for more information or a little extra help with what you've learned in *The Writer's Guide to Psychology*, here are a couple of suggestions. First, in the back pages of this book you'll find a bibliography listing the many references upon which I relied. Second, you can visit my **ArchetypeWriting.com** site, which includes additional psychology and writing help, as well as a Q&A section where you can submit your own psychology in writing questions!

# Glossary

**Affect**: Emotional state

**Agoraphobia**: Literally, "fear of the marketplace"; fear of being trapped somewhere from which escape will be difficult or embarrassing, *not* fear of open spaces

**Antipsychotics**: Medications that reduce psychotic symptoms like hallucinations, delusions, and thought disorganization; may also be used to treat *bipolar disorder*

**Antisocial Personality Disorder**: Personality disorder marked by persistent and pervasive disregard and violation of other people's rights; not synonymous with *sociopathy* or *psychopathy*

**Anxiolytics**: Anti-anxiety medications; include both *SSRIs* and benzodiazepines

**Avoidant personality disorder**: *Personality disorder* marked by persistent and pervasive fear of being criticized or rejected and tendency to avoid others; symptoms overlap with social phobia

**Bipolar disorder**: Mood disorder characterized by extreme ups (*mania*) and downs (depression)

**Borderline personality disorder (BPD)**: Personality disorder marked by persistent and pervasive inability to modulate one's own emotions

**Brief psychotic disorder**: Sudden appearance of psychotic symptoms, often triggered by a severe stressor

**Comorbid**: Two or more distinct disorders in the same person at the same time; each disorder makes the other worse

**Conduct disorder**: Persistent violation of others' basic rights or consistent violation of ethical and legal norms in children or adolescents

**Culture-bound syndromes**: disorders that appear in limited cultural settings; some clearly overlap with diagnostic categories in the *DSM* and others do not

**Cyclothymia**: Mildest form of *bipolar disorder*, often undiagnosed unless it develops into a more serious version of the disorder

**Delusions**: Unrealistic beliefs that are maintained despite logic or evidence to the contrary; cultural beliefs, e.g. in deities, are not considered delusional

**Dependent personality disorder**: *Personality disorder* marked by persistent and pervasive passivity, neediness, and subservience

**Depersonalization**: Dissociative experience during which one feels disconnected from one's body; individual may also feel as if she watching herself from the outside

**Derealization**: Dissociative experience during which one's environment or surroundings seem surreal or unreal

**Dialectical Behavioral Therapy (DBT)**: Specialized treatment for *borderline personality disorder*

**Diathesis-stress model**: Theory that states that genetic vulnerabilities to a disorder must be triggered by environmental stressors for the disorder to actually manifest

**Dissociation**: Partial or complete "split" in normal conscious functioning or identity

**Dissociative amnesia**: Inability to remember important information about oneself or one's experiences for psychological reasons; people with amnesia following head injuries are not diagnosed with dissociative amnesia

**Dissociative fugue**: Inability to remember important information about oneself or one's experiences coupled with travel away from home; typically occurs following a major stressor or trauma

**Dissociative identity disorder (DID)**: At least 2 different personalities take control of the body at alternate times; typically due to extreme childhood trauma; amnesia is a hallmark symptom of DID

**Dopamine**: *Neurotransmitter* that regulates emotion, motivation, and feelings of pleasure and reward, and which is particularly involved in addiction, *schizophrenia*, and Parkinson's Disease

**DSM**: *Diagnostic and Statistical Manual of Mental Disorders*, which provides information on diagnosing psychological disorders

**Dual relationship**: Unethical situation in which a therapist has both a non-therapeutic relationship and a therapeutic relationship with a client or patient

**Duty to warn/Duty to protect**: Therapist obligation to warn/protect an individual or party she believes may be in danger from a client or other party; one of the few times that confidentiality does not apply to the client-therapist relationship

**Dysthymia**: chronic, low-grade depression that lasts more than two years

**Ego-dystonic**: Values, behaviors, and feelings are inconsistent with how one sees oneself; most disorders are ego-dystonic in that the individual feels that the disorder is causing problems for them; contrast with *ego-syntonic*

**Ego-syntonic**: Values, behaviors, and feelings are consistent with how one sees oneself; in psychology, usually used to refer to the way individuals with personality disorders do not recognize that they have a disorder that is contributing to their problems; contrast with *ego-dystonic*

**Electroconvulsive therapy (ECT)**: Treatment for individuals with depression, *psychosis*, *mania*, or suicidality when other treatments have failed; modern ECT is very different from the typical outdated media depiction

**Etiology**: Cause or origin of disorder

**Exposure therapies**: Treatments during which clients are slowly and methodically exposed to feared stimuli, usually while they are practicing relaxation; typically a very effective treatment for anxiety disorders

**Eye movement desensitization and reprocessing (EMDR)**: Treatment for PTSD that helps individuals process and deal with traumatic experiences and move on with their lives

213

**False memory syndrome**: Caused when memories, usually of a traumatic nature, have been implanted by an unscrupulous therapist

**GABA: Gamma-AminoButyric Acid**: a neurotransmitter involved in relaxation, sedation, and sleep

**Generalized anxiety disorder (GAD)**: General, "free-floating" anxiety

**Hallucination**: Sensory experience without sensory stimulus; that is, seeing (visual hallucination), hearing (auditory hallucination), feeling (tactile hallucination), smelling (olfactory hallucination), or tasting (gustatory hallucination) things that aren't really there

**Histrionic personality disorder**: *Personality disorder* marked by persistent and pervasive dramatics, flirtatiousness, and other demonstrative behavior; typically strike others as shallow, vain, and immature

**Iatrogenic disorders**: Disorders caused or induced by an unwitting or unscrupulous therapist; DID is believed by skeptics to be iatrogenic most if not all of the time

**Impulse-control disorders**: Disorder in which feelings of tension can only be relieved by performing an act that is harmful to the individual or others; seem to be related to obsessive-compulsive behavior

**Intake or Intake Interview**: First meeting with a client during which the clinician gathers information on the client's concerns, problems, and background

**Interpretation**: Psychodynamic technique in which a therapist draws a client's attention to a psychological process that may have gone unnoticed by the client

**Lobotomy**: Obsolete "treatment" in which the frontal lobes of the brain were permanently destroyed, sometimes to make difficult patients more manageable

**Major depressive disorder**: Mood disorder characterized by extreme episodic depressions, often accompanied by feelings of guilt and hopelessness and suicidal thoughts

**Mania**: Abnormally extreme euphoria or irritability due to *bipolar disorder*; sometimes people who are manic experience psychotic symptoms

**Martha Mitchell effect**: Therapist unwittingly diagnoses a client who's telling the truth with a delusional disorder

**Mood stabilizer**: Medication used to reduce manic and depressive symptoms in *bipolar disorder*; sometimes used to help antidepressants work better

**Monoamine Oxidase Inhibitors (MAOIs)**: Older antidepressant class sometimes used for treatment-resistant depression; can be dangerous to combine with certain foods and beverages

**Multiaxial system**: Diagnostic system endorsed by the *DSM*

**Narcissistic personality disorder (NPD)**: *Personality disorder* marked by persistent and pervasive self-centeredness and self-aggrandizement and little if any empathy toward others

**Nervous breakdown**: Colloquial term for an extremely upsetting experience during which the individual felt unable to cope

**Neurotransmitters**: Chemicals colloquially referred to as "brain chemistry;" neurotransmitters pass messages from one neuron (nerve cell in the brain or spinal cord) to the next

**Norephinephrine**: *Neurotransmitter* involved in concentration, motivation, and alertness

**Obsessive-compulsive disorder (OCD)**: Disorder characterized by overwhelming feelings and thoughts of dread, which are relieved by ritualistic behaviors

**Obsessive-compulsive personality disorder (OCPD)**: Personality disorder marked by persistent, pervasive, and extreme perfectionism, dogmatism, and stubbornness; unlike *OCD*, does *not* involve obsessive thoughts or compulsive ritualistic behaviors

**Paranoid personality disorder**: *Personality disorder* characterized by paranoia in every aspect of the individual's life

**Paraphilia**: Sexual urges or behaviors that cause problems because they involve non-sexual objects, human suffering or humiliation, or non-consenting partners

**Personality disorder**: Rigid, narrow, inflexible approach to life that causes interpersonal problems; individuals with personality disorders typically blame others for problems rather than appreciating their own contributions to the situation

**Phototherapy (light therapy)**: Intensive light treatment for people with low mood during the colder, darker months of the year

**Post-traumatic stress disorder (PTSD)**: Abnormally extreme and persistent anxiety symptoms resulting from trauma

**Predisposing Factors**: Stressors, problems, family constellations, or genetics that make one more likely to develop a disorder

**Presenting Problem**: Chief complaint or symptoms; the problem the client says needs help

**Professional counselor**: Typically a licensed master's-level counselor; cannot prescribe medications

**Psychiatrist**: Medical doctor who specializes in mental health; can prescribe psychological medications

**Psychologist**: Doctoral-level researchers and practitioners in psychology; typically cannot prescribe medications

**Psychopathy**: Specialized term for someone with a dangerously extreme *antisocial personality disorder*, and who has no qualms about violently violating others' rights; psychopaths are thought to have brain abnormalities that make them incapable of fear, empathy, or love; different from *psychosis* and *sociopathy*

**Psychosis**: Loss of contact with reality as most people experience it, usually characterized by hallucinations and/or delusions; different from *psychopathy*

**Selective serotonin reuptake inhibitors (SSRIs)**: Most commonly used class of antidepressant drugs; has fewer side effects and lower toxicity than older antidepressants like *tricyclics* and *MAOIs*

**Serotonin**: *Neurotransmitter* that regulates mood, appetite, and sleep; depression is often blamed on inadequate levels of serotonin in the brain

**Schizoaffective disorder**: Both *schizophrenia* and either a *major depressive disorder* or *bipolar disorder* are present at the same time

**Schizophrenia**: Psychotic disorder characterized by hallucinations, bizarre delusions, disorganized behavior and speech, and sometimes paranoia or catatonia; not the same thing as multiple personalities or *dissociative identity disorder*

**Social workers**: bachelor's-, master's-, and doctoral-level counselors who specialize in helping people function better in the community; cannot prescribe medications

**Schizoid personality disorder**: *Personality disorder* marked by persistent and pervasive reclusiveness, detachment, and indifference to others

**Schizophreniform disorder**: Symptoms are the same as with schizophrenia, but have only lasted between 1 and 6 months

**Schizotypal personality disorder**: *Personality disorder* marked by persistent and pervasive odd ideas, speech, behavior, and appearance; may be a mild version of schizophrenia

**Shared psychotic disorder (folie à deux)**: Delusional beliefs are shared by two people who have a relationship with one another; the French translates to "madness shared by two"

**Sociopathy**: Extreme version of *antisocial personality disorder* due to severe abuse or neglect; *psychopathy* is thought to be biological in origin, whereas *sociopathy* is acquired due to environment

**Threat/Control Override delusions**: unrealistic beliefs that someone or something is controlling one's mind or otherwise persecuting her; sometimes associated with increased levels of violence

**Transcranial magnetic stimulation (TMS)**: Noninvasive magnetic treatment used to improve the moods of people who have not responded to antidepressants

**Tricyclic antidepressants**: Older type of antidepressant used when *SSRI* antidepressants fail; easy to overdose on

**Vagus nerve stimulation (VNS)**: Implantation of a pacemaker-like device below the collarbone that stimulates the vagus nerve every 3 to 5 minutes; used in individuals whose depression is treatment resistant

**V code**: "Problem of living" rather than a disorder; many V codes refer to relational problems, such as ongoing conflict between siblings, parents and children, and romantic and sexual partners

# Note About the *Diagnostic and Statistical Manual of Mental Disorders* (DSM)

As *The Writer's Guide to Psychology* goes to publication, the *DSM-5* is slated for a May 2013 release. The date has repeatedly been pushed back over the last few years, and though I've kept a close eye on the papers and suggestions produced by the *DSM-5* Work Groups (www.dsm5.org), the predictions for what we'll see are ever-changing. At the APA Conference in August 2010, even researchers on overlapping workgroups were providing contradictory information.

Whether psychopathy will be recognized as its own disorder, whether schizophrenia will continue to have recognized subtypes, and how a dimensional model of personality disorders might look still remains to be seen, but there are a few things I do know.

First, change takes time. Just because disorders are reorganized, renamed, and moved onto or off of the list of disorders "for further research" in the back of the *DSM*, that doesn't mean that everyone's internal understanding of psychology will shift in the same way, or at the same time. In other words, if the list of personality disorders is pared down from 10 to 5 or 6, many clinicians will continue to think of those 10 categories as valid for years to come. The authors of college and graduate-level textbooks can also be resistant to change—more than a few were still referring to *dissociative* fugues as *psychogenic* fugues 10 and 12 years after the change was made for the *DSM-IV*. When I (having been trained after the proper term became *dissociative* fugue) pointed this out to textbook publishers, I was told that it's the authors' prerogative to use whichever terms they prefer.

Second, while the *DSM* is an official guidebook produced with the help of many thousands of professionals, it is also part of a political and cultural discourse. In other words, the book is not produced in a vacuum. It is produced by people, all of whom have biases, and many of whom have agendas. So we must ask ourselves—does a disorder exist or not exist simply because the *DSM* says so? That's a slippery question, particularly when we're looking at a *DSM* that may be updated much more frequently than older editions. (Much of the reason the next *DSM* is being referred to as *DSM-5* rather than *DSM-V* is that many hope the new edition will be more fluid and include more regular changes, leading to updates like *DSM-5.1*, *DSM 5.2*, and so on.)

Despite all of this upheaval and change, it's important to point out that the core of clinical and counseling psychology is not figuring out the proper labels for the problems suffered by people who need our help. It's how we interact with those people and what we do to make their lives better. Likewise, *The Writer's Guide to Psychology* is about more than finite categories of psychological disorders—it's about how psychological professionals understand people, and how they help those who need it. It's about breaking down myths and misconceptions, many of which have been around since long before the *DSM-IV*, let alone the *DSM-5*. It's about getting your psych right—and telling a great story because now you have the tools to do so!

# Bibliography

American Psychiatric Association. (2000). *Diagnostic and Statistical Manual of Mental Disorders DSM-IV-TR Fourth Edition (Text Revision)* (4th ed.). Arlington, VA: American Psychiatric Publishing.

Antonuccio, D.O., Danton, W.G., & DeNelsky, G.Y. (1995). Psychotherapy Versus Medication for Depression: Challenging the Conventional Wisdom With Data. *Professional Psychology: Research and Practice*, 26(6), 574–585.

Babiak, P. & Hare, R. D. (2007). *Snakes in Suits: When Psychopaths Go to Work.* Harper Paperbacks.

Barlow, D. H. (2007). *Clinical Handbook of Psychological Disorders, Fourth Edition: A Step-by-Step Treatment Manual* (4th ed.). New York: The Guilford Press.

Baumeister, R. F., & Beck, A. (1999). *Evil: Inside Human Violence and Cruelty.* New York: Holt Paperbacks.

Beck, A. T. & Freeman, A. (1990). *Cognitive Therapy of Personality Disorders.* New York: The Guilford Press.

Beck, J. S. (1995). *Cognitive Therapy: Basics and Beyond.* New York: The Guilford Press.

Berzoff, J. (2007). *Inside Out and Outside In: Psychodynamic Clinical Theory and Practice in Contemporary Multicultural Contexts* (2nd ed.). Northvale, New Jersey: Jason Aronson.

Beyerstein, B. L., Lilienfeld, S. O., Lynn, S. J., & Ruscio, J. (2009). *50 Great Myths of Popular Psychology: Shattering Widespread Misconceptions about Human Behavior.* Malden, MA: Wiley-Blackwell.

Bezchlibnyk-Butler, K., Jeffries, J., & Virani, A. S. (2009). *Clinical Handbook of Psychotropic Drugs* (18th Revised ed.). Cambridge, MA: Hogrefe Publishing.

Blair, R. J. (2003). Neurobiological Basis of Psychopathology. *British Journal of Psychiatry*, 182, 5-7.

Blair, R. J. (2010). Neuroimaging of Psychopathy and Antisocial Behavior: A Targeted Review. *Current Psychiatry Report*, 12, 76-82.

Boddy, C. R. (2006). The Dark Side of Management Decisions: Organisational Psychopaths. *Management Decision*, 44(10), 1461-1475.

Bornstein, R. F., & Weiner, I. B. (2009). *Principles of Psychotherapy: Promoting Evidence-Based Psychodynamic Practice* (3rd ed.). New York, NY: Wiley.

Boyd, M. A., Niemiec, R. M., & Wedding, D. (2009). *Movies and Mental Illness: Using Films to Understand Psychopathology* (3rd Revised ed.). Clare, MI: Hogrefe & Huber.

Butcher, J. N., Hooley, J. M., & Mineka, S. (2010). *Abnormal Psychology* (14th ed.). Boston: Allyn Bacon.

Cashdan, S. (1988). *Object Relations Therapy: Using the Relationship*. New York: W.W. Norton & Co..

Coffey, C. E., D., M., T., J., Beale, M., & Pritchett, M. (1997). *Handbook of ECT*. Washington D.C.: American Psychiatric Association.

Cormier, S., Nurius, P. S., & Osborn, C. J. (2008). *Interviewing and Change Strategies for Helpers: Fundamental Skills and Cognitive Behavioral Interventions* (6th ed.). New York: Brooks Cole.

Corsini, R. J., & Wedding, D. (2010). *Current Psychotherapies* (9th ed.). New York: Brooks Cole.

Costa, P. T., & Widiger, T. A. (Eds.). (2002). *Personality Disorders and the Five-Factor Model of Personality* (2nd ed.). Washington: American Psychological Association (apa).

Coverdale, J., Nairn, R., & Classen, D. (2002). Depictions of Mental Illness in Print Media: A Prospective National Sample. *Australian and New Zealand Journal of Psychiatry, 36,* 697-700.

Edney, D. R. (2004). *Mass media and mental illness: A literature review*. Ontario: Canadian Mental Health Association.

Flaherty, A. W. (2005). *The Midnight Disease: The Drive to Write, Writer's Block, and the Creative Brain*. Mariner Books.

Fleming, M. (1987, July). Through A Lens, Darkly—Mental Illness and Psychiatry in Motion Pictures. *Psychology Today*. Retrieved March 8, 2006, from http://www.findarticles.com/p/articles/mi_m1175/is_v21/ai_503838/print

Gabbard, G. O. (1999). The Cinematic Psychiatrist. *Psychiatric Times*, XVI(7), 1. Retrieved August 26, 2006, from http://www.psychiatrictimes.com/display/article/10168/50141

Gabbard, G. O. (2002). *The Psychology of the Sopranos: Love, Death, Desire and Betrayal in America's Favorite Gangster Family*. Basic Books.

Goodwin, F. K., & Jamison, K. R. (2007). *Manic-Depressive Illness: Bipolar Disorders and Recurrent Depression, 2nd Edition*. New York: Oxford University Press, USA.

Gorman, J. M., & Nathan, P. E. (2007). *A Guide to Treatments that Work* (3rd ed.). New York: Oxford University Press, USA.

Grinfield, M. J. (1998). Psychiatry and mental illness: are they mass media targets? *Psychiatric Times*, XV(3).

Hare, R. D. (1999). *Without Conscience: The Disturbing World of Psychopaths Among Us*. The Guilford Press.

Hawk-Carpenter, Sharon. Personal interview. 10 May 2009.

Heide, K. M., & Solomon, E. P. (2006). Biology, Childhood Trauma, and Murder: Rethinking Justice. *International Journal of Law and Psychiatry*, 29, 220-233.

Hyler, S., Gabbard, G. O., & Schneider, I. (1991). Homicidal Maniacs and Narcissistic Parasites: Stigmatization of Mentally Ill Persons in the Movies. *Hospital and Community Psychiatry*, 42(10), 1044-1048.

Hyler, S. (2003). Stigma Continues in Hollywood. *Psychiatric Times*, XX(6).

Ivey, A. E., Ivey, M. B., & Zalaquett, C. P. (2009). *Intentional Interviewing and Counseling: Facilitating Client Development in a Multicultural Society* (7th ed.). New York: Brooks Cole.

Jackson, H. (1994). *Using Self Psychology in Psychotherapy*. Northvale, New Jersey: Jason Aronson.

Jamison, K. R. (1995). *An Unquiet Mind: A Memoir of Moods and Madness*. New York: Vintage.

Jamison, K. R. (1996). *Touched with Fire: Manic-Depressive Illness and the Artistic Temperament*. Free Press.

Kaylor, L. (1999). Antisocial Personality Disorder: Diagnostic, Ethical, and Treatment Issues. *Issues in Mental Health Nursing*, 20, 247-258.

Kessler, R.C., Berglund, P., Demler, O., Jin, R., Merikangas, K.R., & Walters, E.E. (2005). Lifetime Prevalence and Age-of-Onset Distributions of DSM-IV Disorders in the National Comorbidity Survey Replication. *Archives of General Psychiatry*, 62, 593-602.

LaBrode, R. T. (2007). Etiology of the Psychopathic Serial Killer: An Analysis of Antisocial Personality Disorder, Psychopathy, and Serial Killer Personality and Crime Scene Characteristics. *Brief Treatment and Crisis Intervention*, 7(2), 151-160.

Larsson, H., Viding, E., & Plomin, R. (2008). Callous-Unemotional Traits and Antisocial Behavior: Genetic, Environmental, and Early Parenting Characteristics. *Criminal Justice and Behavior*, 35(2), 197-211.

Leszcz, M., & Yalom, I. D. (2005). *The Theory and Practice of Group Psychotherapy* (5th ed.). New York: Basic Books.

Levin, A. (2001). Violence and Mental Illness: Media Keep Myths Alive. *Psychiatric News*, 36(9), 10. Retrieved March 8, 2006, from http://pn.psychiatryonline/cgi/content/full/36/9/10

Levin, A. (2005). People with Mental Illness More Often Crime Victims. *Psychiatric News*, 40(17), 16.

Linehan, M. M. (1993). *Skills Manual for Treating Borderline Personality Disorder*. The Guilford Press.

Matsakis, A. (1994). *Post-Traumatic Stress Disorder: A Complete Treatment Guide*. Oakland, CA: New Harbinger Publications.

Matzenbacher, D. (2006). *The Blockbuster Approach*. Columbus: Pearson.

McWilliams, N. (1994). *Psychoanalytic Diagnosis: Understanding Personality Structure in the Clinical Process*. New York: The Guilford Press.

McWilliams, N. (1999). *Psychoanalytic Case Formulation*. New York: The Guilford Press.

Millon, T., Simonsen, E., Birket-Smith, M., & Davis, R. D. (Eds.). (2002). *Psychopathy: Antisocial, Criminal, and Violent Behavior*. New York: The Guilford Press.

Phelps, J. (2006). *Why Am I Still Depressed? Recognizing and Managing the Ups and Downs of Bipolar II and Soft Bipolar Disorder*. New York: McGraw-Hill.

Pies, R. (2001). Psychiatry in the Media: The Vampire, the Fisher King, and the Zaddick. *Journal of Mundane Behavior*. Retrieved August 26, 2006, from http://www.mundanebehavior.org/issues/v2n1/pies.htm

Pirkis, J., Blood, R. W., Francis, C., & McCallum, K. (2005). *A Review of the Literature Regarding Film and Television Portrayals of Mental Illness*. Melbourne: The University of Melbourne Program Evaluation Unit.

Pomerantz, J.M. Focused Psychotherapy as an Alternative to Long-Term Medication. *Drug Benefit Trends*, 11(7), 2-BH-5-BH.

Preston, J. D., O'Neal, J. H., & Talaga, M. C. (2010). *Handbook of Clinical Psychopharmacology for Therapists* (6th ed.). Oakland: New Harbinger Publications.

Price, M. (2009). *A Pacemaker for Your Brain? The Monitor on Psychology*, 40(3), 36-39.

Putnam, F. W. (1989). *Diagnosis and Treatment of Multiple Personality Disorder*. New York: The Guilford Press.

Swinson, R. P., Antony, M. M., Rachman, S., & Richter, M. A. (2001). *Obsessive-Compulsive Disorder: Theory, Research, and Treatment*. New York: The Guilford Press.

Takats, J. M. Personal interview. 26 Aug. 2009.

Tilley, J. Personal interview. 17 Apr. 2009.

Twenge, J. M. & Campbell, W. K. (2010). *The Narcissism Epidemic: Living in the Age of Entitlement*. Free Press.

Viding, E., Blair, R. J., Moffitt, T. E., & Plomin, R. (2004). Evidence for Substantial Genetic Risk for Psychopathy in 7-Year-Olds. *Journal of Child Psychology and Psychiatry*, 46(6), 592-597.

Wahl, O. F. (1997). *Media Madness: Public Images of Mental Illness*. New Jersey: Rutgers University Press.

Walter, G., & McDonald, A. (2004). About to Have ECT? Fine, But Don't Watch It in the Movies: The Sorry Portrayal of ECT in Film. *Psychiatric Times*, XXI(7), 1-3. Retrieved April 10, 2006, from http://www.psychiatrictimes.com/display/article/10168/48111

Weiner, R. D. (2001). *Practice of Electroconvulsive Therapy: Recommendations for Treatment, Training, and Privileging (A Task Force Report of the American Psychiatric Association* (2nd ed.). Arlington, VA: American Psychiatric Publishing, Inc..

Wilson, C., Coverdale, J., Nairn, R., & Panapa, A. (1999). Mental Illness Depictions in Prime-Time Drama: Identifying the Discursive Resources. *Australian and New Zealand Journal of Psychiatry*, 33, 232-239.

Yankelovich, D. & the Daniel Yankelovich Group (1990). *Public attitudes toward people with chronic mental illness: final report*. Princeton, NJ: Robert Wood Johnson Foundation, Program on Chronic Mental Illness.

Zimmerman, M. (1994). *Interview Guide for Evaluating DSM-IV Psychiatric Disorders and the Mental Status Examination*. East Greenwich: Psych Products Press.

Zuckerman, E. L. (2010). *Clinician's Thesaurus, 7th Edition: The Guide to Conducting Interviews and Writing Psychological Reports (The Clinician's Toolbox)*. New York: The Guilford Press.

# Index

# ABOUT THE AUTHOR

**Carolyn Kaufman, PsyD** was pursuing a bachelor's degree in writing when she discovered how much an understanding of psychology could add to her stories. By her senior year, she'd not only subjected most of Shakespeare's plays to psychodynamic analysis, she'd decided to pursue her doctorate in clinical psychology.

Kaufman received her Bachelor of Arts in English/Writing from Otterbein College and her clinical Doctorate of Psychology (Psy.D.) from the APA-accredited Wright State University School of Professional Psychology. She completed her internship at the University of Pittsburgh in Pennsylvania.

As a therapist, she has worked with individuals, couples, and groups, with specialized training in issues relevant to college students, crisis intervention, domestic violence, media psychology, and relationship problems. Her areas of interest include crisis and trauma, relationships, creativity, business psychology, and media psychology.

Kaufman is an assistant professor at Columbus State Community College and occasionally teaches at her alma mater, Otterbein. She always emphasizes the practical application of psychology to everyday life, which has transferred well into her work with writers.

In addition to her job as an assistant professor, she works with writers and serves as an expert source for journalists.

# More practical books for the working writer from Quill Driver Books

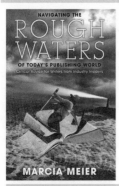